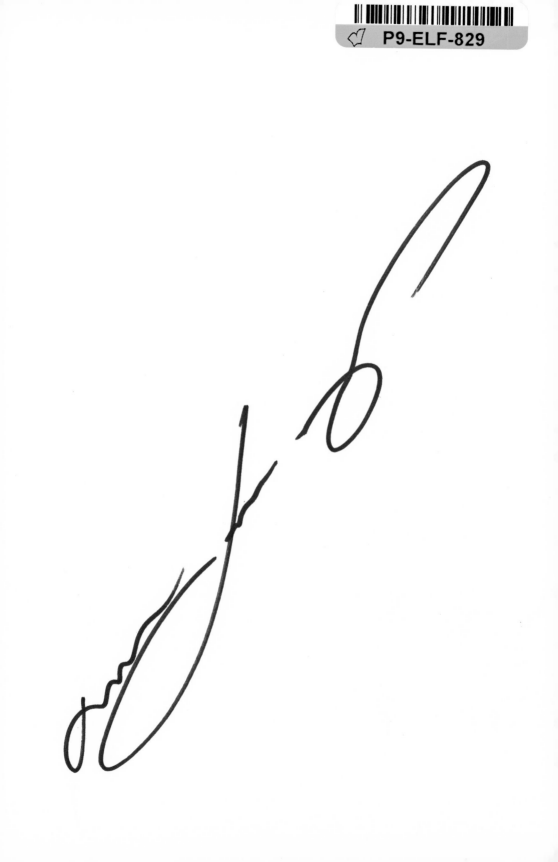

OFF THE PLANET

OFF THE PLANET

Surviving Five Perilous Months
Aboard the Space Station *Mir*

Jerry M. Linenger
U.S. Astronaut/*Mir* Cosmonaut

McGRAW-HILL

New York   San Francisco   Washington, D.C.   Auckland   Bogotá
Caracas   Lisbon   London   Madrid   Mexico City   Milan   Montreal
New Delhi   San Juan   Singapore   Sydney   Tokyo   Toronto

McGraw-Hill

A Division of The **McGraw·Hill** Companies

16 17 18 DOC/DOC 0 9 8

ISBN 0-07-137230-X (pbk)
ISBN 0-07-136112-X (hc)

McGraw-Hill books are available at special quantity discounts to use as premiums and sales promotions, or for use in corporate training programs. For more information, please write to the Director of Special Sales, Professional Publishing, McGraw-Hill, Two Penn Plaza, New York, NY 10121-2298. Or contact your local bookstore.

To my children:
John, Jeff, and (newly arrived!) Henry.
May their lives be full of adventure.

Contents

Preface   ix

PART ONE: ON THE PLANET

1. Looking Upward   3
2. Becoming an Astronaut   5
3. Hello, Russia   16
4. Hanging Out in Star City   28
5. Training, Russian Style   38
6. Tomorrow, *Mir*   48
7. Crew Quarters   57
8. Off to Work   64

PART TWO: OFF THE PLANET

9. Docking a One-Hundred-Ton Space Shuttle   75
10. My First Days on *Mir*   88
11. The Arrival of Vasily and Sasha   92
12. "Fire!"   99
13. An Attempted Coverup   111
14. Cosmonauts, *Da!* Mission Control, *Nyet!*   118
15. The Glories of Earth Gazing   135
16. Profound Isolation   149
17. Escaping a Near-Death Collision   160

18. Housekeeping in Space   178
19. Hurtling Into Nothingness   184
20. Broken Trust   194
21. Taking a Stroll   203
22. Going Home   211
23. Even the Air Tastes Sweet   220

PART THREE: BACK ON THE PLANET

24. Home at Last   231
25. Getting Back on My Feet   237
26. Aftershock   241
27. "Are You Glad You Flew on *Mir?*"   246

    Index   255

Preface

ON THE LAST LINE of my astronaut application form, I paraphrased a quote that had once caught my eye, and that I tried to live by. My variation on the original read: "Specialization is for insects. Man should be able to change a diaper, run a marathon, build a house, write a book, appreciate good music, and fly in space."

I have now flown in space, traveling around the planet more than two thousand times. On my last trip, I lived on the Russian Space Station *Mir* for nearly five months and traveled the equivalent distance of one hundred ten round trips to the moon and back. Although I was single when I filled out my first astronaut application, I now have three boys. I know how to change diapers. I have run a marathon or two, my stereo is always blasting, and while I have not yet built a house, I have built additions and turned a fixer-upper house into a livable home. And now I have written a book.

I wrote this book mainly because five months in space aboard *Mir* was one great adventure. I want my children to be able to read about it someday, to know what their father did, stood for, and was willing to sacrifice. I want them to be able to *feel* what it was like up there. My goal was to take them there with me.

Living in a former KGB-guarded compound in Russia for a year and a half while preparing for my *Mir* flight was difficult. Russian did not come easy to me. Trying to unravel the political undercurrents of post–cold war U.S.-Russian relations, which oftentimes drove irrational decisions at NASA, was never straightforward. Working in space on a rapidly deteriorating space station—fighting fires, tumbling uncontrollably in utter darkness in an electrically power-dead space station, watching a spacecraft moving at eighteen thousand mph nearly collide with us—proved the ultimate challenge. In retrospect, now that I am firmly planted back on the earth, it was one incredible experience. Specialization is for insects.

Under the "Manual Skills" section of my astronaut application form I had listed "woodworking, drafting, carpentry, small engine repair, electrical wiring, sprinkling system installation, heavy cement work, plumbing, and bricklaying." I explained to the astronaut selection board during my interview that some of these skills were rudimentary, but that I could get by.

With the exception of the cement work and bricklaying, all of these skills proved indispensable on *Mir*. The crew of two cosmonauts and myself were cut off—not merely away—but off the planet. Whenever the oxygen generator broke down—as it often did—we had to fix it using only the tools and supplies onboard and our ingenuity. Competence counted for everything. Skills acquired earlier in life were put to use. The work was never-ending.

In the accomplishment section of my astronaut application form I stated that I had read *War and Peace* from cover to cover. The interview board found that entry amusing, following as it did a list of my academic degrees and military decorations. I simply told them that it was a long book and that I made it to the end. They understood, I think, the implication. My stab at subtlety and humor proved almost prophetic. In the novel the Russians, thoroughly overwhelmed by Napoleon and his forces, were nearly crushed and sent retreating. Both sides suffered through the hardship of an unforgiving Russian winter. The Russians endured, counterattacked, and ultimately triumphed, driving Napoleon from Moscow. Moscow lay in ruins; life there would never be the same.

My endurance and that of my fellow cosmonauts was similarly tested. *Mir* proved a harsh environment that nearly overpowered us. Facing defeat, and at times death, we reached deep into our reserves, rose to the occasion, and worked together. In the end we triumphed. The experience changed my outlook on life forever.

I now read simpler books, mostly children's books, to my boys as bedtime stories. I enjoy them. They all have happy endings.

Jerry M. Linenger
Suttons Bay, Michigan
May 1999

PART ONE

ON THE PLANET

1

Looking Upward

YES, I ALWAYS WANTED to be an astronaut. Didn't every kid growing up during the time of the space race?

Of course, as a youngster growing up in East Detroit I vacillated in my career choices. I wanted to be a cowboy one day and a fireman the next. I was enjoying a family vacation at Ipperwash Provincial Park, Canada, in July 1969 when I decided that someday I would become an astronaut. I was fourteen years old.

Nestled on the eastern shore of Lake Huron, Ipperwash is an unusual combination of a family vacation park and a Canadian army training base. Typically we would camp close to the lake, which I remember was cold even in the summer, but clear, blue, and refreshing. Swimming, shivering, and hiding in foxholes—that is how I spent my days at Ipperwash.

After finishing dinner at the campsite one evening, my older brother, Ken, and I returned to the beach. Our bellies were full of hot dogs and baked beans. We plopped down on a sand dune and watched as Lake Huron gulped the last rays of the sun. The moon came out.

"Isn't it amazing? Two astronauts are up there now," Ken said.

"Yup. Absolutely incredible," I replied, awestruck.

We then grew quiet, thinking our own profound boyhood thoughts, imagining what it must be like up there on the moon. I wondered whether the astronauts were looking down at us on the shore of Lake Huron.

I broke the silence between us by suggesting that we go back to the campground and find a television. Arriving at the campground, we noticed that twenty or thirty people were gathered around a picnic table on which one of the more enterprising campers had placed a small black-and-white television set. A noisy gas generator powered the television.

Kenny and I squeezed our way to the front of the assembly, plopped down on the sand, and watched Neil Armstrong and Buzz Aldrin plant an American flag in the Sea of Tranquility on the surface of the moon.

Although the noise from the gas generator overpowered the voice of Walter Cronkite's commentary, we could see by the look on his face that he was as awestruck at that moment as we were. In fact Mr. Cronkite, to me a "grown man," had a tear in his eye. He was so overwhelmed with emotion that he was rendered speechless.

Even at age fourteen I knew that I was seeing something rare. It was an event that made campers leave their campfires and put down their beers to watch. And it was at that moment that I made up my mind to be an astronaut someday. Like the astronauts bounding across the surface of the moon, I, too, wanted to do something special.

2

Becoming an Astronaut

WHEN I LOOK BACK at the decisions I made after that evening in Canada, I can't say that my choices were always made with the sole purpose of trying to become an astronaut, but the dream always remained in the back of my mind.

I applied to the U.S. Naval Academy in part because I knew that the majority of the astronauts had graduated from Annapolis. And there was also, admittedly, a practical reason for that choice. My brother and my two older sisters had beaten me to college. Dad, a telephone man, was struggling to come up with enough money just to keep them in school, let alone send me. One more college student in the family might not have been financially possible. So when Congressman Lucian Nedzi offered me an appointment to Annapolis, and when Dad and Mom discovered that they did not have to pay tuition or room-and-board expenses (and that, in fact, I would actually get *paid* while at Annapolis), well, the decision essentially became a nondecision. I was either going to the naval academy or going to work.

During the first days I hated the "boat school." I think that I would have left after the first week except that I had been given such a severe buzz haircut that, looking the way that I did, I was too embarrassed to return home and face my friends. Over the course of a few months, however, I began to like Annapolis. In particular, I found the academics first rate. While I can now admit without embarrassment that I enjoyed the coursework, back then I would never have said so.

In addition to the classes in engineering, math, and science, I also enjoyed learning new skills: how to drive a ship, how to fire weapons accurately, how to take a fix on a star, how to navigate the seas. While I do not claim to be particularly smart, I am "off-scale high" curious—and curiosity is a great motivator. Throw in some self-discipline, a skill I developed under the tutelage of some top-notch officers, and I did all right academically. After the completion of my plebe year, with few demerits and straight-A report cards, I was selected along with nineteen other midshipmen to participate in a newly introduced major—bioscience.

We took premed courses in addition to the standard engineering classes required at Annapolis. If those of us in the major were able to get accepted into a medical school, the navy would send us directly to that school after graduation.

Three years later, in June 1977, graduating third in my class of more than a thousand midshipmen, I tossed my cap into the air, put on my ensign shoulder boards, and headed off for Wayne State University medical school in Detroit.

My name is now properly written: Jerry Michael Linenger, M.D., M.S.S.M., M.P.H., Ph.D. After completing the medical degree, I went on to complete two master's degrees and another doctorate. Since returning from my flight on *Mir*, I have been awarded three honorary doctorate degrees in science from three separate universities. So now I am now formally Doctor, Doctor, Doctor, Doctor, Doctor Linenger, but I still prefer Jerry.

Whenever anyone teases me about the number of academic degrees I have accrued, I generally respond that I was a rather slow learner—I had to keep going to school until I got it right! Their next comment is invariably along the lines of "Every nook and cranny in your brain must be totally filled up." I respond that one should never underestimate the brain. In the worst case, one can always write over what has already been imprinted.

Curiosity has always gotten the better of me. It is a trait that I cannot seem to keep under control. No, I am not a geek. I never wore a slide rule or calculator on my belt, although I admit I regularly carry a briefcase. I am actually more of a jock. As my official NASA biography states, I "enjoy running marathons, triathlons, and ocean swim-racing; downhill and cross-country skiing, scuba diving, and backpacking." I am married to a beautiful woman and we have three wonderful little boys. I suppose my quirk is that I prefer technical journals to television and hate sitting still. I cannot resist trying new activities, and really enjoy squeezing as many projects into my life as possible.

DESPITE my plebe-year reservations about Annapolis, navy life suited me well. I traveled around the world. I worked in a variety of fields with differing responsibilities. And in spite of changing locations and jobs, my career moved along with promotions in rank.

I completed a surgical internship in San Diego and received aerospace medicine training in Pensacola, Florida. I served a two-year stint as a flight surgeon at Cubi Point in the Republic of the Philippines. That job was followed by work as a medical adviser to a three-star admiral in San Diego.

Admiral Jim Service was in command of U.S. Navy aviation assets for half of the world. His purview of responsibility covered navy operations in the entire Pacific and Indian Ocean basins. His task was to keep U.S. Naval air stations and aircraft carriers equipped and ready to fight. As his medical advisor, I advised him on any medical issues that would affect the readiness of those forces. In addition, I was involved in direct support of the admiral's aviation operational medical forces, which included flight surgeons on aircraft carriers, physiologists running decompression chambers, and clinic doctors stationed at naval air stations in isolated locations throughout that region of the world.

Admiral Service was a real people person. He cared deeply for the well-being of all the naval personnel under his command, including their long-term health. Therefore, the admiral ordered me to develop and implement health-promotion programs for all the ships and naval air stations under his command.

The health programs that the admiral and I finally put into place were all-encompassing. They ranged from sailor-education programs focusing on the threat of AIDS in East African ports of call to cutting down on the fat content of navy diets. We built the program on the premise that if the barriers leading to healthy lifestyles were lowered sufficiently, the majority of people would choose to live in this manner. For example, a sailor might choose to ride his bicycle to work, but after almost being run off the road by a passing vehicle, that same sailor would drive to work instead. As part of our program, bicycle paths were added to any road being repaired or newly constructed on naval air stations. Weight rooms were added aboard ships. Beer vending machines were removed from living quarters, and salad bars were included in wardrooms and cafeterias.

In fact, we not only put the salad bar front and center in the mess hall, but we also moved the ice cream and dessert area to less conspicuous and, therefore, less tempting spots. On the advice of an observant and street-smart sailor, we also moved a young female worker who had previously worked behind one ice cream counter to the salad bar. That sailor had informed me that the reason the ice cream bar on his station was so popular had nothing to do with ice cream or its nuts and toppings. The sailors had frequented the ice cream bar simply for the opportunity to talk with this particularly attractive worker. After relocating the salad bar and the young woman, ice cream consumption dropped precipitously, and we could hardly keep up with the demand for lettuce!

As a consequence of the work I was doing in health promotion, I realized that preventive approaches could make a significant difference in people's health. I applied for out-of-service training in preventive medicine at the University of North Carolina, Chapel Hill.

The navy gave me two years to complete the preventive medicine residency. It required the completion of a master's degree in public health in addition to clinical training. Not one to waste time, I was also able to quietly finagle my way into a doctoral program—studying epidemiology. Once I was enrolled, and because I was able to keep up with all the other requirements necessary for preventive medicine certification, the navy did not object.

I finished all three programs—the master's degree, the preventive medicine residency, and the doctorate in epidemiology—in two years. I was later informed by university administration that this was the shortest time on record for any student in the history of the university to have earned the epidemiology doctoral degree alone.

As you can see, I do not enjoy sitting around idly. When I find something worth doing, I give it everything that I have. And when I start something, I finish it.

BY THE summer of 1989 and at age thirty-four, after watching two great Tarheel basketball seasons at the University of North Carolina, I was back in San Diego and working at the Naval Health Research Center. I headed up a research program that examined the problem of soft-tissue injuries in navy and marine recruits as well as in special forces (SEAL) team members.

I was living on Coronado Island, across the bay from downtown San Diego. In keeping with what I had been preaching, I decided to fall into an even healthier lifestyle than the one I had been following.

At dawn I would drag my kayak down the street, put on my wetsuit, and paddle for forty-five minutes across the San Diego Bay to the Naval Recruit Training Center marina at the foot of the Point Loma peninsula. I then mounted my ten-speed bicycle and pedaled to work over mostly uphill terrain for the next half hour. After a shower I changed into my khaki uniform, microwaved oatmeal, and began my workday. On the rare occasion when I was late for work, I would apologize by honestly admitting, "There was a lot of traffic out there this morning: two destroyers and an aircraft carrier!"

At noon I would run a few miles down to the naval submarine base, do forty-five minutes of lap swimming in the base pool, followed by a return run up the hill. Lunch consisted of a can of tuna fish dumped into Minute Rice, a healthy meal whose overpowering aroma was, very likely, of great annoyance to everyone else occupying the building. Back in my office, I would eat while working at the computer. After work, I was only a bicycle ride, paddle, and short walk away from a quick dinner. Following dinner, I would go to night classes. I was enrolled in a master's degree program in systems management at the University of Southern California.

Weekends were more relaxed. Besides getting my homework done and flying a hop in the backseat of a navy jet in order to meet the flying hours required to stay current as a flight surgeon, I would usually run a race—a triathlon or ocean-swim competition—with some of my SEAL team friends.

The SEALs are an elite group of very physically fit navy personnel trained to do the impossible. When the United States needs to rescue downed American pilots behind enemy lines or infiltrate terrorist operations, the SEALs are sent in. One of my former Annapolis roommates became a SEAL officer. Without even asking me if I cared to participate, he would sign me up for any race that his men planned to enter.

To compete against members of a special forces team like the SEALs required me to be willing to hang up my ego. In these contests, I expected many opportunities to cultivate the virtue of humility, so I always got a special thrill and, admittedly, a perverse sense of pleasure whenever I was actually able to beat some of the SEALs in a race. "A navy doctor beating *you,* a SEAL," team members would good-naturedly rib whoever finished in my wake. I was never good enough as an athlete in these up-to-one-thousand-person triathlons to win the race, but, much to my surprise and satisfaction, I performed quite respectably. I could usually pick up a medal or trophy for placing as one of the top three finishers in the thirty- to forty-year-old age group.

These competitions taught me a lesson. I realized that human beings could be motivated to go to great extremes and endure much personal hardship in order to achieve a goal. For me the motivation to continue another week of strenuous training came in the form of a token race T-shirt. An even stronger motivation to work hard often took the form of conversations overheard among SEALs raising eyebrows over the physical performance of a navy doctor. Based on such trivial rewards, I would paddle the kayak all the harder the next morning, run an extra mile, or swim despite the icy Pacific water.

AFTER I had worked at the Naval Health Research Center for a month, the commanding officer ordered all personnel to the beach one Friday afternoon for a traditional navy "Hail and Farewell" party. Newcomers to the center, myself included, were being introduced and hailed, while the people that we were replacing were being bade farewell. Also being honored was a group of public health graduate students from San Diego State University who had completed their practical rotations at the research center over the past semester.

I joined in a game of beach volleyball. During the game I noticed that a young woman dressed in baggy sweats and a big straw hat kept taking pictures of the action. As the game wore on, I began to take more notice of her because it seemed that she was not merely taking pictures of the volleyball players in general, but of me in particular.

She was a blue-eyed brunette with "legs that go all the way to the floor" as I would have put it back then. I was beginning to discount her attention to me—thinking that it was probably just wishful thinking on my part—until I dived headfirst to return a hard spike near the endline. Spitting dirt and somewhat perturbed—I had missed the ball—I looked up to see a camera in my face. As I stood to wipe the sand from my sweaty body, I counted two more clicks of the camera. I looked at her and she smiled an absolutely gorgeous smile at me. She then tipped her hat and returned to a blanket where bikini-clad graduate students were sunbathing. To my disappointment, she kept her baggy sweats on.

She left the beach party without my getting a chance to talk to her. The volleyball game broke up. While I was washing off in the ocean one of the guys who had worked with her told me that she was a grad student named Kathryn Bartmann and that, yes, she looked *very* good under all those baggy clothes. She was twenty-four, smart, friendly as could be, and unattached as far as he knew. "Definitely worth pursuing" was his assessment.

Normally somewhat shy in dating, I was cocky-confident. I called her for a date. She hesitated and said she would call me back. I was dumbfounded. Had she not taken at least a roll of pictures of me at the beach? I pursued and finally she agreed to a friendly daytime walk and some boogie boarding in Coronado.

I later learned that yes, she had singled me out, but it wasn't her camera. A different graduate student had a mad crush on me and asked Kathryn to take some inconspicuous photos. She had told Kathryn that I was a great catch and described me as a "single navy flight surgeon who lives in Coronado with some SEAL team guys. He runs triathlons and wins, and you ought to see him in uniform!" Kathryn commented to her that I did not seem all that friendly to her and appeared to be too serious.

She eventually found my softer side, and we grew to love each other. After two years I took her to a place where my parents had met—a small resort town on the shores of Lake Michigan named Saugatuck. We stayed at a cottage with the parents of my former Annapolis roommate, Mark Clark. His parents, too, had met while on vacation in Saugatuck. I considered the place charmed.

After discussing my secret proposal with Mr. Clark, a grandfather with too many grandchildren to count, I left the cottage early in the morning and headed to town. I later called the cottage and asked Kathryn to meet me in town at Wilkin's Hardware Store. I explained that Mr. Clark had sent me there to pick up a part for the hot water heater and I needed his help.

Five minutes later, Kathryn and Mr. Clark arrived at Wilken's Hardware Store. I wasn't there, but there was a note and a flower for Kathryn, the desk clerk told her. The note said, meet me at Billy's Boat House.

At Billy's was another note and flower, but no Jerry. The note said, "Kathryn. Did you know . . ." followed by "Meet me at Round the Corner ice cream shop."

The flowers and the notes continued until, at the Butler eatery, where a glass of champagne accompanied the new note, they read, when strung together, "Kathryn, did you know that I love you, and that I want to spend the rest of my life with you? Will you . . . Meet me at Chequers."

Kathryn, Mr. Clark later told me, did not take the time to drink the champagne but ran immediately to Chequers. There, in the foyer of the restaurant, was the final flower in the bouquet and the final two words of the message, ". . . marry me?"

She burst into the restaurant, we hugged, and she cried. Through the tears I heard her say yes. We sat down to a candle-lit dinner. A few minutes later, I saw Mr. Clark, panting and trying to catch his breath, as he peeked in, unable to resist seeing what the answer was. He saw us hugging and kissing. He smiled and left.

On a surprisingly sunny day in March, in her hometown of Chicago, Kathryn and I were married. The altar girls thought the wedding was "so cool"—with me dressed in my formal navy choker whites along with some of my sword-carrying friends. Kathryn wore a white full-length wedding dress that was tight at the waist but blossomed into a two-foot bell at the bottom. She was gorgeous under her veil. I had a hard time leaning over the hoop skirt and around her bouquet of tulips and calla lilies to kiss the bride. We left the church under an arch of swords, with rice and pink balloons flying.

THE SEALs were having a problem. During their initial training, recruits were "bilging out" in droves, not from a lack of motivation or desire, but from tibial stress fractures. They were fracturing their lower leg bone, the tibia, at rates ten times higher than any other group reported in the medical literature. This was not surprising. Most normal people do not carry telephone poles, jump from fifteen-foot walls carrying sixty-pound knapsacks, or run in the surf for miles at midnight. I assembled a group of sports medicine experts to look into the problem.

While I was working on the SEAL project in late 1991, I decided to submit an application to become an astronaut. There are literally thousands of applicants applying for each new astronaut class, so I knew that my chance of selection was slim, but if I didn't try, I knew that I had no chance. I did not even tell Kathryn that I had applied.

Selection was a two-step process. My application went first to the U.S. Navy astronaut selection board, which screened all prospective navy candidates and then sent a list of fifty names to NASA. A preliminary astronaut selection committee at the Johnson Space Center in Houston screened and compiled a similar list of qualified civilians. NASA's list was then combined with the lists submitted by the armed forces. These two hundred or so applications were then sent to the full astronaut selection board for review. The board then invited half of these applicants—twenty at a time for five consecutive weeks—to Houston. I was one of those invited.

After completing a week of interviews and medical tests, I had a sense that my chances for selection were good. When elementary school classmates, past girlfriends, college roommates, former landlords, and present neighbors started calling me to tell me that a government special agent had stopped by and was asking all kinds of questions about me, I knew that NASA was running a security background check on me. A good sign.

When I received a phone call from the selection committee chairman, and not from a member of his administrative staff, I figured I had been selected even before he said, "Commander Linenger, we would like you to report to Johnson Space Center for astronaut training if you are still interested in joining the new astronaut candidate group."

While jumping up and down, I dropped the telephone. Regaining my composure, I told Mr. Donald Puddy that yes, indeed, I was still interested in becoming an astronaut.

Why was I selected? It is difficult to determine why one person is

selected over another since thousands of applicants, many of whom
are fully qualified, are vying for a few available places in the astronaut office. Other than pure luck, which I do not discount one bit in
my case, I can guess at some of the aspects of my application that
allowed my packet to remain on the consideration table when others
were being discarded.

The members of the selection committee consisted of senior astronauts, high-level NASA managers, and a scientist in the same disci-
pline as the candidate being interviewed. That scientist might be a
specialist in the field of astrophysics, material science, or, in my case,
the field of life science. Since no one has any past experience doing
spacewalks or releasing satellites, the selection committee is forced to
look at life experiences that might translate to, or at least give an
indication of, potential astronaut skills.

I was a "proven quantity." Because of good performance, I had
been promoted early—deep selected—to the next navy rank on two
occasions. I had managed a million-dollar research program and had
gotten results. Furthermore, my SEAL stress-fracture research had
relevance to space travel. The demineralization and softening of
bone in astronauts exposed to weightlessness is a documented phenomenon that may prove to be a show-stopper for lengthy missions
to other planets. I knew about the dynamic processes of bone. Being
an expert in this area probably did not hurt my chances.

Having varied experiences, and adapting well to them, is a desirable characteristic for an astronaut. I had a solid educational background in several very different fields. I had performed a variety of
jobs in various settings around the world. I had gone to the extremes:
from flying at high altitude in high-performance tactical aircraft to
scuba diving.

I was also psychologically sound—and was proven so under
stress. I had lived without difficulty in many isolated duty stations
and onboard the closed quarters of ships. I had been the only physician within a thousand miles when living on the island of Diego
Garcia in the middle of the Indian Ocean. I had been lowered from
hovering helicopters onto disabled fishing vessels in the Sea of Japan
to render aid. I had flown on recovery missions searching for
downed pilots. I had picked up the pieces and led the accident investigation of an F-14 fighter that, flying too low in cloudy weather, met

a mountain. Having displayed competence, self-reliance, and the ability to work effectively even under the most gruesome conditions strengthened my application. I suspect these traits were considered both relevant and necessary for work as an astronaut.

And finally, I *really wanted* to be an astronaut. I had wanted to become an astronaut since that night on the shore of Lake Huron when, on a generator-powered television perched atop a picnic table, I had watched astronauts place an American flag on the moon. The selection board could feel confident that if, for virtually my entire life, I had set my sights on flying in space, then I probably would not bail out during the arduous and demanding astronaut training program.

MY DAD was no longer alive to celebrate my selection as an astronaut with me. But I was thinking of him on the day that I received the telephone call from the Johnson Space Center. Silently, I thanked him for all that he had done for me.

I figured that Dad would have been proud of his boy, a boy to whom he had hit hundreds of fly balls over the years, a boy whose baseball games he had cheered and honors banquets he had proudly attended.

"So you want to be an astronaut? Why, sure, son . . . why not?"

I made it, Dad.

3

Hello, Russia

WHEN THE ASTRONAUT selection committee chairman told me that I had been selected he also asked me to not tell anyone about it until the next day because the official NASA press release would not be issued until then. Indoctrinated with "loose lips sink ships," I decided to consider the information top secret and tell no one.

As I hung up the phone, the people in surrounding offices at the research center wanted to know what I had been screaming about. I told them that some of my research data looked really good and I was excited about it; the looks they gave me said they thought that I must be working too hard. Kathryn and I were heading to Colorado the next day to meet my sister's family for a ski vacation. I would hold off telling even her until then.

As we boarded the airplane the next morning, I quietly asked the flight attendant to pass a note to the pilot, assuring her that it had to do with my being in naval aviation and not with hijacking. Once we reached altitude and leveled out, the pilot made an announcement.

"Would Kathryn Linenger please identify herself to the flight attendant."

Kathryn gave me a bewildered and concerned look, then she waved her arm. The flight attendant asked us both to stand.

The pilot continued, "Kathryn, we have an official news release from the Johnson Space Center in Houston. I hope that you like spicy food and cowboy hats, because it says here that Commander Jerry Linenger has been selected to become one of our astronauts, and it looks like you two will be moving to Houston. Congratulations!"

Kathryn hugged me and cried. The flight attendant handed us a bottle of champagne from first class. The other passengers applauded and congratulated us. As we left the airplane, I thanked the pilot for the favor. I had guessed correctly, both were former navy pilots and were glad to help out a navy flight surgeon. We had a great vacation celebrating and skiing.

SIX MONTHS later, in August 1992, at age thirty-seven, I reported to the Johnson Space Center in Houston, Texas, along with twenty-four other astronaut candidates. Throughout the years groups of newly selected astronauts have reported for training together. Ours was the fourteenth group of astronaut trainees since the so-called Original Seven astronauts had first arrived more than thirty years earlier.

It is an in-house practice at the astronaut office for the previous astronaut class—now fully trained and beginning to fly missions—to christen the new recruits with an affectionate, if disparaging, nickname. Since our class was one of the largest astronaut classes ever selected, the more senior astronauts thought it meant that we would be hogging much of the T-38 flying time, simulator training, and, eventually, space shuttle seats. The senior astronauts nicknamed us the "Hogs."

At first, I was rather displeased at being called a hog. But I figured that we were let off easy after learning that astronaut candidates before us were referred to as "Hairballs" and "Maggots."

Unlike the "Original Seven," we arrived at the space center without fanfare. Although there was a press conference, we were by no means mobbed by a gaggle of *Life* magazine photographers. In fact, most of us felt that, although being an astronaut sounded good, we were, in essence, being demoted from the perks and privileges of our previous jobs. Those jobs included the classic astronaut mold—military test pilots—but among the Hogs were also physicists, astronomers, physicians, a business executive, a veterinarian, and a deep-sea diver.

After hiking each morning from a parking space that was closer to the cow pastures than to the simulator and classroom buildings—we did not yet rate assigned parking spaces—we were imprisoned in a classroom for eight or nine hours of nonstop lectures. A different engineer would enter our cell every two hours. In excruciatingly painful detail, and with uniformly monotone voices, the experts would explain how rockets work and what each of the two thousand switches in the shuttle do. After class we were often scheduled for simulator training that lasted until midnight. So much for the glamour of being an astronaut.

In spite of my having to listen to engineers dryly lecture for hours on end, astronaut training suited me well. I was fortunate, lucky really, to be the first person in my group of astronaut candidates to actually fly in space. My first shuttle mission took place in September 1994—a mere two years after we initially reported to NASA for training. Learning all the skills necessary to work competently in space takes time. While two years might seem like a long time to train, it was actually a record pace—at that time, the shortest period from the start of training to blasting off for any astronaut. In the past some astronauts, fully trained and ready to go, had to wait ten years before getting the opportunity to fly in space.

THE SPACE shuttle mission to which I had been assigned was complex and multifaceted. Mission highlights included: the first use of lasers from space for environmental research; deployment and retrieval of a solar science satellite; robotic processing of semiconductors; use of a shuttle arm-attached boom for impingement-reactive thruster research; and an untethered spacewalk to test a self-rescue jet pack—the first in ten years.

Luckily for me, and probably by NASA design, I was placed on a crew consisting of some very experienced and, for the most part, respected astronauts. Yes, there are occasional squabbles among those within the corps of astronauts that are better not discussed in public. As in any profession some astronauts are more respected than others by their peers. Do anything to tarnish the astronaut image, professionally or personally, and one falls down a rung or two on the ladder.

Being the only rookie flier among them, I learned a great deal under their guidance. While every astronaut candidate undergoes extensive formal training from expert instructors based upon a formal syllabus, the most important aspect of preparation for a space flight takes place as a sort of apprenticeship during which the veteran space travelers share their knowledge and experiences with the rookies. The pros had a lot to teach me.

Captain Richard "Dick" Richards, naval aviator extraordinare, commanded the mission. He was a cool, unflappable redhead in his forties who exuded confidence and who would burst into an unrestrained hearty laugh easily. The laugh usually followed a joke he himself had told or an undoubtedly jazzed-up story from his past. When on a roll, he could make the crew (sitting together in a shuttle simulator) and the eight-member training team (listening in on the radio and seated behind consoles in a separate control room) laugh so hard that we were lucky we were strapped securely into our seats.

Dick was not one to enjoy the medical experiments being performed upon us "lab rat" astronauts. Emerging from the toilet area, his still-warm urine sloshing in a clear plastic collection bag that he thrust high into the air, Dick would scream at the top of his lungs, "Science!" This declaration was inevitably followed by his laugh. Even when in orbit, I swear that I was awakened in the middle of the night from my tenuous sleep (sleeping strapped to the wall horizontally, stacked three people high) by the cry of "Science!" booming through the otherwise quiet shuttle.

Dick Richards also knew when to get serious, and was as competent as they come. He knew that he had an experienced and dependable crew. He did what many in the same position cannot seem to do: assign responsibility and corresponding authority, then turn the crew loose and let them do their jobs. Since it was my first flight, he kept me under his wing, made sure that I was both comfortable and competent, and eased me from astronaut candidate to full-fledged astronaut. By the time we were sitting on the launch pad, we were a team, confident and ready to go.

The laser was our main payload. Our goal was to prove that lasers could be used to map the clouds on the dark side of the earth. By flying the shuttle *Discovery* inverted, and by beaming the payload bay–mounted laser down toward the earth, we were able to plot the topography of the clouds in the darkness below. Given our success, a series of satellites may someday be launched equipped with similar lasers. Armed with the other half of the weather picture, meteorologists of the future should be able to predict the weather more accurately.

We released a solar-observing Spartan satellite from the payload bay. The satellite flew independent of the shuttle for two days before we retrieved it. While free-flying the satellite was able to point very accurately at the sun and record images of its corona and solar flare activity.

In order to detect the effect of shuttle thruster firings on regions surrounding the spacecraft, we mounted pressure-sensitive detectors on the end of the shuttle's robotic arm. We then fired *Discovery*'s steering thrusters and recorded the disturbance felt by the detectors. The information gathered would later be used to plan docking approaches of the shuttle to space stations—space stations from which broad-winged and delicate solar panels project.

We also flight-tested a newly designed Buck Roger's–style jet pack. The jetpack was attached to the back of the spacewalking suits. Should an astronaut become inadvertently detached from the shuttle during a spacewalk, firing the thrusters in the jetpack would fly him back to the spacecraft. The jetpacks worked well and are now used routinely as an added safety feature during most U.S. spacewalks.

The mission aboard Space Shuttle *Discovery* was, well, awesome. The incredible power of launch, the freedom of floating and flying in weightlessness, the earth as a whole unfolding below, and, finally, rumbling through the turbulent fireball of reentry. It was everything that I expected. I was anxious for more.

AFTER returning to Houston from the landing site at Edwards Air Force base in California, navy captain Robert "Hoot" Gibson, chief of the astronauts, summoned me to his office. Hoot was a veteran of four space shuttle flights and would later command the first shuttle-*Mir* docking flight. Carefree and laid back, Hoot was highly respected among astronauts as someone with the right stuff but without the ego to match. He played lead guitar in the all-astronaut rock band Max Q. (Max Q is the engineering shorthand term for maximum dynamic pressure, signifying the maximum stress loading on a structure. Max Q does not occur at maximum shuttle speed, but rather sometime between thirty seconds and a minute into a shuttle launch. At Max Q there are extreme "breakup" forces placed on the structure of the shuttle, as airspeed rapidly builds in the still dense atmosphere.) He always used an amplifier given to him by a member of the rock group the Eagles. And so, despite his top position, when mellow Hoot summoned me to his office it did not cause me any anxiety.

As I entered his office, Hoot jumped to his feet, flashed a boyish grin, and reached out and shook my hand.

"Jerry, great flight! Welcome back to the planet. Congratulations, Astronaut Linenger. Well done."

Coming from him, someone whom we all respected, the *astronaut* part sounded good.

"Thanks, Hoot. Being up in space was fantastic, as you know."

After some small talk, Hoot got to the point. "Have you thought more about what we talked about before your shuttle mission?"

"You mean flying on the *Mir* space station?"

I told him that Kathryn and I were still game. My wife had a strong sense of adventure, wanting to travel and live in different parts of the world. I understood her restlessness. I used to feel the same way before my navy lifestyle tempered that desire in me. I told Hoot that I thought working with the Russians would present quite a challenge for me, a U.S. naval officer, but added that I believed it would be a worthwhile experience.

"Great!" Hoot said, "Because you are still our top choice for the job. You had better take your postflight vacation quickly, because you need to start up on Russian language soon. My plan is for you to be the prime crew member for the NASA-3/*Mir*-22 mission. Because of the limited time until the flight, you will not be a backup for anyone—just go there and do it, first time through."

"Sounds great. Thank you, sir."

"Again, Jerry, you did a great job on your flight. You have served our navy and our country well. Good luck."

And so, just back from a whirlwind tour of the planet, I was heading to Russia.

AT THAT time, September 1994, most of America and, to a surprisingly similar extent, the astronauts knew little about the Russian space program. We only knew that a new cooperative undertaking, politically inspired, was shaping up between the Americans and the Russians. The program was called shuttle-*Mir* or *Mir*-shuttle, depending upon what side of the earth one lived on.

I was able to piece together some scattered facts concerning the program and the Russian *Mir* space station. In March 1995 an American astronaut, Norm Thagard, would launch to *Mir* with two cosmonauts in a Russian Soyuz capsule. He would return 115 days later with the same cosmonauts, but this time aboard the space shuttle. Then, starting in March 1996, a series of shuttle flights would take four American astronauts, one immediately following the other, to *Mir.* At that time the planned sequence called for Shannon Lucid to fly first. She would be replaced by me, who in turn would be replaced by John Blaha. John's replacement was not yet selected.

We would each ride up and down on our space shuttle, while our Russian counterparts would get to and from the space station in the Russian Soyuz capsule. Once on *Mir,* the crew would consist of two Russian cosmonauts and an American astronaut. The flight duration of our missions was to be between three to five months. Later, John and I switched positions in the sequence in order for me to do a spacewalk. Much later, two additional long-duration missions were added.

The *Mir* was an old space station. The first module, termed the base block, was put into orbit in February 1986. Three other modules were added over the years. The final two modules, U.S.-financed Spektr (spectrum) and Priroda (nature) were still to be added. Over its lifetime the *Mir* was, at times, kept in orbit unmanned, but this was no longer deemed possible because of the increased operational complexity of the station. The three-seat Soyuz capsule had been used from the start to transport the cosmonauts back and forth.

While the typical stay times for cosmonauts to live on *Mir* were from three to six months, two cosmonauts had remained on *Mir* continuously for over a year, setting an endurance record. Beyond six months neither did much purposeful work—they were too worn out. The Russian controllers deferred all critical tasks to fresh crewmates who kept coming and going. Regardless of the fact that they did little for the second half of their stay, they nevertheless persevered and proved that it is possible to stay in space for a year.

The economic crisis in the Soviet Union almost forced the Soviets to abandon *Mir* in the early 1990s. Only by partnering with the U.S. space program were the Russians able to financially keep the space station in orbit. The partnership was one forced by necessity, not desire.

GOING to Russia was not something that every astronaut, or even most of the astronauts, wanted to do. The shuttle-*Mir* program was new and it was yet to be seen whether the flights could be carried out without delay. Russian technology was viewed as inferior and crude. And although the extent of the danger would not be known until after American participation in the joint flights began, the *Mir* space station was suspected by most astronauts to be outdated, possibly unreliable and unsafe, and a definite step backward in technology from the space shuttle. Astronauts who already were assigned to shuttle flights, or who thought that they would be assigned to a flight in the near future, viewed commitment to the program as a disruption to their prospects of getting back into space quickly.

Many astronauts, though thrilled to be doing ten-day missions, had no desire to be in space for months on end. Shuttle pilots were, for the most part, disinterested since they would not be able to pilot anything while traveling to or from the space station. That task would be left to the shuttle crew, not to the long-duration American *Mir* astronaut. Furthermore, since there were no jets available for the aviators to fly while training in Russia, their aviation skills would become rusty.

Astronauts with young children also opted out. Could one really expect youngsters to enjoy living on an isolated base for nearly two years and speaking only Russian? And finally, to be frank, some military officer astronauts just could not stomach the idea of cooperating with our former cold war foes.

But for me, the opportunity to be among the first Americans to live on the Russian space station sounded like just the type of adventurous undertaking that had driven me to become an astronaut in the first place. I could participate in the early colonization of space. I could set aside my animosity toward our former military foe and instead work with them toward achieving a common goal. As a physician always fascinated by the adaptability of the human body, I was thrilled at the prospect of being able to observe how my own body and psyche could adapt to long-duration space travel. How would I hold up in the face of profound isolation? Furthermore, the prospect of running my own laboratory in space held great appeal. I would be responsible for executing the work of top researchers from around the world.

As a professional astronaut, the opportunity to view and study the earth for months at a time, to learn new spacecraft systems, to fly in a Soyuz capsule during a flyaround, and to do a spacewalk, was exceedingly attractive. So what if the Russians were still using a capsule that was no more advanced than the American Gemini space-craft? So what if the *Mir* space station was no more capable than our vintage 1970s *Skylab?* This would be one glorious adventure.

I always enjoyed talking with John Young, an American legend who flew two Gemini missions (1965, 1966), two Apollo missions (including a moon-buggy ride in 1972), and two space shuttle missions (commanding the first shuttle flight in 1981). Still serving our country as senior astronaut at NASA, John is the person whom *astronauts* look up to. Whenever Captain Young would, almost shyly, with eyes turned downward, tell me about the days of living in cramped capsules and of the can-do attitude of those times, I would feel a pang of regret, sorry that I had not been around then. Going to Russia seemed like my one chance to experience at least a sliver of that groundbreaking era.

The timing was also good for me personally. Since we had no children at the time, making a move to Russia would be comparatively easy for Kathryn and me. She was the perfect mate for such a venture—she was actually more thrilled about the adventurous aspects of our journey to Russia than I was. Practical career reasons also applied. I had one shuttle flight under my belt, a flight to which I was quickly assigned partly in order to qualify me to be able to go to *Mir.*

Wisely, the deputy director of the Johnson Space Center, George Abbey, decided that anyone sent to Russia had to be flight tested and fully trained on shuttle systems before being assigned to one of the more demanding *Mir* flights. If nothing else, I learned from my first trip into space that I am one of the lucky 10 percent or so of people who feel physically perfect in space from the get-go. George Abbey was able to assure himself that I was reliable and could be counted on to get the job done.

I was now very likely at the end of the waiting line in my Hog astronaut group for the next chance to fly a shuttle mission. That wait would surely be long—at least two years, and probably longer. A mission to *Mir* was a concrete flight opportunity, one that assured me another ride into space. I was thrilled at the prospect of being assigned to another mission so quickly, even though, in all honesty, I had very little idea of what exactly that mission would entail.

Within a month of my conversation with Hoot, I left the Johnson Space Center and headed off to the Defense Language Institute in

Monterey, California, to begin a five-week crash course in the Russian language.

IN SPITE of all of my formal education, I had never mastered a foreign language beyond a few phrases of Tagalog acquired when living in the Philippines for two years—and some of those phrases are best not repeated. Having to learn the Russian language—we would speak only Russian on *Mir*, and communicate only with mission control in Moscow, not Houston, during the entire mission—was perversely appealing. I always felt guilty and lazy, rather an egocentric American, for not mastering a foreign language. My sister Karen, who had been valedictorian in her high school class and a straight-A student in both college and at graduate school at the University of Michigan, taught high school French and Spanish. When I told her what I was about to undertake, she told me that, for her, learning languages had come almost naturally. "It must be in our genes, Jerry. You'll do fine," she assured me. She did warn me that Russian was one of the more difficult languages.

The Monterey peninsula was blanketed in fog when I arrived at the Defense Language Institute, which is run by the army. Situated near the base of the peninsula and perched on the hillside overlooking Steinbeck's Cannery Row, the institute consists of a motley collection of buildings. A few Spanish-style, stately structures with red tile roofs, sit on the hillside. The next tier is made of newly constructed cinderblock buildings found in duplicate and triplicate on military bases around the world. At the lowest tier are the classrooms: cream-colored, 1950s-era standard-issue military barracks, stacked in neat military rows one after another.

During the heyday of the cold war, the Russian language department at DLI was the largest at the school. With the end of the cold war, however, it was pared down to less than half its previous size. The remaining instructors, tenuously clinging to their jobs, were grateful to have work from NASA.

Protocol came first. After a restless night in an unfamiliar bed in the unfamiliar surroundings of the concrete-block bachelor officers' quarters, I reported at 7 A.M., as instructed, to the DLI Commandant's office. I was greeted by a stern, barrel-chested colonel whose last name was simply unpronounceable, but ended with lots of "skis." He looked to be more suited to run a tank battalion in the former East Germany than to be teaching language in sunny California.

In a thick accent the colonel told me that the institute had been training students since the 1940s and had experimented with a number of curriculums over the years to try to improve their efficiency. Based on that historical experience, it was found to take six months to train a person to be proficient in French or Spanish. It takes two years of dedicated, full-time training to become proficient in Japanese or Chinese. There are no shortcuts, he emphasized. More difficult than the Romance languages, but less challenging than the Eastern languages, Russian required a full year and a half of intense study. He again reiterated that he knew of no shortcuts.

He then rose from behind his desk and stood rigidly, as if at attention. I had never been offered a seat so I had never sat down; but at his rising, I threw my shoulders back and stuck my chest out further, more closely approximating his posture. With a bone-crushing grip, he shook my hand and told me, without a hint of a smile, "Good luck, Commander Linenger, learning the language in five weeks."

I almost asked for permission to shove off, a phrase left over from my naval academy days, but instead just nodded, turned, and left. I ambled down the hill to the classroom buildings, already beginning to doubt that this Russian thing was such a good idea after all.

I faced a dilemma. I had only a year and a half until my flight. In addition to learning Russian, I had to master the *Mir* space station systems, the Soyuz spacecraft, and the U.S. science program planned for the mission. I also had to train for a spacewalk in a Russian spacesuit, setting a precedent as the first American astronaut to conduct a spacewalk from a Russian spacecraft. Someone at NASA decided that, while it might take a year and a half for everyone else to learn Russian, Linenger was both smart and trainable. More likely, since the time period simply did not fit the schedule, NASA just ignored DLI's fifty years' worth of experience in teaching foreign languages and designed my schedule to fit the predetermined timetable.

Despite my sister's encouraging words, I was not gifted in learning languages. I stumbled my way through the Cyrillic alphabet during one-on-one language lessons with my somewhat schizophrenic instructor. (Some days nice enough; other days nearly a raving lunatic, shouting at me in, thank goodness, totally incomprehensible

Russian. Hey, he was under the gun to make me competent in five weeks and would panic from time to time.) I quickly surmised that I would defy my genes. After five weeks I packed my bags, said *zdrastvutye* and *dosvedanye,* hello and goodbye being the only two words I could say with confidence in Russian, to the fog-shrouded barking seals along the Monterey shore, and headed to snowy Moscow.

4

Hanging Out in Star City

STAR CITY, RUSSIA, is where cosmonauts have been training since the sixties. Carved into the woods, thirty miles northeast of Moscow, the former top-secret military base was patrolled by KGB guards and only recently positioned on Russian maps. All phones were tapped; most still are. Star City residents live and work on the base. Nine-story apartment buildings are stuffed with people, four or five or six to a room. The heat for the entire compound is supplied from a central furnace, pumped out as steam to the outlying buildings. In order to save money, the furnace is not fired up until the temperature drops well below freezing, the rationale being that people can tolerate the cold for a few weeks. In the summer, hot water to all residents would be cut off for weeks in order to save on the Star City fuel bill. While uncomfortable, the conditions proved to be good training for space station *Mir,* where I would go nearly five months without a shower.

The residents rely on the half-dozen or so shops in the complex for their sustenance. The grocery store is about the size of a small-town IGA grocery store in America, but is stocked with about one tenth of the goods. The produce is not stacked deep in columns, but rather spread out horizontally across the shelves in order to make the shelves appear less bare. Bread is the most popular item, twenty-five cents a loaf, bring your own bag. Vodka also sells well. The compound is entirely self-contained. Everything is within walking distance.

Until recently, a Russian was considered lucky to live in Star City. The cosmonauts were national heroes, the town of Star City a Soviet showcase. Residents lived better than most other citizens of the Soviet Union did. The military complex was at the top of the communist food chain, assuring first dibs on groceries, liquor, and clothing. And when economic conditions got particularly frightful in the Soviet Union, the remaining bread was shipped off, by military convoy, to places like Star City.

But the situation has changed dramatically. With the fall of communism and the advent of private enterprise in Moscow, many Star City residents, mainly spouses and children of the Russian military officers, are forced to work second jobs. They board a crowded train situated just outside the main gate of the compound and commute to Moscow. As the influence of the military has waned, the stores are now better stocked in Moscow. Instead of feeling privileged to live in Star City, many feel trapped. With no means to buy or rent an apartment elsewhere, the residents are stuck in their government-furnished apartments. Since the apartment comes with the job, it is almost impossible to change jobs. Disgruntled and unmotivated workers trudge to work, often receiving their meager paychecks only after months of delay.

Even the job of cosmonaut is no longer looked upon with awe and reverence by the Russian people, nor are the pay and perks associated with the job what they once were. Despite what might be expounded by some, the average Russian on the street is more concerned with getting bread on the table than with what the cosmonauts are up to. The propagandist government newspaper *Pravda* no longer has a stranglehold on the news. Upstart newspapers no longer trumpet the triumphs of the Soviet space program nor try to hide the failures—in fact, the writers are quickly learning that bad news sells.

Many, especially among the young, take no pride whatsoever in their country's space program and barely know anything about it. Even the better-informed new rich—businessmen, bankers, entrepreneurs, and, dare I say it, members of the Russian Mafia who are the rich among the rich—often view the Russian space program as an economic burden that is no longer justified.

While I truly believe that our U.S. space program more than pays for itself in technological spinoff, as well as providing inspiration for us all to go beyond what is deemed comfortable and to embrace change, it is difficult to argue with hungry people, people whose technology needs to move into the 1980s or 1970s before seriously pushing the limits in the new millennium.

KATHRYN and I arrived at Moscow's Sheremetyevo airport in January 1995, thoroughly jet-lagged after the eighteen-hour flight from Houston. Dark, cavelike, more like a gulag than the entryway to a country, Sheremetyevo is a gloomy greeting to Russia for the weary visitor. Standing in what appeared to be the shortest of three lines weaving toward the customs officers, I counted forty other poor souls in front of me before I became too frustrated to count any further.

Peering down the line, I saw Russian soldiers holding machine guns at the customs booth. The soldiers were dressed in green-gray uniforms with big black snowboots pulled to the knee. The drab uniforms were adorned with the insignia of communism: red star, hammer, and sickle. It seemed that the military was not so fond of the new world order and decided to defiantly hold out against adopting the new Russian Republic tricolor red, white, and blue flag and the double eagle shield of freedom.

With my U.S. Navy armed forces identification card tucked in my pocket, I felt as if I were standing in line for execution. Looking up at the black ceiling, I noticed that only every fifth or sixth light bulb, each without a fixture, was lighted. I squeezed Kathryn's hand, trying to reassure her. Two hours later we received our passports stamped by an unsmiling customs agent, then stood in a different line for another hour to make a claim for our missing baggage.

Welcome to Russia.

We would later learn that the baggage of an American traveling on an official U.S. passport would always be missing. Someone had to rifle through it carefully and then, the next day, charge an exorbitant fee for the service of "holding the bags overnight." Pay or never see your underwear again. We always received similar or worse treatment on subsequent trips in and out of Sheremetyevo.

In fact, I once had to pay a two-hundred-dollar "penalty fee" in order to be allowed to leave. A gentleman wearing an ill-fitting suit—not the uniform of a customs agent—informed me that the stamp on my visa, although present, was not precisely in the spot where it should be. It would cost me two hundred dollars to fix it. Not deemed relevant was the fact that Russian customs agents had put the stamp on the visa in the first place.

After I explained that I was a guest cosmonaut in their country training for a cooperative spaceflight, the fee remained unchanged at "two hundred bucks," as he put it. An appeal via phone by a Russian general from Star City fell on deaf ears. Evidently, this airport operation was outside the influence of the military. Nor could a representative from the U.S. embassy, speaking directly to the agent by telephone, sway him. His operation was obviously outside the government. He ignored them all; he wanted two hundred bucks; and, oh yes, he informed me, you can pay by credit card.

Two minutes prior to departure, furious but with no options, I gave in to his demand. I was hurriedly ushered into a back room where four or five Mafia or former KGB or whoever they were—all big, suspicious-looking men who appeared more than capable of taking me out—accepted my credit card payment of the blackmail money. One of the men, using a walkie-talkie, talked directly to someone in the airplane and told him or her to hold the plane.

This incident generated a letter from the U.S. embassy in Moscow suggesting that if the Russians want to join the civilized world, then they had better start acting as such in their dealings with Western guests in their country. I doubt that the letter had any effect.

FINALLY free from customs and empty-handed, we were greeted by our Russian driver who would take us to Star City. NASA had permanently hired him to transport astronauts and their gear back and forth. He spoke no English. My five weeks of Russian had paid off, though, as I was able to determine that his name was Ephim and that he had something to do with *cosmos* (space). So, having no option, I entrusted our lives to this stranger. I told him *nyet,* no baggage, then we tromped our way through the foot-deep snow to his Chevy Astro van. The cold of a Russian winter reawakened me and provided me with my third wind, but after five minutes of driving, the warmth of the heater in the van, the inability to converse with the driver, and the twenty-one hours of sleepless travel overtook me and

I passed out. An hour later I was shaken awake by Ephim. He escorted Kathryn and me to our quarters: an apartment in a three-story, rectangular building unattractively named the Prophylactorium.

We awoke twelve hours later, sweating. Although it was winter, the room felt like a sauna. There was no thermostat or valve on the radiator to control the heat in the room. Apparently, every room gets the same amount of steam flowing through the radiator, and if the room is situated near the beginning of the steam pipeline, well, one gets lots of heat. I got up and opened a window to regulate the temperature.

Awake, we took a look around. The living quarters consisted of a bedroom, a living room, and a bathroom. The furnishings were gaudy, but adequate. The bathroom looked like an institutional bathroom—the walls and floor lined by aqua-blue tile squares, dingy along the grout lines. The building had been built in the seventies, using American money, as a place to house American astronauts during the first Russian-American joint space venture, the Apollo-Soyuz program. It appeared that not much had been done to modify the building or its furnishings since then.

In the summer and even into early winter, the place proved to be mosquito-infested. Because there were no screens on any of the windows, we would sleep at night with the windows closed in spite of the summer heat. But dive-bombing mosquitoes still attacked. I would get up at least three times a night to stage a counteroffensive. Armed with a fly swatter and temporarily blinded by the overhead light, I would try to locate and then take out the particularly pesky mosquito that insisted on buzzing near my ear. We eventually concluded that the mosquitoes lived in greater density inside the ducts of the building than outside the building, so we opted to leave the windows open with the hope that the mosquitoes would fly *out*. We eventually resorted to sleeping with a mosquito net draped over our bed.

THROUGHOUT Star City and the Moscow region the people speak only Russian. Even my language teacher spoke no English, although she could blurt out a word now and then if I became stuck on the Russian word. The signs in the stores are handwritten in Russian. The prices of the goods were not, however, displayed in rubles but in American dollars. Because the ruble became worth less and less on an almost daily basis—five thousand rubles to the dollar when I first arrived—shopkeepers opted to list the cost of items in stable dollars. Then, at the checkout counter, the dollar cost was converted to rubles and the payment was made in rubles. This system proved easier for the shopkeepers than trying to change the price tags on the goods daily. Soaring inflation was especially disheartening for pensioners who had seen their life savings become worthless in less than a year. Seeing prices in dollars was about the only thing familiar to Kathryn and me.

Most of the residents of Star City were crammed into single-room apartments. Husband, wife, and children lived on top of one another. Our apartment was considered spacious and luxurious by Russian standards. But I could not help myself. I complained. We had been promised Western-style duplexes. The duplexes, already paid for by NASA, were supposed to be ready before we arrived. But like so many things in Russia, what was promised was often not delivered. As weeks passed, then months, we could see that very little was being done to complete the construction of the new housing.

As Kathryn approached nearer to her due date, her condition a direct result of those long, cold Russian winters I contended, we complained even louder. NASA flight surgeons advised us that the Russian hospital facilities were not up to Western standards, and that Kathryn should return to the United States for the delivery. Kathryn was flexible and brave, an angel. She was nervous and concerned, a first-time mother-to-be. We still were not in our promised quarters when she had to depart for Houston at the last possible moment allowed by the airlines for a pregnant woman to travel. I was too swamped with training and could not leave with her. She stayed in Houston for the final months of her pregnancy with astronaut Ellen Baker and her family. I would eventually join her in Houston a few days before the expected due date.

After many delays and excuses from the Russian builders and Star City officials, and after I finally said that I would not return from the States after the baby's birth unless I had a decent living quarters for my wife and newborn, the duplexes were finally completed. After seven months and with Kathryn safely back in the States, I moved into the new rooms.

The experience introduced us to two realities beyond that of the frustration with Russian builders. First, paying the Russians for a service or product in no way guaranteed that the service or product would be delivered. Managers at NASA would discover this fact only after numerous abortive attempts. The worst case concerned buying a Russian-built service module for the upcoming International Space Station. When U.S. representatives traveled to the factory to view the "almost complete" module, contracted for a year earlier, they found an empty shell. They also discovered that the money was gone. (Some say into the pockets of Russian space officials and generals, who were building half-million-dollar dachas outside the gates of Star City).

NASA shuttle-*Mir* management seemed at best reluctant to confront the Russians. Duplexes not built as paid for? No problem. Training materials not provided? Not to worry, our astronauts will figure out a way to get by. This approach by NASA management made the astronauts training in Star City feel that they had been abandoned. No one, not even *our* guys, seemed to want to make our training or living conditions any better.

The astronauts at Star City accepted the fact that we were pioneers and that there would be a lot of rough edges. On the other hand, none of the astronauts in training could believe that no one at NASA seemed interested in making incremental improvements to ensure things would be better for those who would follow us. The shuttle-*Mir* program was advertised as a transition program, preparing the way for later work with the Russians in building the International Space Station together. Many astronauts would have to train in Star City in the future. Why not work to correct the deficiencies now?

Maybe the managers back in Houston gave it their best shot and failed. Maybe someone had tipped them off early on that shuttle-*Mir* was more about politics than space exploration, that the Russians never really needed to deliver, and that we only needed to stay engaged. The astronauts in Star City saw easy fixes to problems that would improve how we did business with the Russians, but we were continually frustrated by NASA's failure to support our efforts.

THERE was a pleasant surprise when I finally moved into our new quarters: a baby's room complete with crib and rocking chair. I sent some E-mail to Kathryn to let her know that her "nest" was ready. Whenever someone from NASA would arrive at Star City, they would drop off a suitcase full of disposable diapers and baby formula. Kathryn and Ellen Baker, back in Houston, were making sure that we would be ready for the baby. Disposable diapers and baby formula could not be readily found in Russia. The baby's room began to fill with books of Russian fairytales and teddy bears as Kathryn's Russian girlfriends dropped by with gifts.

I flew back to Houston a few days before the baby was expected. I had delivered fifty or sixty babies myself, but there is nothing like your own flesh and blood. I was as nervous as any new father.

A beautiful boy kicked and screamed his way into our lives. Kathryn looked absolutely radiant and joyous. We felt blessed.

A day later, I invited cosmonaut Valeri Korzun, with whom I would later fly on *Mir*, to the hospital to see Kathryn and to show off our new son. Valeri was in Houston for U.S. science training. He found the invitation to visit unusual—in Russia, men other than the father rarely visit the mother and her newborn during the week or two that she recovers following delivery. I assured him that it was okay with Kathryn. Valeri was genuinely thrilled to see our boy, and offered a lot of name suggestions from Vadim to Vladamir to, of course, Valeri. But Kathryn declined his choices and decided that a namesake from the hospital itself, St. John, was fitting. We then left the hospital carrying our newborn son, John.

I stayed in Houston for two weeks, then had to fly back to Russia. Kathryn came back after John's six-week medical check-up. As small consolation to her traveling for eighteen hours with the baby, upon arrival at Moscow's Sheremetyevo airport, the baby-loving, machine-gun toting Russians whisked her to the front of the line at customs.

WHILE our new quarters allowed for a good night's sleep, the duplex also set us apart from the Star City natives, who probably resented the new residents who lived in the best housing in town. We tried to live quietly, unpretentiously, inviting only close Russian friends over for visits and an occasional dinner. The demands of my training schedule and of our newborn son also predicated this keep-to-yourselves lifestyle.

On the other hand, our duplex neighbors, the household of British-American astronaut Mike Foale—who was my backup as well as the astronaut who would eventually be named part of the crew to follow my tour on *Mir*—took a different tack. Far more gregarious and with fewer reservations than me about just how far the cooperative spirit between the Americans and Russians could be pushed, the Foales would throw large parties, routinely inviting thirty or forty lesser-known Russian acquaintances from around Star City.

Mike was the perfect diplomat. He must have gotten a better briefing than I did to the effect that the program was not primarily concerned with doing good science or advancing our expertise in space operations, but rather was conceived and thrust down NASA's throat by the Clinton administration as a form of foreign aid to Russia. ("If you can get something for the money, fine, but the money will be given [funneled] to the Russians in any case," must have been the content of a private directive sent from the president and vice president to the NASA administrator.)

Unfortunately, many Russians were not enamored with the idea of cooperating with the Americans living well in Star City while they were crammed into one-bedroom apartments. When the Foales left Star City for the Christmas holiday, their duplex was ransacked. Not only were items stolen, but upholstery was slashed, food was removed from the freezer and left out to rot, candle wax was dripped over the carpets, and toilets were plugged with balls of wadded-up duct tape. The intruders knew the house. They wanted not only the goods; they wanted the Americans out. After we had completed our tours of duty in Russia, Mike would tell me that one of his biggest disappointments was that, despite his efforts, he never really felt befriended by the Russians in Star City. I can attest that outgoing, friendly Mike Foale had given it his best shot.

The break-in was not an isolated event. Two of the NASA-purchased Astro vans were stolen one night from outside the Prophylactorium—within the walled and guarded gates of the Star City compound. Strangely, the incident was quietly accepted by program managers back in Houston. Neither the Russians nor the Americans made a serious investigation of the theft. We were advised to just keep quiet about it; replacement vans would be bought. To those of us living in Star City, our own security became suspect.

Since NASA management seemed more concerned with hushing up any negative news in our Russian partnership than addressing the issue, I let the word leak into the rumor mill—a rumor from Russia could somehow reach America faster than I could find a working telephone—that I desired a permit to keep a weapon in my apartment. Even though I did not own a gun, I thought the ploy would get someone's attention.

Security alarms were wired into our duplex the next week. No gun permits were issued. Rumor had it that the Russian Mafia was involved in the theft of the vans. Within a week, NASA bought two brand-new Chevy Astro vans.

EVEN though it wasn't easy and despite the dive-bombing mosquitoes, the empty shelves in the grocery store, and the ambivalent feelings that some Russians displayed toward us, Kathryn and I had a memorable time living in Star City. There is something pleasant about not having to jump in a car in order to get a gallon of milk and about not having fifty television channels to choose from.

Life was much simpler. Cars and televisions and shopping malls did not crowd out simple pleasures. We found the compound a good place to stroll with our baby, and to have the Russians, all wild about children, echo what we already felt as parents—that our boy was precious and beautiful. We took plenty of walks in the woods. We spent more time talking face-to-face with our Russian friends and less time on the telephone.

Kathryn, much more outgoing and friendlier than I will ever be, made lifelong friends of the Russians. Perhaps she made up for my inability to find many spare moments outside of training and family demands to forge meaningful relationships with the Russians. She was the perfect diplomat. As time passed, we saw many of the barriers between us fall. I personally found many of my misconceptions about the Russians clarified, and I think that many of the Russian misconceptions about Americans were cleared up.

We went on numerous excursions to Moscow. We so thoroughly explored the Moscow region that I honestly do not care if I ever see another museum or art gallery or the spire of a Russian Orthodox church for the rest of my life. I am borscht'd out, but satisfied that I know Russia—not with the superficiality of a tourist, but really, deep down, her frustrations and struggles as well as her beauty. I found that the Russians were not much different than us. They cared about family, friends, and a peaceful existence, much as we did. It was a privilege for us to be their guests.

5

Training, Russian Style

To get to work I would take a five-minute walk from my living quarters to a walled training-center compound within the outer walls of Star City. To pass into the inner sanctum—where the simulators and classrooms were located—I had to show my cosmonaut-in-training card to the military guard stationed at the entrance. This always annoyed me.

It meant nothing that the crumbling concrete block wall surrounding this compound within a compound had gaping holes around the perimeter through which anyone could pass, or that there was nothing inside the training center requiring any additional security. The typically illogical bureaucracy and paranoia that had once smothered the Soviet Union was obviously still alive and well at Russian military bases. I would intentionally try to walk by without showing my ID in an act of defiance of the absurdity of it all. Sometimes the bored and apathetic guard, who knew everyone in town, would let me pass unchallenged.

The training center consisted of four or five large and architecturally unremarkable three-story buildings. In the summer, dandelions bloomed everywhere among the patches of uncut grass. The weeds were, I think, considered flowers. I never walked too close to any of the buildings because, with everyone sneezing from the pollen, I was fearful that another brick might fall from one of the crumbling buildings at any moment.

Entering the classroom building, I would wave to yet another guard sitting in a glass booth in the foyer. The building was always too warm in the summer, and either absolutely freezing or sweltering in the winter. The corridors were universally dark. I would look far down the hall to where a window let in some light, and then walk toward it. It was a rare day when I would not kick loose a sickly green linoleum tile from the deteriorating floors.

The classrooms resembled those found in American schools built in the 1960s—wooden desks placed neatly in rows with a black chalkboard in the front of the room. My instructors expected me to wash the blackboard before each session. There were no audiovisual materials or computers.

Restroom facilities in the building were primitive. Toilet paper could never be found. On a fortunate day, I might discover some torn-up newspaper in a wire basket hanging on the wall of the stall. The odds were against the toilet flushing properly. Eventually I found the "foreigner's bathroom." French cosmonaut trainees of years past must have demanded a civilized commode. I would subsequently go out of my way—walk through a blizzard if I had to—to use this restroom. I even stashed some real toilet paper in a cabinet there.

I should add that most public restrooms in Russia are disgusting—as bad as I have seen anywhere in the world. When touring Moscow, we found that it was less important to be able to find Red Square than to know the location of the handful of marginally acceptable bathrooms.

LEARNING aeronautics, technical systems, and general rocket science is difficult enough when the material is taught in English, but learning the same subjects in Russian becomes a nightmare. A year and a half is a very short time to prepare for a space mission. As a matter of fact, for space shuttle missions the assigned crew is together for at least a year of mission-specific training, and that training occurs only after all of the assigned astronauts have studied shuttle systems for at least two years. While I could draw on my past experience and knowledge of U.S. space systems and operations—the laws of physics and orbital mechanics are no different in Russia than they are halfway across the world—the technical nature of the material being taught in a foreign language made learning a huge challenge.

Instead of listening to American engineers rattle on for hours about shuttle systems as I had during astronaut-candidate training, I was now trapped listening to equally dry Russian experts. As an added complication, I had to first decipher the meaning of the Russian words before trying to deduce how the technical system actually worked. I found myself behaving as a sort of language detective—piecing words together in order to solve the puzzle. I would try to make sense of what was being discussed by combining an understood phrase or two with my prior knowledge of the subject matter.

My only savior was oftentimes an outdated, hand-drawn engineering diagram hanging in the classroom beside the instructor's blackboard. Wiring diagrams, plumbing diagrams, and computer logic charts are universally understandable to engineers and astronauts. During many of my one-on-one lectures, I would block out entirely what the instructor was saying and memorize the diagram hanging on the wall. The diagrams themselves were outdated—showing only the original configuration of the *Mir* and not the myriad modifications made over the then eleven-year lifespan of the station—but so were the lectures. Most of the instructors looked as if they had been teaching the subjects since the time of Yuri Gagarin. They had not kept abreast of the changes on *Mir*. Furthermore, I had the impression that my understanding the material presented was almost irrelevant to the lecturer. What was important was that they got through the canned lecture word for word, just as they had for the past ten years.

What struck me as different about the training sessions, as compared to all of the schooling I had ever received, was the lack of written materials or handouts. All of the material was presented orally. All exams were oral exams. The scarcity of paper in the past, and of copying machines in the present, resulted in a paucity of published training materials. Furthermore, instructors realized that their job security, to a large extent, hinged on their knowledge of a system or component of the space station. Write the information down and their corner on the market would be lost.

For a fledgling language student like myself there is no more difficult way of learning space systems than by lectures delivered entirely in Russian. I would be exhausted after a day of morning language class followed by a series of afternoon technical lectures. Admittedly, I learned very little during the 4:00 P.M. to 6:00 P.M. lecture time-slot, other than how to appear attentive while daydreaming. I spent much of my time asking myself, "What am I doing here?"

My ONLY reprieve during the day was two hours of scheduled daily physical training conducted in the cosmonaut gymnasium. The gym was ancient but adequate. The complex included a swimming pool, sauna, massage therapy room, and a small loft filled with weight machines imported from Eastern Europe. A separate ramshackle building housed a small gymnasium, used mainly to play indoor soccer or badminton. I was assigned a trainer, a smoking forty-five-year-old former athlete with a marine's mentality. He imposed this attitude not upon himself, but on me.

Weight training I enjoyed. Swimming laps in the pool was refreshing. I took up badminton—quite a popular sport in Russia—and found it to be not bad at all. I passed on indoor soccer. Occasionally we would play tennis outdoors on a birch tree–rimmed court. And after a good workout, there was nothing better than a massage by strong-handed Olga.

But this was *cosmonaut* physical training, embellished beyond mere sport. Although I never saw a cosmonaut being tested, all foreigners training for space had to undergo physical fitness testing every month or so. While the cosmonauts sat in the sauna, sometimes accompanied by Star City colonels and generals who usually smuggled in a bottle of vodka for their "workout," I would be doing my fitness test. Timed run, timed swim, pull-ups, push-ups, balance on one foot with eyes closed, sit-ups, and timed leg extensions on the parallel bars. Pedal on a stationery bicycle while a doctor kept an eye on the EKG.

Being a jock, I did not mind the tests. In fact, I preferred them to sitting in the sauna drinking vodka. What I did mind were some of the inner-ear training sessions.

We started on a trampoline. Up and down, up and down. Oh, you want me to do twists? Okay, no problem. Flips next? Are you sure that I will not break my neck? Flips, spins, sit-downs; a whole choreographed sequence was required to qualify me for space. Although

I never really saw how doing flips on trampolines would help me adjust to space, I did feel like a kid again, playing. After the completion of a flip, I would think "I wonder what my old Annapolis friends are doing now? I bet that none of them have flipped on a trampoline in years!"

Next came the strap-you-to-a-circular-ring-and-spin-you training. Faster and faster until the room was a blur. Dives from the high dive and backflips from the low dive into the too-shallow pool. Splash! Qualified for spaceflight!

I drew the line at a series of spinning chair sessions after hearing reports from other victims that the chair not only made everyone sick during the ride, but left them with a dull headache for the rest of the day. I was too busy and too challenged to be saddled with an aching head. The chair torture was scheduled as a series of runs, each one, in theory, desensitizing the subject to motion sickness. The endpoint was a ride without vomiting.

NASA flight surgeons had already determined that the training, done in a similar form years before at NASA for the first groups of astronauts, in no way affected who would suffer from space motion sickness. I told my trainer this fact. I explained that I had *already been* in space and that I felt fine the entire time. Wouldn't it be more fun to play tennis? He remained unconvinced. I finally resorted to a firm "no thanks" whenever he invited me to a spin session, until he gave up on me.

I did agree to a centrifuge run. Since NASA had already paid for it, I figured I might as well do it. Hooked to the end of a long arm, I was strapped tightly to the seat while the capsule began turning in a long arc around the circular-shaped building. Faster and faster I spun as the Gs increased. The G-force was felt primarily in the direction from my chest to my back, so my heart did not have a particularly difficult time keeping blood flowing to my brain. I therefore had no sensation of grayout or pending blackout that I had occasionally felt when pulling Gs in navy jets where the Gs are felt primarily in the head-to-foot direction. I did feel my face flattening, the skin being pulled taut and toward my ears as the Gs continued to build.

I had a cut-off trigger in my hand. As long as I continued to push down on the trigger, the test would continue. Should I lose consciousness and my body go limp, I would loosen my grip and cease pulling on the trigger, which would open a circuit causing the centrifuge to come to a stop. A good design, I thought.

The capsule itself, on the end of the arm, then began to rotate, making for quite a disorienting ride. Shortly afterward, the capsule stopped spinning and the centrifuge began to decelerate. I could feel my face returning to its previous shape, the pile of bricks coming off of my aching chest, and my breathing becoming less labored.

Coming to a stop, a technician opened the door to the capsule and unhooked me from my seat. I got out, feeling wobbly and flushed. As the doctor removed the ECG leads from my chest, I told him, in a small lie, that I felt just fine. He told me that there was nothing unusual in my EKG tracing, test passed. I was relieved that the chest discomfort I had felt was not a heart problem. I reasoned that the pain was probably caused by a bit of costochondritis—as the rib to sternum joint contorted under the strain.

I have never gotten ill in space. For five months on *Mir*, I never took any medication, not even an aspirin. In spite of not spinning in chairs and vomiting in Russia, I did quite well. Maybe the trampoline helped.

AFTER hearing pleas for assistance from every astronaut training in Star City, NASA shuttle-*Mir* program managers finally sent over American trainers to help produce some translated, written materials. The trainers listened to us to determine our needs, then approached the Russians.

The Russians were uniformly uncooperative. The Americans offered to help produce training manuals in collaboration with the Russian instructors. They would write the proposed manuals in dual-language format and distribute them to all cosmonauts and astronauts in training. The work would be done at no expense to the Russians.

The Russian administration in Star City was not interested. Change was not welcome. The goal of helping cosmonauts and astronauts better prepare for a mission was not a shared goal. Making money off the Americans seemed to be the overriding consideration.

The Russians were being paid to train the American astronauts. Each minute of training was paid for. If written materials—clear, understandable, and readable—were made available, we would eventually require less instructor time. Less time, less money. The Russians finally agreed to at least explore the possibility of making training manuals, but insisted that they be paid handsomely for their "vast knowledge and experience."

The material that would be useful was nothing extraordinary. For example, I told a visiting American trainer that it would be helpful for us to have a copy of the engineering diagrams that hung in the classrooms to study at home. He asked his Russian counterpart for permission to photograph the diagrams so that he could work from the photos.

His Russian counterpart welcomed the idea, but told the American that he must first, of course, get permission from the training center management. Management refused the American's request. No one would be allowed to photograph the outdated diagrams. A week later the Russians presented NASA a proposal: They would provide the diagrams, but only after NASA paid an exorbitant five-digit fee. The scenario would be repeated time and again.

We astronauts training in Star City were not naive. We knew, a priori, that Russia would not be an easy or comfortable experience. The program was hastily thrown together under the guise of political expediency. There would be rough edges. None of us in training expected change overnight.

What we did expect was a willingness to at least begin the process of change. We were not pushing for change for our own sake, but for the sake of the multitude of astronauts who would come to Russia, beginning in two years, to train for the planned International Space Station construction missions. We hoped to see incremental improvements being made from the way that visas were being handled at Sheremetyevo to more comfortable, mosquito-free housing and decent handouts to study by.

We also understood that other astronauts back home in Houston did not uniformly share our trailblazing enthusiasm. A number had refused to go to Russia. Many in the future would not be thrilled at the prospect of training in Russia. They would be less suited to tolerate inefficiencies and needless bureaucracy than the present group of volunteers. We all knew that, while we could tolerate the situation presently, the same template could not be applied to less-flexible astronauts two years in the future.

Yet we were unable to convince those who had never been to

Russia, or who had visited briefly—usually staying at a Western-style hotel in downtown Moscow—that big changes needed to be made and that we had better begin making them now.

As stubborn and hardheaded as I was—never too shy to tell NASA shuttle-*Mir* management during their periodic visits to Russia that all was not well—I failed miserably. After I had left NASA, Frank Culbertson, program manager for the shuttle-*Mir* program, told a writer that "I dreaded going to see Linenger. He always complained about how things were not right." It seems to me that a program manager should be interested in what is "not right" with the program he is managing. Astronaut John Blaha really butted heads with Culbertson, saying that Frank, and NASA shuttle-*Mir* management in general, not the Russians, was the biggest problem he faced throughout his Russian tour of duty.

In all fairness, Culbertson's office was undermanned, and he was not granted sufficient authority to get the job done. He also fell victim to advice given to him by people who had no Russian experience and did not understand that Star City and the *Mir* space station were not the Johnson Space Center and the shuttle. Comments made by his deputy manager in interviews conducted at the conclusion of the shuttle-*Mir* program make it apparent that his assistant, in spite of the events that actually took place on *Mir,* never did get it.

When the initial International Space Station crews came to Russia in early 1998, little had changed. They reported back to NASA the same frustrations that we early *Mir* astronauts had described two years before. In fact, they threatened, as a group, to leave Russia—they had become so frustrated in their first few months of dreadfully inefficient training in Star City.

Hearing the news of the near mutiny, I regretted that I had not been even more hardheaded. I felt that I had let my fellow astronauts down. That the lessons we in the trenches learned during the shuttle-*Mir* program translated into little positive change for the International Space Station program, in my opinion, was our greatest failure. To the point of being labeled complainers and whiners, I can only say that the astronauts in Star City tried to create positive change and to move the space program forward. We failed, not from lack of effort, but from being eventually worn down by butting our heads against a brick wall too often.

EVERY six weeks or so judgment day would arrive. A board of ten to
fifteen examiners would grill me for two hours about the space station systems that I had been studying. The examiners included controllers from mission control in Moscow, researchers from the
Russian Biomedical Research Institute, cosmonaut training-center
experts, and engineers from Energia, the company that built the
space station modules.

As I stood before the experts, I was, in fact, being tested not only
on my knowledge of space systems, but also on my Russian language
skills. The questions were not superficial but technical and often per-
tained to subtle points. On responding, I was never sure that I had
answered the question.

When I was done, I was asked to leave the room. I knew that my
answers lacked the sophistication that they would have had were they
spoken in English, so I always stepped out into the hall feeling disappointed in my performance. While waiting for the pass-fail verdict I
could not help but think that the examiners must have considered me
intellectually weak. In fact, the examiners probably got the impression that all American astronauts were not as knowledgeable about
space technology and operations as their cosmonaut counterparts. I
knew better, but the thought of being judged inferior still nagged at
me. After waiting nervously in the hall while the examiners discussed
my weaknesses and my merits, I would eventually, sometimes a half-
hour later, be called to reenter the room for sentencing.

I passed all of my examinations the first time through. But regardless of the examination topic, whether discussing emergency medical
procedures—a subject on which I was more knowledgeable than the
examiners—or thruster fuel composition, after the interrogation I
always felt drained and thankful that I was done.

As WEEKS passed and the training wore on, my language skills
improved. I began to understand the lectures the first time through.
Armed with better language comprehension skills, I found myself
reviewing all of the technical material that had been covered early-
on in the training, but that I had not fully understood. As launch day
approached, the intensity of training increased. More examinations,
more Soyuz simulator sessions, more bottom-of-the-pool spacewalk
training runs. It would be an understatement to say that I was very
busy the last few months of training in Star City.

I had never balanced so many conflicting demands on my time in my life. I actually surprised myself with how many different responsibilities I was able to juggle. But the question that bothered me was: How long could I sustain the tempo? I began to worry that I would be so burned out from all the training that I would have few reserves left to endure the hardships of five months in space.

I completed my last examination on Friday morning. I was blessed by the Russian powers that be and declared ready for flight by four o'clock that afternoon. After nearly two years in Russia, I was to leave the next morning to return to Houston, join the space shuttle crew, fly to Florida, and blast-off into space.

At the duplex, John, now just over a year old, greeted me with outstretched arms. I hugged him and felt the tension of the day drain. Kathryn and John would fly back with me for launch, and then return to Russia alone. Kathryn was working for a subcontractor of NASA helping to coordinate all of the life science experiments that would be conducted on *Mir.* She was also told that if she stayed in Russia during my flight, she would be able to talk to me more often via radio while I was on *Mir.*

As if she needed more concerns to add to the unsettled nature of things, she was also pregnant again—the culprit being those long Russian winter nights. Her due date was two weeks after my scheduled landing. She never complained to me about her situation. She was as brave as any astronaut or cosmonaut. She did, however, let me know that I had better land on time or I would be in big trouble!

I spent the night organizing my training materials and packing up my belongings. I was still awake for John's 2 A.M. feeding and when I heard my driver beep his horn at five the next morning to take us all to the airport. We swaddled John in four or five blankets—it was December 1996 in Russia—and I carried him out to the van. On the drive to Sheremetyevo, I could not stop thinking about how much I loved our little boy, and how much I would miss him.

6

Tomorrow, *Mir*

JOHN LIKED FLYING in airplanes—so much so that he did not want to miss a moment of it. He would inevitably fall asleep just before landing. Kathryn and I took turns entertaining him. We arrived in Houston exhausted.

We would be in Houston for three weeks. I would receive individual refresher shuttle training—primarily emergency drills—along with final cockpit simulator training with the full American Space Shuttle *Atlantis* crew that would take me to *Mir*. The final week would be spent with the crew in medical quarantine. Two days before launch, we would fly down to the Kennedy Space Center, Florida, and remain quarantined in Kennedy Space Center crew quarters until launch.

Arriving at our temporary quarters from the airport at midnight, a message light on the answering machine was blinking. "Jerry, welcome home. Report to building ten for emergency egress training tomorrow morning at o-seven hundred. Hope you had a nice trip."

AFTER two weeks of nonstop training, it was time to go into quarantine. The dietitians—very strict sanitation measures are taken in preparing all crew meals in the final week before launch—had prepared a nice dinner for us to share with our families. After dinner, Kathryn and I spent some quiet moments together. I told her that I loved her and I was sorry that I had to leave right in the middle of her pregnancy. I assured her she could ask for help when she needed it—we had lots of good friends who would do anything for her. I said that I would be just fine—the only thing that worried me was leaving her and John behind.

At the end of the evening, I carried John to his carseat. He reached out for me, but I had to leave him. I stood in the rain as I watched the car pull away, John looking over his shoulder to see why his father was not coming along. I stood out there for a long time, feeling miserable. When I had regained my composure I went back to the crew quarters and joined my crewmates. After a few more days of final preparation the crew flew to Florida for launch.

THE WIND screamed through the convertible as the sun began to rise over the Atlantic. I was alone and feeling restless and reckless. The blacktop road was gray, the hot Florida sun having leached the oil out of its tar long ago. Sand dunes began to blur as I pressed harder on the accelerator.

I was half-hot, half-cold. The heater blew hot air onto my feet, but the saltwater-laden January air was frigid as it struck my upper body. I pulled up the hood of my XX-large, NASA-issued gray sweatshirt and fumbled with the drawstring, but I was too preoccupied dodging potholes and trying to keep the car on the road to tie the knot one-handed. In places the sand, always drifting, always blowing, had won the battle and covered half of the two-lane road. The car was no longer gripping and rolling but gliding and sliding across the loose sand. I felt a familiar, yet unexplainable, sinking sensation deep between my legs. I didn't know and didn't care to know exactly what was going on down there, but I liked the feeling. I liked being on the edge again. I always have.

The astronaut beach house, standing alone and barely visible from the road, whizzed by on the right. I let off the gas pedal and started turning the wheel to mimic the darting of downhill ski turns. I weaved back and forth along the road as the speedometer wound down. At fifty miles per hour I slammed on the brakes just to make the ride interesting. I skidded and felt more of that between-the-legs fight-or-flight sensation. I turned into the skid, like anyone raised on the icy roads of Michigan would, and the car partially recovered. I was half off the road with the left wheels spinning wildly in the sand.

At thirty miles per hour I was in a spin. By the time I stopped I was just about facing in the direction I wanted to go—back toward the beach house—and just about feeling the way I wanted to feel—adrenaline spent.

If I were a king, I would live at a place like the astronaut beach house rather than a palace. A solitary hermitage, it was built in the late fifties, and is the only building along a ten-mile stretch of the Cape Canaveral beach. Its neighbors are launch pads and satellite-tracking antennas—most of them outdated, no longer used, and rusting. The exterior wood siding of the hideaway beach house is mottled, worn, and long ago stripped of its paint by the sandblasting it takes from the onshore Atlantic breezes. The wood siding looks more like driftwood than lumber and is falling apart nicely.

There is no air conditioning, the floors creak, and the walls only hold out part of the wind. Sand permeates everything. Beyond the house, while seagulls are flying and diving, endangered-species turtles show Sisyphian determination to crawl and mate. The sound of the surf provides constant background music. Despite its missing boards and occasionally protruding and rusting nails, the back deck is this venerable beach house's most-used area.

The dunes block the view of the house from the road. I drove slowly and carefully, but still missed the turnoff, which was not a road but more of a sandy path leading to the beach house. I continued to back up all the way to the side door, spinning my wheels in the sand. What the heck! What can anyone do to me? It's 5:30 in the morning. I am leaving for space tonight aboard the Space Shuttle *Atlantis* . . . well, actually, tomorrow, at 4 A.M. And besides, no one is around.

Although the probability was slight that any security person would show up, I relished the thought. Suppose a security guard had seen my driving or believed me to be an intruder.

For the entire week before launch, I had been quarantined from other germ-carrying people. No one, with the exception of medically screened primary contacts, was supposed to get within twenty feet of me. While I could drive the car alone, I could not stop to get gasoline or to pick up a bite to eat. I had to warn the approaching security guard to stay away from me. But even at a distance, what could the security guard have done to me? Could he or she have put me in jail? Held up the launch of the Space Shuttle *Atlantis?* Risk an international incident because the American astronaut did not show up to join his Russian crewmates aboard the space station *Mir?* What was the most this security guard could have done to me? The guard would simply have had to deal with me when I returned from space—in five months!

SITTING alone on the beach, I recalled the time my brother Ken came to visit me in Russia. Ken and I care about each other a lot, and we know we can depend upon each other. Despite the fact that we are brothers, we are different. Ken likes a certain amount of stability and security in his life and, in that regard, is perhaps like most people. He lives close to where we were born, got married early on, and has four kids. He is a homebody who vacations every year on Mackinac Island, Michigan—no cars, only horses—an ideal place for a bicycle built for two. But *every year?* Well, he is just not all that adventurous. He would hate my life, and I would not be happy living his life.

While Ken was visiting me in Russia, I decided that he and I should explore the Russian woods on mountain bikes. Following a whirlwind tour of Moscow, we returned to Star City in late afternoon. He was ready to nap; I was ready for a workout. I convinced him to delay his rest for a pleasant excursion into the surrounding woods. "Just a little ride," I assured my rather sedentary brother. Mounting two NASA-supplied bicycles, we left my apartment.

What I had in mind was not a slow ride down well-marked roads, but rather a mountain bike adventure. Concrete walls and barbed wire surround the Star City cosmonaut training complex. But no matter. Upon reaching the wall we heaved the bikes over it and crawled under the surrounding barbed wire on our bellies. We then bicycled through birch and pine woods over narrow paths or by blazing our own trail. We ate wild strawberries along the way, and I was having a grand time. Ken only seemed to tolerate it.

As darkness fell I continued to pedal vigorously, weaving through the shadowy figures of the trees, purposely going fast to give Ken the idea that he might lose me if he did not keep up the pace, speedy enough to feel that I might just run smack into a tree. As we biked through the underbrush of an ancient trail, we came upon a deserted complex of two or three aging buildings. I pedaled more slowly until I brought my bicycle to a halt and signaled to Ken to do the same.

I turned to him and gravely warned him that for the next few minutes of our journey, we had to be quiet. "Don't say anything Ken. We have crossed into an old KGB base and, if we get caught, I am not sure what they would do to us. Probably the gulag." I also told him that we were "sorta lost," and asked him what his best guess was as to the way back. I knew he was clueless as to our whereabouts, but I enjoyed asking him the question nonetheless, just to see the bewildered look on his face.

Ken didn't really know whether he should believe me, but the prospect of his being lost in the middle of a country whose people did not speak English and who were, very possibly, still not that fond of Americans, was unsettling enough for him to decide not to take any further risks. He would keep quiet, and when the tires of his bicycle broke twigs in the course of that twilight journey he grimaced, not because he might be thrown head-over-heels from the bicycle, but because breaking twigs on the path could possibly alert the KGB assassins.

We finally escaped from the woods and I breathlessly exclaimed, "Ah, we made it!" Having not dared stop for fear of falling behind, Ken, panting heavily, rode up to me.

"Ken, you have a flat tire," I said in dismay.

Ken looked down at the wilted spokes of his bike and replied, "Oh that's what the problem was. This bike has been riding pretty rough for the last ten minutes or so." In true "gotcha" brotherly fashion, I could not help but snicker, just a little. Ken vowed he would never ride with me again.

While I never admitted it to Ken, we were, in fact, lost, and we were, indeed, inside a Russian military base. But for me such excursions were nothing new.

In fact, jaunts of this type would occur often for me after a serious evening's study of the "conspects," my *Mir* training manuals. The conspects were written entirely in Russian, and they were boringly, monotonously, dry. They were also technically outdated. And, because the conspects were printed on paper of very poor quality, and because individual editions were copies of copies, the conspects, in addition to being tedium incarnate, were also barely readable.

The conspects were, however, the only source of material available on the space station's life support, guidance and control, electrical, and you-name-it systems. Therefore, night after night, I had no choice but to try to decipher and study these manuals.

To motivate myself through the evening's study hours, I would tell myself that I could go cross-country skiing only after memorizing, for example, the configuration of the electrical wiring. Consequently, many nights, after long hours of studying, I would put on my favorite extra-extra-large-with-lots-of-holes University of Michigan hooded sweatshirt and head out for some midnight cross-country skiing in the woods. I would ski forty-five carefree minutes or so, not particularly concerned about the direction I was taking. Then I would try to determine the way back home. Sometimes I would get so lost in the unfamiliar forests that I would not get home until three in the morning.

But during these nighttime ventures I made a few worthwhile discoveries. I learned, for example, that it is best not to take shortcuts over half-frozen lakes. It was a conclusion to which I quickly came after falling through the lake ice one night. I emerged waist-deep in slush, shivering, and barely able to lift my seemingly concrete-laden legs out of the clinging sludge.

I discovered that, in this part of the world, dressing in layers—a number of layers—was best. During my own lifetime I have braved many raw, snowbound Michigan nights. But Russian winters, especially at midnight, are brutal in a way Michigan winter nights never were. As I skied through the Russian woods during the late night and early morning hours, I came to understand why the vastly superior armies of Napoleon and Hitler were decimated less by opposing Russian soldiers than they were by the fierceness of the bitter Russian cold.

But in the glacial woods of Russia I had also learned much more about myself. I learned that I liked the feeling of being lost in the woods, of being alone and waist-deep in slush, and of scratching my face on unseen branches as I skied recklessly downhill in the midnight darkness. It reinforced what I had always felt: that I liked living on the edge and relying on myself to work my way out of difficulties. And in the frigid air of a clear, snow-laden winter night, it occurred to me that I was the right kind of person to go out in the frontier of space, to go out and live on *Mir,* and I would do okay once I was out there.

AT THE NASA beach house in Florida, I unlocked the rusty padlock of the door to the storage area. Though unlocked, the door still required a solid yank to separate its rusted hinge parts. The warped door swung open, its lower edge scraping along the concrete. Partially hidden behind an old-fashioned, eight-foot surfboard that was probably used by the "Original Seven," or at least by the "Next Nine," stood a rust-colored bicycle. Or more accurately, spokes, tubes, handlebars, all were solid rust. The chain was corroded.

I pushed the surfboard aside, found a bicycle pump and some WD-40, and went to work. Miraculously, the balloon tires still held air and the rusted chain loosened its frozen grip. After ten minutes or so, I clanked onto the road, leaving a trail of rust flakes behind me, and pedaled over to the Titan launch pad. I ignored the Keep Out signs, and got up close to the Titan rocket, which, towering above me like a skyscraper in the middle of a field, was apparently ready to go.

By getting close to the rocket, standing at its base, and looking up, I could truly appreciate its size. The Titan is huge. The shuttle is bigger yet. That it takes millions of pounds of thrust just to get these rockets to move should be of little surprise.

In technical terms, the shuttle stands 184 feet tall from the base of the solid rocket boosters (SRBs) to the tip of the external tank (ET). Gross weight at liftoff of the shuttle stack (two SRBs, one ET, and one orbiter) is about four and one-half million pounds. The orbiters themselves—*Atlantis, Columbia, Discovery,* and *Endeavor*—weigh 200,000 pounds apiece. Each solid rocket booster generates 3.3 million pounds of thrust, 6.6 million pounds of thrust combined. The three main engines on the orbiter each generate an additional 393,800 pounds of thrust to supplement the SRBs and to keep the shuttle accelerating after the SRBs drop off at the two-minute mark of the flight.

In human terms, and simply put: the shuttle, like the Titan, is a monster. When the supercooled liquid oxygen and liquid hydrogen are filling its tanks in the hours before liftoff, the shuttle seems almost alive as vapors billow out of vent lines and, like an awakening dragon, it seems to moan. Standing at its base is a humbling experience. One almost feels compelled to kneel down and worship the thing.

On launch morning, when I would climb out on the scaffolding on the pad at the 195-foot level to enter the orbiter, I would be so high up that I would have a grand view of the entire cape and part of the Florida coastline. It will be reassuring, I thought to myself, to see the steady stream of cars heading out to the causeway to be there for the launch, to see our crew off, to witness history in the making, and, perhaps, to say some prayers for us.

Still traveling by means of that rickety old bicycle, I clunked back to the beach house. By now the sun had fully risen. "Red sky in morning, sailors take warning; red sky at night, sailors delight," ran through my mind. Scrutinizing the horizon, I could not detect even a smidgen of red in the blue, clear morning sky. "Looking good to go," I thought. I bent down, swept away stray spiderwebs, and gulped some water directly from the outdoor spigot. Then I headed off for a run on the beach.

The waves were low and regular, not too challenging to dodge as they lapped up on the shore. In and out I weaved, trying to stay close to the surf but not get caught by it. "Mary and Molly and someone and May went down to the beach one day to play. La la la la la la la la la lee, it's always yourself you find at the sea," I sang, and thought it accurate. Enjoy the things of the earth while you still can, Jerry. Five months will be a long time. God, I will miss running, the fresh air, riding a bicycle. I'll be trapped and cooped up—like a prisoner in a cell.

After my run on the beach, and deceived by my revved-up metabolism and sweat, I decided that a swim was appropriate. I stripped naked, entered the surf at full speed ahead, with knees pumping and legs jumping incoming waves, all the while hoping not to step on the back of a stingray. With the water above my knees, I did a backward flop over the next incoming wave. "You are alive!" the frigid water screamed at me. "Alive!"

I washed myself, swapping the salty sweat for the even saltier Atlantic Ocean water. Without my triathlon wetsuit, and unable to exhale fully because of the cold, I decided against an offshore ocean swim. I headed back toward the shore and dried off, using my sweaty T-shirt, this time exchanging the saltwater droplets for my own salty sweat once again. Along with the NASA T-shirt, I put on the rest of my clothes.

On the beach directly in front of the beach house I found a shovel, a sandpit, and a few logs. Was it yesterday or a week ago that someone had prepared for a beach fire, only to abandon the idea? I grabbed the shovel, piled up a mound of sand, and began sand sculpting. The sand was wet and good for packing. I topped off the figure of a spacesuit-wearing astronaut with a clump of seaweed for hair. It felt good getting my hands dirty, molding the sand with my fingers.

I GOT BACK into the convertible and headed for crew quarters. Although it was only eight in the morning, it was time to go to bed. In order to be alert at liftoff, and to assure that our biological clocks would synchronize with the sleep-wake cycles of those waiting for us aboard the orbiting *Mir*, our crew was sleep shifting, which meant that we were staying up at night under banks of bright lights and sleeping during the day in windowless rooms.

This time, I drove like a law-abiding citizen. I arrived at the fastidiously clean, but stark astronaut crew quarters building, opted to run up the backstairs instead of using the elevator, entered my spartan room, and showered.

Clean and lying in bed, I reflected upon the fact that my journey to *Mir* would begin tomorrow. It would begin with over six million pounds of thrust—a virtual volcano exploding underneath me. I would be accelerating from zero to 17,500 mph, twenty-five times the speed of sound, in just over eight minutes.

Content with these thoughts, I slept soundly.

7

Crew Quarters

THE ALARM WOKE ME from a deep sleep. I put on my crew shirt and headed down the hall to breakfast. In the old days, the astronauts would typically eat steak and eggs. I settled for three glasses of fruit juice: cranberry juice followed by cranberry-apple juice followed by plain apple juice. I felt a little guilty about disappointing the friendly kitchen staff, who enjoyed doing their part in preparing astronauts for launch, but I stuck with the clear liquid diet.

There was a good reason for me to consider a light breakfast on launch-day morning. Immediately after entering earth orbit, many astronauts and cosmonauts, about half of them, experience various degrees of nausea. Of those not feeling well, 10 to 20 percent will vomit.

No one is immune to space motion sickness, and who it will strike is difficult to predict. Even the fighter pilot who never felt nauseous when flying a supersonic jet inverted or when performing a series of loops and spins may nevertheless vomit heavily in space. Other astronauts, who never particularly liked aerial acrobatics, might feel fine in space. The only reliable predictor of how well a person will do seems to be how that astronaut felt during his or her previous flight. If they were unaffected during the first flight, they will probably feel fine during their subsequent flights. As for astronauts who became ill during their first flight, their symptoms during their second mission will sometimes, but not always, be milder. Seldom will they be cured completely.

Given the tendency toward nausea and vomiting, astronauts always come prepared. We carry a rather nifty space vomit bag in the front leg pocket of our spacesuits. The bag is equipped with a quick-seal band to prevent any added contents from floating out into the spacecraft, a built-in cloth flap to wipe the victim's lips, and a Velcro fastener to help temporarily secure the bag to the bulkhead after use.

By the second day in earth orbit practically everyone feels better—either on his or her own or with some help from the crew doctor. As designated crew doctor, I would first give my suffering crewmate oral anti-nausea medication. If ineffective—which it usually was—I would administer the injectable form of the drug. It makes for quite a scene: me floating after an astronaut who, with pants lowered, waits to get stuck with a needle in the backside—not the heroic picture of space-traveling adventurers that one usually conjures up when thinking of astronauts in space.

The other advantage of the clear liquid diet, besides an empty stomach, is a relatively empty intestine. Relieving oneself can be a somewhat time-consuming and complicated procedure in space. I know of some astronauts who eliminate bulky foods from their diet for up to a week before launch in order to minimize the number of times that they will have to use the space commode.

Urinating is not particularly difficult. When the need arises, the astronaut simply grabs the urine-collecting hose, hooks their personal funnel to its free end, turns on a fan to create some suction, opens a valve, and proceeds. The urine is collected in a waste tank. But defecating in space is a much more demanding and time-consuming process. Not all astronauts are successful on their first try. In fact, because of the rather strange environment and also perhaps because the bowel does not at first function normally with the intestines floating inside the weightless astronaut, many come out of the middeck toilet area mumbling, "Another misfire."

The astronaut in need of serious relief enters the toilet area, pulls the accordion-like door shut, and sits all propped up on a cold, high commode. The throne is equipped with spring-loaded thigh-hold-down bars—a good seal is critical to success—as well as footholds.

The restraining devices also serve to keep the user from being thrust away from the toilet when what could tactfully be described as digestive gas thrusters are fired.

In the center of the seat is a four-inch, covered orifice. To the right of the seat is a stick shift. When it is shifted forward, the sliding cover over the hole opens. Alignment by the user is critical. After the job is complete, the stick shift is moved back to its original position, closing the orifice. The toilet vents odors to the vacuum of space; tissues are placed in a different wet-trash compartment similarly vented.

It feels strange sitting all propped up on the throne. The commode is cold. Quiet conversations can be heard coming from the adjacent middeck, and any noise that one might generate can be downright embarrassing. Many a first-time user is forced to call "misfire," move the stick shift back to the original position, and try another time.

AFTER breakfast, photographers came into the dining room and took the traditional launch-day photos of the crew. We smiled, even though it was the middle of the night. We then went back into our rooms and began putting on our cooling garments. The cooling garment bears a strong resemblance to traditional long johns, but the fabric is laced with a weave of plastic tubing. Water circulates through the tubing to keep us cool inside the suit. Thus fashionably attired, we made our way down the hall to the suit-up room.

Ready to begin the ritual of suiting up, two suit technicians greeted me. Everything is done deliberately and methodically, much as a knight of old might have put on his armor before heading off to battle. All of my personal gear—parachute-lanyard cutting knife, sunglasses, vomit bag, survival radio, signal mirror, and other survival gear—had been neatly arranged on a table. The suit techs and I triple-checked every item to make sure that no item was missing and that everything was in good condition. The techs then stuffed the gear into the pockets of my launch-and-entry space suit.

I then climbed into the orange suit. The spacesuit is intentionally designed to be too orange, too bright. Should the crew have to parachute into the ocean because of a shuttle rocket engine failure during launch, the less-than-subtle color is designed to increase the odds of search-and-rescue crews finding us bobbing in the ocean. Once I was zipped up in the suit, we began pressurizing the suit to test its airtightness.

After passing the leak test, I deflated the suit by opening a pressure-release valve built into the suit's chest area. The techs then helped me smooth out wrinkles in the undergarment. Wrinkles create uncomfortable hot spots when lying flat on one's back in the shuttle during the two-hour countdown period prior to launch.

Lumbering along in our oversized orange suits and bearing a remarkable resemblance to Pillsbury Dough Boys, we made our way down the hall to the elevator. The crew quarters staff lined the hallway waving good-bye and wishing us well. We entered the elevator at the end of the hall, descended two floors, and marched out single-file toward the astronaut van that would drive us to the launch pad and to the Space Shuttle *Atlantis*.

Flashing cameras and a wildly enthusiastic crowd of reporters lined the walkway to the van. The reporters were stacked four-deep behind the rope that kept them separated from our quarantined crew. There were so many flashing cameras that I had to feel my way blindly into the Astro van. These reporters, representing the media from all over the world, were cheering as if we had just won the Super Bowl. They were obviously as excited about the night launch as I was. It felt good knowing that they, and the world they represented, were pulling for us.

While driving out to the launch pad I was filled with strong, but mixed, emotions. The months of arduous training were over, and I was about to head off to work. I felt excited and pumped up, but, at the same time, I also recognized that the venture ahead was not without risk to my own life. I was intoxicated by the special thrill of space-flight anticipation, but I also thought about my pregnant wife, our one-year-old son, and family and friends from Michigan. More than a thousand strong, they were standing on the causeway a few miles away praying for my safety.

Along the route to the pad, Kennedy Space Center employees waved wildly at the van, giving us the thumbs up, and experiencing vicariously the thrill of space flight. Despite the chill and darkness of the early morning hour they were out there, eager for launch. They were the men and women who had put together that tremendous rocket sitting on the launch pad. Our lives depended on their competency. The countdown had begun and I could feel their pride. I wanted to represent them well.

Looking out the windshield of the van I could see the shuttle stack—orbiter, external tank, and solid rocket boosters—sitting on the launch pad. Arranged in a circle around the pad, xenon lights brilliantly lit the stack against the backdrop of a dark, cloudless night. *Atlantis* was on display. What a rocket! "Can it get any better than this?" I thought.

We drove by the final security checkpoint. The security guard rendered us his sharpest salute. The Astro van climbed the gentle rise of the concrete structure that forms the base of the launch pad, and stopped just short of the pad superstructure. We ambled out of the van. The elevator, which is built into the middle of the scaffolding, then lifted us up to the 195-foot level where the hatch to *Atlantis*'s cockpit was located.

We had a six-person crew, all of us Americans. We boarded the shuttle two at a time. I happened to be in the middle group of the entering crew, so I had time to prophylactically relieve myself of my fruit-juice breakfast at the crude but workable 195-foot-level head. During the countdown on my first flight, bad weather had delayed the launch. I can attest to the fact that it is impossible not to have a tremendous urge to urinate when your legs are elevated above your head for three hours. Whenever one of the crew began to whistle softly, we all knew what he was up to. And no, we do not wear diapers; we wear MAGs. To be sure, no *Right Stuff,* red-blooded American astronaut would admit to wearing a diaper, so the personal equipment specialists came up with a different name—MAG. By now, no one remembers what the first two letters of the acronym stand for, but the G stands for garment. Once in orbit, any wet MAG is removed, placed into a sealable plastic bag, and stowed in the wet trash compartment for the duration of the mission.

After waiting twenty minutes—during which time astronaut John Grunsfeld and I enjoyed looking out over the nearly endless stream of headlights weaving their way over the causeway to view the launch—I was called into the White Room located at the end of the gangplank hugging *Atlantis*. Three technicians—two men and a woman—were there to assist me with getting into my parachute harness. They triple-checked everything. I told them that I would see them next summer. It was January, and although the shuttle would return in ten days, I would not be on the return leg. I would instead be delivered to *Mir* to join two cosmonauts who had launched from Russia in a Soyuz capsule months earlier. The technicians told me that they didn't know how I could do it—five months aboard *Mir*—but that they were real proud of me. "Good luck, Captain Linenger." After shaking hands, I crawled on my hands and knees through the hatch and into *Atlantis*.

Another astronaut, Pam Melroy, dressed not in a spacesuit but in a clean-room "bunny suit," greeted me inside *Atlantis*. The bunny suit resembles a surgeon's garb and is worn by anyone working inside the orbiter as a precaution against contaminating it. Pam had been working inside *Atlantis*, making sure that all switches were properly configured. She greeted me with a smile and led me to my seat.

Being careful not to step on any of the switches in the vertical spacecraft, I walked on what would be the aft bulkhead but was now the floor. As I pulled myself up into my seat, Pam handed me my communication cable and oxygen hose, which I plugged into my suit.

Once secured to my parachute and fully strapped into the seat, I closed my visor and began communication checks. I responded to calls from two people at launch control at the cape and then with mission control in Houston. There, fellow astronaut Kevin Kregel was working as capcom, the capsule communicator, the person through whom all controllers funnel their instructions to the crew.

Kevin and I knew each other well. We were both members of the Hogs and had trained together frequently. It was reassuring to hear his voice.

"Houston, MS four. Good morning, Kevin. How do you read?" I asked.

"Loud and clear, Jerry. How about me?" Kevin replied.

"Loud and clear, going to *Mir*," I ad-libbed.

"Good luck, Jerry. We're all pulling for you."

Communication check completed, I reopened my visor and squirmed to get comfortable in the rock-hard seat. After the entire crew was properly situated, Pam removed the remaining ground-use only items, such as switch covers and protective plates, from the orbiter. She then wished us all good luck and gave astronaut Marsha Ivins and me a friendly peck on the cheek. Shortly afterward, I heard the side hatch closing.

Everyone on the pad cleared out. No rational being wants to be too close to a rocket that takes off with more than six-and-one-half-million pounds of thrust. Besides the crew, the closest people to the rocket at launch are a bare-bones rescue crew stationed more than a mile away, buried in a bunker. We were abandoned to our fate.

Alone in *Atlantis,* we lay flat on our backs, uncomfortable and confined, during the two hours until liftoff. During the wait, technicians at the launch control center at the cape were busy making their final adjustments, but they only occasionally needed to call the crew to move a switch or read an indicator. I closed my eyes and rested.

The two hours passed quickly and my MAG remained dry. When we got the call for "APU [auxiliary power unit] start" at T-minus-five minutes, the adrenaline began to flow. At T-minus-two minutes, the call came to "close and lock visors, initiate oxygen flow," followed by, "have a good flight, *Atlantis.*" I let out a sigh of relief. All was well and we were heading to space. I rechecked the position of my restraining harness, closed my visor, switched on my oxygen, and braced for liftoff. Ten, nine, eight . . .

8

Off to Work

WHEN THE SPACE SHUTTLE boosters light for liftoff, there is an explosion of so much raw power that it is almost impossible to comprehend how we can actually funnel and direct that energy. Although Kathryn and John are located three miles away, and my invited guests are standing seven miles away on the causeway leading to the cape, they still feel the awesome power of the shuttle launch. They are overwhelmed first by the blinding light, then hit by the heart-pounding wall of sound seconds later. Their sense of pride in country merges with their nervous concern for the crew onboard. Tears fill their eyes and, as if they were at a football game and cheering for the home team, some of them begin to chant "Go, Jerry, Go!"

Miles away from the actual launch, my friends not only command a view of the liftoff, but actually experience the forces of the launch, which, quite literally, shakes their insides. Sitting within *Atlantis* itself, we are really rocking and rolling!

At T-minus-six seconds the three main engines ignite in quick succession and the whole space shuttle stack—the two solid rocket boosters, the external fuel tank, and the orbiter *Atlantis*—sways nose-down forward and then backward again. At T-minus-zero the shuttle is once again in a near-perfect vertical position with its nose pointing toward the sky. The two solid rocket boosters ignite.

Simultaneous with the ignition of the boosters, small explosive charges free the eight hold-down bolts (located on the aft skirt of the boosters) from the mobile launch platform. (Months later, after I returned to earth, the Kennedy Space Center launch team sent me one of the severed nuts as a souvenir of my launch. That nut was about eight inches in diameter and made of solid metal.) Once released from the hold-down bolts, the enormous thrust of the boosters merges with the powerful thrust of the three main engines, and the shuttle is free to fly. Nothing can hold it back! We explode off the pad, leaping into the sky.

I get slammed into my seat and, within seconds, I am flying upside down. The shuttle, after clearing the pad, rolls so it is inverted as it begins its journey up the East Coast. It is as if I were in the middle of a herd of charging buffalo. For the first two minutes of flight, with the massive boosters firing away, I also feel as if the shuttle would go wherever it wanted. Along merely for the ride, we were following the stampeded herd.

Inside the orbiter *Atlantis,* it feels as if the computers were having a hard time keeping the shuttle moving in the intended direction. When the shuttle hits the edge of the trajectory envelope—an imaginary tunnel in which the shuttle must fly in order to end up at a precise location in space at engine cutoff—there is nothing subtle about the spacecraft's steering. Abruptly and roughly, the crew gets whipped back into a different direction. And if the winds aloft are unusually strong, the crew gets jerked around even more severely.

The shuttle's two thousand switches are tough to make out as the whole vehicle rattles and shakes violently. To an astronaut, these switches represent two thousand ways to screw up. Reading the labels by the switches is almost out of the question because of the vehicle's shaking. Therefore, before changing the position of a switch, astronauts do their best to get their hand up to the proper lever, and then, when they think that they are fingering the appropriate switch, they yell to the person next to them to "verify." Only after both astronauts agree that it is, indeed, the proper switch does the astronaut proceed to throw the lever. Unintentionally turning off, for example, the main engine power switch could be the last mistake the crew ever makes.

At about one minute into the flight, the vehicle goes through maximum dynamic pressure (Max Q), which simply means that if the wings of the shuttle are going to fall off, they will probably do so at this time. At Max Q, the atmosphere is still thick and resistant and the vehicle speed is still increasing. The main engines throttle back automatically to temporarily ease the load on the structure of the vehicle, then the engines smoothly run back up to full speed.

On the space shuttle, full speed is actually 104 percent–rated thrust. How one can run an engine at more than 100 percent never made a lot of sense to me, either. But the bottom line is that the shuttle's main engines turned out to be more powerful than the designers thought they would be. Consequently, we can actually run the main engines at 4 percent greater thrust than what was originally thought to be full speed ahead. And we do!

At two minutes into flight, the solid rocket boosters are fully spent. Bang! Separation thrusters fire to separate the boosters from the external fuel tank. The two boosters briefly continue coasting upward, and then fall back toward the ocean. As the boosters near the surface of the ocean, parachutes deploy to break the impact of the booster's fall. The solid rocket boosters splash into the ocean about 140 miles down-range from the launch site, are recovered by specially designed recovery ships, and are later refurbished and used again.

Onboard the shuttle, we always breathe a sigh of relief after the boosters are released. A leaking O-ring in one of the solid rocket boosters was the cause of the *Challenger* disaster, and, though redesigned, they are still powerful and dangerous elements. The crew is glad to be rid of the boosters at the appropriate time.

After booster separation, the shuttle ride changes dramatically from a buffalo stampede to one more akin to the glide of an eagle. After six and a half minutes of this pure acceleration, which ultimately results in increasing the speed of the space shuttle to Mach 25 (twenty-five times the speed of sound), the three main engines cut off and the external tank, now depleted of fuel, separates from the orbiter *Atlantis*.

At this point during the mission, I felt the 3-G gorilla leap off of me. The acceleration force had rested heavily upon me for two minutes of powered flight and felt as if two people were sitting on my chest. Not only had the two bodies flown off, but the weight of my own body left me. I began to float from my seat, with only the seat harness holding me loosely in place.

Checklists float. Tethers holding pencils become taut as the pencils float. Loose items that were lost while preparing the shuttle for launch—nuts, washers, an occasional screw—sneak out from nooks and crannies and casually float by us. Until the air filters effectively began operating, the air became dusty. Crew members sneezed.

We then checked on each other to see who was not feeling well and tried to assist anyone who was nauseous. I unstrapped myself from my parachute and harness and began to float freely. Moving slowly and deliberately, and pushing off the seat using only my fingertips, I felt once again the exhilaration of pure freedom of movement in all directions.

My space legs came back quickly. Within a few minutes, I was comfortably moving around the cabin, paying close attention to controlling my body position so as not to inadvertently bump into any switches. Everyone had big smiles on their faces, happy to be back in space.

We had made it safely into earth orbit and breathed a sigh of relief. We all realized that during launch, technology is being pushed to its limits and there is simply no room for human error. Launch is a high-risk enterprise no matter what safety features the engineers design into the launch system and precautions management has taken, no matter how thoroughly and meticulously the rocket has been prepared, and no matter how well-trained and competent the crew. Sitting on top of a bomb is and will always be a dangerous venture.

LAUNCH is dangerous, no doubt. Astronauts know the risks and are willing to accept them. On the other hand, should something go awry, there are some specific actions that the crew can take to save the spacecraft or, short of that, themselves.

For example, suppose the shuttle was already moving at a pretty good clip and suddenly two of the main engines fail. While there might be insufficient velocity to get into orbit, we might still have enough speed to make it to an emergency landing site in Africa or Spain.

A fellow astronaut is prepositioned prior to the launch at these sites. This prepositioned astronaut flies practice approaches to the runway and reports visibility and weather at the site to NASA. If the weather conditions across the Atlantic do not support the landing of the space shuttle should an emergency occur, the launch is delayed, regardless of the weather in Florida.

In another scenario, suppose the engines fail before we have enough oomph to make Africa. We would then be forced to perform a return to launch site (RTLS) abort, and attempt to return the shuttle to Florida. To perform such a maneuver, the shuttle essentially has to do a flip-turn. That is, the crew flips the shuttle, pointing the engines in the direction of movement toward Africa to slow the shuttle down until, at one point, the vehicle actually comes to a brief halt before accelerating back in the other direction.

That brief halt, where we would slow to a zero-velocity point before picking up speed in the other direction, concerns most astronauts. Experience in jets tells us that if one stops, one drops. Although computer models show that such a maneuver is theoretically possible, I do not know of a single shuttle commander who cares to test that theory in a real-life emergency.

While every astronaut is prepared for a possible emergency bailout, so, too, are the search-and-rescue teams, who are on alert status and standing by during all launches. If we were fortunate enough to have survived an explosion that caused a failure, to have bailed out without impacting any part of the shuttle, and to have managed the wind-blast or parachute-opening shock so that we could climb out of the icy North Atlantic Ocean and into our life rafts, then our lives would depend on the search and rescue team's competence.

These shuttle escape options were added to the spacecraft's capabilities after the *Challenger* accident. While offering some hope under certain scenarios, they did not assure survival. Most experts say that even if these new capabilities were in place during the *Challenger* accident, survival of that crew would have been questionable at best. During the *Challenger* solid rocket booster failure, severe G-forces were imparted to the orbiter. Furthermore, the wings-level flight needed to accomplish a bailout was probably not achievable. While the new escape capabilities improve the chances of survival in the case of some failures, the bottom line is that going from zero to 17,500 mph in eight and a half minutes will never be without risk.

BESIDES the risk to the crew, NASA recognized that part of the launch risk could extend to population centers, particularly along the coast. Long ago, NASA considered and essentially eliminated these risks to the population centers. The space shuttle carries explosive devices on the SRBs that can be remotely activated to destroy the shuttle should the vehicle suddenly veer toward the big urban centers of the East Coast during launch.

The U.S. Air Force has the responsibility of tracking the shuttle and pushing the destruct button should the shuttle become uncontrollable. Astronauts always make it a point to stop by and say hello to the air force technicians who exercise control over our fate during a shuttle flight. We show them pictures of our families. We autograph our official NASA portrait photographs for them. We try to make sure that they know us not only as professional astronauts, but also as people. We hope that they have slower than normal reflexes and will not get trigger-happy. We want to stay on their radar screens until the last possible moment.

"Have I ever shown you a picture of my wife and son?"

I ONCE dated a woman whose father was a former marine aviator. He had fought in Korea in the same fighter squadron as did astronaut John Glenn. It was difficult for me to imagine my date's father as he once was, a swaggering U.S. Marine fighter pilot, for now he was stooped and slow moving, almost fragile looking. His remaining hair was thin and gray, his drooping eyelids obscured his now-gray eyes.

One night at his home in Dallas, while waiting for my date to get ready, I came upon his military flight logbook in his study. I thumbed through it until I got to the section recording his combat missions over Korea. As a young fighter pilot, he had recorded a number of sorties and had sometimes described them in fascinating detail. Following one fight, he was forced to limp back to the air base with his low-oil light flickering all the way. After inspecting the plane, it was determined by the ground crew that a bullet had penetrated his plane's oil line.

An asterisk marked another entry. Next to it he had written the word "kill," followed by a question mark. Because I wanted to find out more about that suggestive entry, I left the study and walked into the living room, where my date's father was reclined on his leather lounger and reading the newspaper.

"Excuse me, sir, but I happened across your logbook, and there sure are some interesting entries in it," I said.

He smiled, took the book, and began reminiscing. I asked him specifically about the entry with the question mark next to it. His eyes lost their heaviness and became young again. He spoke with the authority of the marine colonel that he had once been.

Detail by minute detail, he described how he had spotted his North Korean opponent trying to maneuver in on another American fighter plane in his air group. In an attempt to save the life of his marine buddy, the colonel flew in behind the opponent and fired his guns.

"Jerry, after I fired, I saw my bullets penetrating the enemy's fuselage. I saw him begin to fall toward the ground, but then his plane entered a cloud below. At that very moment, my attention was diverted to other enemy fighters, and I had to pull up and get ready for the next guy attacking us. Eventually the North Koreans backed off and we broke away, but, by that time, it was too late to see what had happened to the first enemy fighter. You see, the rules were such that unless we saw an enemy fighter plane hit the ground, we could not call it a confirmed kill. But I know that I got that guy. I should have taken credit for it."

In his voice, in his demeanor, in his sense of conviction, I could see that his actions during that particular military engagement were still very real to him. The dogfight had been a defining moment in his life. In resurrecting its memory, the events of that battle over Korea were as fresh to him, some thirty-five years later, as they had been during the moments in which they had actually occurred. He could recall every detail. In fact, his mind had recorded every split second of that dogfight. He was not really telling me a story—rather, he was replaying the film in his head and simply supplying me with the narrative. The entire time his eyes were focused on the replay, not me. The dogfight was unforgettable.

ON MY deathbed someday, I will probably once again recall my launch to *Mir* aboard *Atlantis*. Launching into space will always be one of the highlights of my life. For eight and a half minutes, I was riding atop an enormous controlled explosion. The acceleration was awesome, the power overwhelming. During those moments of ascent, I was so alert, so pumped up, that my mind recorded the events, not vaguely or haphazardly, but precisely and permanently, split second by split second, breath by labored breath.

The dramatic contrast—one moment pulling three Gs and the next moment losing all sensation of body-weight encumbrance—is so shockingly abrupt that I will never forget that moment of transition from earthling to spaceman. And the joy of knowing that "We made it! I am here in space!" is one that made me scream at the top of my lungs.

PART TWO

OFF THE PLANET

9

Docking a One-Hundred-Ton Space Shuttle

ONCE THE SHUTTLE is established in orbit around the earth, the spacecraft's flight path resembles that of a hula-hoop encircling a basketball. The space shuttle flies around the same orbital ring, again and again. To alter the tilt of this imaginary hula-hoop relative to the basketball is very costly, propellant-wise, because changing the angle of the shuttle's orbital path relative to the earth requires an enormous amount of thrust. It is not so costly, however, to increase the diameter of the loop; that is, the shuttle's orbital path can be adjusted by going up higher, an operation which is achieved by firing thrusters to increase the orbital velocity slightly. While this maneuver requires additional fuel, the fuel cost is much less than that incurred by trying to redefine the tilt of the shuttle's orbit.

Because changing the tilt of the orbit (or, in orbital mechanics terminology, changing the inclination of the orbit) proves impractical once the space shuttle follows a given flight path on a given hula-hoop ring around earth, it is important to launch the shuttle into the proper orbital ring initially. To do so can be especially critical if the goal is to rendezvous with another spacecraft—such as the *Mir* space station.

How is the orbit determined? To make sure that the shuttle will properly rendezvous with the *Mir*, the launch is timed so that the shuttle is propelled into the same tilted ring around the earth in which the *Mir* is traveling, but also slightly behind, and at a lower altitude. With respect to the space shuttle then, the *Mir* flies ahead and higher than the shuttle's initial orbit.

Propellant margins are such that the shuttle can make up the distance should it launch slightly late, but that margin is slim. If, for example, the shuttle is launched more than six minutes late, then it will not have the capability, that is, the fuel reserve, needed to catch up to *Mir*. This particular six-minute launch window is inflexible. Delays beyond six minutes are unacceptable and require a launch attempt on a different day. These hard-and-fast requirements demand that any technical problems uncovered during the prelaunch check be quickly resolved before the start of the launch-window countdown. Obviously, it is also crucial that weather conditions remain acceptable both at the cape and across the Atlantic at the emergency landing sites during this window of opportunity.

LUCKILY, our mission was going like clockwork. We launched on January 12 at 4:27:23 A.M.—on time and exactly as planned. The shuttle performed flawlessly throughout the entire phase of powered flight and left us at the precise location in space desired at main engine cutoff. We were not only in the exact spot in space as planned, but also at the precise speed needed to begin our chase of *Mir*. Over the next two days, we would play catch-up to *Mir* by periodically firing some of Space Shuttle *Atlantis*'s smaller orbital-thruster engines.

During the journey to *Mir*, our crew was busy converting *Atlantis* from a launch vehicle to an orbital laboratory and delivery vehicle. We opened the hatch that led to the Spacehab module, a bus-sized pressurized module that was resting in the payload bay and attached by an airtight tunnel to the middeck of *Atlantis*. Once Spacehab was powered up, we activated materials processing, fluid physics, and fundamental biology experiments. We continued to actively fire thrusters and to monitor our progress toward closing the distance gap to *Mir*. And in spite of the rather harried timeline, we were able to give live media interviews.

The most memorable and humorous interview was conducted by one of my crewmates, John Grunsfeld. John had spent a number of years in Boston as an undergraduate student at MIT. While in Boston, he worked on his car in a self-help garage run by two MIT grads, who later started the popular radio program *Car Talk*. The format of the program entails people calling in with questions about their car problems and needed repairs.

John is an articulate astrophysicist with a calculating sense of humor and an inventive sense of fun. Prior to our launch, he had arranged with the producers of the show to play a prank on the program's two hosts. While we were in orbit, the producers of *Car Talk* patched in John's "telephone call" to the two unsuspecting radio talk show hosts.

John began by complaining to the show's hosts about a government-issued vehicle that was really giving him a hard time. According to John, this government-issued excuse for a vehicle had horrendous gas mileage . . . a real gas-guzzler. Furthermore, this particular vehicle would run extremely rough for the first two minutes—lots of shimmying and shaking—but then would smooth out and ride beautifully. But at after eight minutes into the trip, the darn thing would die completely!

"No," John replied to a concerned query by one of the hosts, "the acceleration was good, very good."

After more concerned bantering on the part of the show's hosts, John began tipping his hand. "No, the vehicle hits pretty good speeds. About 17,500 miles per hour."

At this point, the astonished, and now clearly suspicious, hosts asked, "Who is this?"

Still controlled but smiling, John responded that he was an astronaut onboard the Space Shuttle *Atlantis*.

BETWEEN running experiments and making calls to Boston, we were rapidly catching up to *Mir*. Aboard the space shuttle, we were loaded to the gills. Our plan was to transfer nearly six thousand pounds of logistical equipment to the space station. Supplies included over a thousand pounds of U.S. science equipment, over two thousand pounds of Russian-supplied cargo—food, clothing, and *Mir* repair parts, and 1,600 pounds of water, which we would make.

In the process of generating electricity onboard *Atlantis*, we combine liquid oxygen and liquid hydrogen in fuel cells. A by-product of the reaction is water. While some of this water is used for personal consumption on all shuttle missions, the excess water produced is normally dumped overboard. This water is saved only if we are going to *Mir,* in which case the water is diverted to portable water-proof sacks. Each sack holds approximately twenty gallons. In such cases, we then physically transfer the sacks from the space shuttle to the *Mir* after docking. The 1,600 pounds of water transferred would later be used by my cosmonaut crewmates and myself onboard *Mir* for drinking or to make oxygen—the hydrolysis of H_2O producing oxygen and hydrogen once again. The oxygen we cosmonauts would breathe and therefore consume; we would vent the hydrogen, an explosive gas, into the vacuum of space.

The only downside of this truly synergistic relationship between *Atlantis* and *Mir* is that we missed out on quite a dazzling show. During water dumps, a blizzard is created as the water instantly crystallizes. The darting crystals are quite a sight through the space shuttle's side-hatch window, one that always gathers a crowd of astronaut "tourists." Of course, since I would be one of the prime consumers of the water on *Mir,* mundanely bagging and transferring this resource won my vote over the snowstorm spectacle.

On the second day of flight, we began to see *Mir* in the distance. "Tally-ho," cried naval aviator turned *Atlantis* commander, Mike Baker. As the solar panels of *Mir* reflected sunlight, the space station first appeared as a very bright star. Eventually, the star became better defined, resembling a Tinker Toy–like monstrosity floating in space. As we moved in closer and closer, we began to see distinctly *Mir*'s six cylindrical modules.

By docking day, as per the plan, we had moved to a point eight nautical miles behind *Mir.* From this position, we began our final approach to the station.

Mir looked more majestic, more magnificent, than I had expected. Overwhelmed by the enormous size and intricacy of the space station, John Grunsfeld, who had formerly taught astrophysics at Cal Tech and had observed some impressive galactic phenomena in his day, blurted out in amazement, "Wow, Jerry! Are you in for an adventure. Look at that thing!"

I nodded in agreement. It was, indeed, an impressive complex.

Before us, the *Mir* space station appeared to be an imposing amalgamation of space modules. In its configuration, *Mir* resembled six school buses all hooked together. It was as if four of the buses were driven into a four-way intersection at the same time. They collided and became attached. All at right angles to each other, these four buses made up the four *Mir* science modules, named Priroda, Spektr, Kvant II, and Kristall. While each of the modules had its own unique features—for example, Spektr had four brilliant, golden solar panels extending from its surface, while the other modules had at most two panels—they were not altogether different in appearance. Priroda and Spektr were relatively new additions to the space complex, and looked it—each sporting shiny gold foil, bleached-white solar blankets, and unmarred thruster pods. Kvant II and Kristall, on the other hand, showed their ten-plus years of age. Solar blankets were yellowed and strewn with propellant stains. Solar panels looked as drab as a Moscow winter and were pockmarked with raggedy holes, the result of losing battles with micrometeorite and debris strikes over the years.

The node of the base block module is the junction where these theoretical buses collided. As if dropped from the sky, another bus—this one larger than all the others and "towing" a smaller bus—was attached at this same point. The falling-from-the-sky bus is called the base block module and the smaller bus in tow is referred to as the Kvant I module. Both of these modules looked battle worn, being the original members of the complex.

Finally, and as we moved closer, some garnishes to the space station could be ascertained. A Soyuz spacecraft, Volkswagen bus–sized, was docked at the only remaining free port of the six-holed node. Following the same imagery, it was attached to the node as if ramming the intersection from underground. A Progress resupply spacecraft, almost identical in appearance to the dull-black Soyuz, was parked at the end of the Kvant I module.

While all of the space station intricacies were of general interest, the only part that mattered to shuttle commander Baker was attached to the end of the Kristall module—the shuttle docking port. An extension to the *Mir* station, added during an earlier shuttle mission, the bright-orange docking module increased the distance between the shuttle and the *Mir* during docking. The bright orange solar blankets wrapping around the extension made our target starkly obvious. The color was not chosen for the purpose of blaring to the Americans, rather insultingly, that "this is where you park," but because the orange solar blanket was found in some Russian warehouse and, in order to cut costs, used instead of manufacturing a new white blanket. In any case, the glowing orange could not be missed.

WITH the eleven-year-old *Mir* dramatically before us, we began the next critical phase of shuttle operations. We would have to carefully rendezvous and dock with the orbiting space station. To do so, *Atlantis* relied upon a number of sensor systems to effect a controlled approach to *Mir.*

The shuttle's approach actually began when the shuttle's rendezvous radar system automatically started to track the station while simultaneously providing range (the distance to *Mir*) and range-rate (the speed of closure) information to *Atlantis.* Another sensor system called the trajectory control sensor (TCS) was mounted in the shuttle's payload bay. This laser device supplemented the shuttle's onboard navigation information by supplying additional data on the range and closing rate. Meanwhile, astronaut Marsha Ivins used a hand-held laser that she aimed out of the overhead window and pinged at *Mir.* Her data was used to verify the distance and closing-rate measurements that the other systems were providing.

The range and closing-rate information was particularly important for rendezvous operations because, in space, it is very difficult to judge accurately the distance and closing speed between two objects. When peering out into the blackness of the void, there are often no other near or far objects with which to place the other spacecraft in context. Without this background, human senses are poorly adapted to accurately define relative motion. Since the tolerance for misinterpretation is so slight—each spacecraft weighing over one hundred tons and moving at twenty-five times the speed of sound—redundant sensors were used. The built-in redundancy, a fundamental safety principle for most critical shuttle operations, assured that the crew was not deceived, that our perceptions were correct.

Marsha looked very much like a highway patrol officer as she shot the laser gun at *Mir.* Firing the gun and barking out the range and range rates, she was almost giddy that she was hitting the target with each shot. That her manual readouts matched that of the other two systems was reassuring to Mike Baker, who was tracking our progress toward *Mir,* ready to take over manually should something go awry. All of the information received from these various sensor systems indicated that the primary motion and distance sensors were working well.

We continued to approach *Mir* from down below, that is, coming up from underneath the space station, with the earth behind us and the *Mir* ahead and above us. As we moved to within a half mile of the station, Mike Baker took over manually.

Meanwhile, I was busy talking in Russian on a specially-rigged VHF line-of-sight radio to the *Mir* crew. I gave my future crewmates updates as to how things were progressing aboard *Atlantis*, echoing our range, range rates, and activities. I assured them that all was going according to plan. As time permitted, I described to them how magnificent their spacecraft appeared, and we chatted a bit about how they were doing and how things were going back on the planet. But by the time I announced the half-mile range, and that Mike had taken over manually, all peripheral chatter ceased and we all got serious.

Using the image from a centerline camera mounted in *Atlantis*'s docking mechanism, Mike tried to keep the docking ring on *Mir* centered. He needed to do very little at this point since we were coming up dead center on *Mir*. At about thirty feet, however, Mike had to fire some braking thrusters. Holding *Atlantis* steady at this distance, Mike awaited word from the ground, that is, from mission control teams in both Houston and Moscow, before proceeding further. Houston was confirming that all of *Atlantis*'s systems were working normally, while Moscow confirmed that the *Mir* was holding steady.

Aboard *Atlantis*, we received the message, "All systems go, proceed to docking," from mission control in Houston. From that moment on Mike was extremely busy. Mike had to negotiate more fine-tuning within our approach corridor the closer we got to *Mir*. The directional thrusters located fore and aft on *Atlantis* sprang to life. Mike was craning his neck out the overhead window, while grasping two thruster control sticks mounted on the aft panel in the cockpit of *Atlantis*. With each twist, push, or pull of the joysticks, the thrusters spewed out yellowish-white vapor bursts.

The closer we approached, the faster and more erratic the tempo of the rhythm became, adding suspense to an already suspenseful event. The tempo continued to increase, until Mike was firing shuttle impulses every second or so just prior to actual contact. As he fought to keep the *Mir* docking ring aligned perfectly, I could see, by glancing at the television screen reflecting the view from the center-line camera, that he had succeeded. We were proceeding right down the intended path toward the station.

Contact! I felt the impact—soft, but definite. Capture! Mechanical hooks and latches swung into place to lock the vehicles together. Damping! The motion between the two massive space vehicles was being calmed down by shock-absorbing springs in the docking device.

We hit the target perfectly. Astronaut Jeff Wisoff, Virginia-bred and plucked from the electrical and computer engineering depart-ment at Rice University for the astronaut corps, floated before the docking mechanism control panel, verifying that nothing was askew. Simultaneously working the switches and monitoring the caution-and-warning lights that would signal any malfunction should it occur, Jeff confirmed that we were, indeed, solidly joined together. As the tension dissipated, we pounded "Bakes" on the back and commended him for his flying skills. We all rejoiced at being locked, firmly and without any scrapes or bangs, to the *Mir* space station. We had arrived.

BEFORE either crew could open any of the multiple hatches between *Atlantis* and *Mir*, John Grunsfeld and I had to make sure that we had an airtight seal between the two spacecraft. We began confirming steady air pressures in various closed vestibules between the shuttle's airtight volume and the airtight volume aboard *Mir*. John worked from the half of the checklist written in English; I worked from the half written in Russian.

In what was a tedious process, I would call the *Mir* crew, telling them the pressure readings we were seeing on the shuttle. After checking their own readings, the cosmonauts would call back with a similar report. If the readings were within a predefined tolerance, we would proceed to verify the airtightness of the next chamber. John and I marched down the checklist in a coordinated fashion. We made sure that our pressure readings aboard *Atlantis* were in synch with the pressure readings that the Russians were getting aboard *Mir*. When John and I were satisfied with the spacecrafts' mutual read-ings, I reported the results to the controllers in Houston, while the Russians on *Mir* reported their results to the controllers in Moscow.

When both mission control in Houston and mission control in Moscow were satisfied that there were no pressure leaks or pressure differential between the two spacecraft, *Atlantis* received word that we had a "go" to open the final hatch connecting us to *Mir*.

Flying down to the hatch I could see John Blaha, the American astronaut-cosmonaut whom I was about to replace, smiling broadly through the porthole. Although the hatch was still closed, the two crews could yell at each other and be understood. A friendly and talkative veteran of four previous space shuttle missions, John looked simply ecstatic to see us. As the hatch was swung open, John greeted us with a hearty "Welcome! Welcome to space station *Mir!*" followed by an uninhibited laugh. Then bedlam erupted, as the six of us blundered our way through the hatch and bumped heads with the much more graceful—being fully adapted to space—threesome of *Mir* occupants.

The scene was one of hugs, shouts, mixed language, and laughter, feet dangling in all directions. Nine space-farers embracing and floating every which way. After the chaos calmed we all migrated single file—heads closely following feet—into *Mir*.

Immediately noticeable was the smell, not of the feet in front of me, but of *Mir*. An unusual odor, although not particularly unpleasant, permeated the cluttered and narrow tubes of all of *Mir's* modules. The smell was somehow familiar. Was it the smell of Great Grandma's basement? Or that of an old wine cellar—musty and mushroomy? Cave-like and dark—the fluorescent lights on *Mir* were inadequate to properly light the space station—the smell matched the setting. One sensed one was entering another realm.

We all finally alighted in the base block module. Supplemental lights were dangling from the ceiling, the light beams aimed at the American and Russian national flags stretched across the far end of the module. In front of this background of red, white, and blue, we all perched for the traditional "Welcome to *Mir*" press conference.

Press conferences were something that we considered a necessary evil. This one would be particularly annoying because what was required of us was to expound on how great it was to be working together as partners with the Russians, how well we got along (even though we had only come aboard five minutes earlier), and how *Mir* was surprisingly in great shape (even though the only American who could possibly know this was John Blaha). Since none of us were poets or philosophers, but rather hard-nosed engineers, test pilots, and scientists, spewing out creative platitudes did not come naturally.

But God, or fate, or a premonition of things to come intervened to save us. Abruptly, the *Mir* master alarm began clanging. The *Mir* commander, looking more embarrassed than alarmed, excused himself and flew to the caution-and-warning panel to check out the source of the problem. He informed us, as he was frantically turning off lights, that there was nothing to worry about, just a low electrical power warning. The news conference would have to wait until we could charge up the batteries once again. As the base block module darkened to match the cavelike ambiance of the rest of the space station, none of the newly arriving guests seemed too disappointed at the change in plans. I glanced at John Blaha, who gave me a knowing look of . . . was it "Be prepared for more to come, Jerry"?

This would be the first of a never-ending stream of master alarms that I would encounter during my fateful months aboard *Mir*.

THE SHUTTLE remained docked to the *Mir* for five days. We transferred nearly six thousand pounds of logistics to the space station. In the reverse direction, from *Mir* to *Atlantis,* we hauled back nearly a third of the weight that we were delivering, an impressive two thousand pounds. Most of what *Atlantis* would be taking back to earth from *Mir* consisted of U.S.–science return material and broken-down Russian equipment. Landing-weight constraints, as well as limitations posed by *Atlantis*'s center of gravity during descent, prevent the shuttle from taking home as much weight as can be delivered. Furthermore, safety concerns forced us to carefully screen what we would accept for transport aboard the shuttle.

We could not accept broken-down equipment that posed toxicological hazards to the shuttle atmosphere. Nor could we transport items categorized as unauthorized for shuttle use, that is, items that did not meet shuttle safety restrictions. For example, because of the potential for breakage and the possibility of shards floating everywhere in the cabin atmosphere (and, of course, eventually into someone's lungs), breakable glass is avoided whenever possible on the shuttle. *Mir*'s rules were obviously less restrictive since glass objects were found throughout the space station.

OVER its eleven-year lifespan the *Mir* had accumulated massive amounts of excess materials, equipment, and, frankly, just plain junk. Everything from obsolete experiment containers and empty water tanks to ancient tools and useless cables were scattered, strewn, and stowed aboard *Mir.* While the space shuttle's ability to carry some of these excess materials away helped the situation somewhat, *Mir* was still cluttered.

The loadmaster of the American crew on the shuttle was Marsha Ivins. She had the daunting task of knowing where everything was stowed on the shuttle, and did. Marsha ensured that all shuttle transfer items were moved to *Mir,* and that all items to be returned to earth were onboard the shuttle and properly stowed before departure. She ruled with an iron fist. She demanded that every item be in its proper place. She was absolutely drop-jaw shocked by the haphazard arrangement and clutter of *Mir.*

Attempting to make her way to the Progress resupply vehicle at the far end of the Kvant I module, she found herself entangled and swallowed in a sea of disarray. The Kvant I module, still touted by the Russians as a research-capable astrophysics module, was now used as a dump. Marsha expected to see high-powered spectrometers and telescopes filling the astrophysics module; what she saw instead was a module stuffed solid with floating garbage bags and busted equipment. Swimming into the module, pushing bags and containers and foul-smelling trash aside, she tried to weave her way through the kelplike bed of stuff, but found herself caught up, entangled. I watched her trying to swim, fishlike, around the obstacles, but one obstacle quickly gave way to the next. Finally, she disappeared from my sight. Backtracking, she returned to the starting point, her eyes widened in disbelief. She was gagging from the smell of decomposing garbage.

"Jerry, do you know if the Progress is at the end of this mess?"

"I think so. Let me help you get through the quagmire."

It took Marsha some time to get over the sight and smells of a module engorged. Recovering, and laughing, she commented how absolutely unbelievable this was—an astrophysics module to boot! We pushed the floating garbage bags out of the way. She got a flying start and fought her way through the mess. About a third of the way down the length of the module, she disappeared behind the intervening obstructions. Having had enough of the smell, I retreated to the base block module.

Upon her return we renamed the Kvant I astrophysics module the "attic."

GENERALLY, the space station resembled an old attic belonging to an eccentric recluse, a perpetual saver of all things, a person who believed adamantly that "You never know when it might come in handy," and who, therefore, had amassed a lifetime of ancient and useless stuff. The accumulated clutter was not the fault of previous space station crews and certainly not the fault of the current crew who, in fact, spent a great deal of time tying to organize and stow equipment to make *Mir* presentable. No, the fault was due to years of accumulated neglect and an inadequate means of removing goods from *Mir*. Concretely, the failure of the Russian Buran program (the Buran being the Russian version of the space shuttle) left the Russians without the means to remove goods from *Mir*.

Items could be brought up, but not returned. The overcrowded condition of *Mir* also resulted from the cash-strapped Russian space agency not being able to say no to flying another paying foreign researcher that wanted to conduct experiments on *Mir*. Science equipment was hauled up, but after the researcher returns to earth in the cramped Soyuz return vehicle—a vehicle with hardly enough space to contain three bodies, let alone extra gear—the equipment remained behind, only adding to the clutter.

AFTER five days docked to the station, the shuttle crew began preparations to leave. John Blaha and I swapped places, with John becoming a part of the shuttle crew and me taking John's place as a member of the long-duration *Mir* crew.

Departing the space station meant, of course, undocking from the station. Undocking is essentially the reverse of docking. Hatches are closed and checked to be airtight. As hooks in the joined docking rings are unlatched, springs built into the docking mechanism push the vehicles apart. The shuttle then begins to fire thrusters in order to move still farther away. The thrusters are specially chosen to enable the shuttle to move in the proper direction, but not to send its exhaust plume toward the *Mir* space station and the station's delicate solar panels.

After closing the hatch, my two Russian crewmates and I did not have much to do other than watch as the space shuttle drifted away from us. On the space station, we were in the free-drift mode, which merely meant that all *Mir*'s steering jets were turned off (they are rarely used, in any event) to avoid any inadvertent firings. An inadvertent firing might cause the space station to twist at an inopportune time, and the undocking was difficult enough to perform without having two spaceships in motion.

About four hundred feet from the space station, *Atlantis*'s pilot, Brent Jett—his actual name—took the controls from Mike Baker and began to fly around *Mir*, circling twice before eventually departing for good.

As the space shuttle departed, I grabbed my camera, moved from window to window, and took some absolutely breathtaking pictures of the world's most advanced spacecraft flying away from us. I found it incredible just how rock steady the shuttle flew.

As *Atlantis* fired thrusters, I saw thruster plumes emanating from multiple jets. The plumes spired, tear-shaped, from the three different thruster pods, two aft and one forward, on the shuttle. I continued taking pictures of the space shuttle with planet earth as a backdrop. I went through roll after roll of film, knowing that I would have to wait five months to see the results. Nearly overwhelmed by the incredible view of shuttle suspended over planet earth, I knew that if the pictures did any justice to the reality that I was seeing, the photos would surely be worthy of a *National Geographic* cover.

I gazed out the window until *Atlantis* was hundreds of miles distant and barely visible. As the earth below darkened, the shuttle stood out all the more distinctly because her altitude allowed her to continue to catch rays from the sun. My final glimpse of the retreating space shuttle was that of a brilliant star, low and near to the curve of the darkened earth. Then *Atlantis,* too, blinked into darkness.

I took a deep breath, felt a pang of loneliness, squinted one more time in a vain attempt to resurrect *Atlantis* and my astronaut friends, now far gone. I closed the cover to the window. My stay on *Mir* had begun. It was now just two Russian cosmonauts and myself, left to fend for ourselves, far removed from home and earth.

10

My First Days on *Mir*

I QUICKLY SETTLED into the routine of living on *Mir*. Valeri Korzun and Sasha Kaleri had already spent five months on *Mir* when I arrived, and had less than a month remaining in their tour of duty. They were well seasoned and already in the mind-set of "count the days until we are back on earth." *Mir* had held up relatively well during their stay; there were no dramatic events, no life-threatening situations. Routine repairs enough to keep them busy, but nothing that overwhelmed them.

Valeri Grigorievich Korzun was the most Americanized of all the cosmonauts that I met in Star City. Forty-something and handsome, he was always dabbling in English, laughed a lot, and had a tendency to admire women beyond what might seem proper for a married man with a son about to enter college. A former military test pilot, he had been working with the cosmonauts since 1987. Ten years later he was making his first flight.

Forty-one-year-old Alexander "Sasha" Yurievich Kaleri, an Omar Sharif look-alike, was a civilian engineer chosen to join the cosmonaut team in 1987. He flew for the first time on *Mir* in 1992. He was serious and soft-spoken, but friendly; admired by women, but a dedicated family man.

My predecessor, John Blaha, had privately warned me that *Mir*-22 commander Valeri Korzun could be an excessive micromanager.

Valeri and John, it seems, had butted heads on more than one occasion. This was probably due to a variety of reasons. First of all, they had never trained together. In fact, it was not until a week before flight that John knew that he would be flying with Valeri. Back in Star City John had to ask me, "Which one is Korzun?" when the Russians announced that the originally assigned cosmonaut crew would not be flying because of a suspected heart problem. This put John in the unenviable position of having to spend months isolated with two virtual strangers. Second, it was Valeri's first flight, John's fifth flight. John had already commanded shuttle missions. Valeri probably felt insecure, perhaps even threatened. Whatever the reason, it was clear that John was glad to be going home.

Luckily, Valeri and I got along fine. In my favor, I had known Valeri before the flight. We trained in simulators and played badminton together, and had even attended plays, accompanied by our families, in Moscow. (While I have always had a hard time understanding the "hidden meaning" behind plays, Kathryn and I were hopelessly lost trying to follow even the plot in these Russian-only productions!) Valeri knew me and trusted me professionally.

Furthermore, by the time I arrived, Valeri was no longer a neophyte—he had five months under his belt—and he probably felt more secure in his position. Most likely, too, he realized the mistakes that he had made in his relationship with John Blaha and did not want to repeat them. While his tendency was still to look over my shoulder, he did so tactfully.

The other member of the crew, Sasha Kaleri, was the Russian onboard engineer (I was designated American onboard engineer). Kaleri impressed me from the start. After five months, he was still on an even keel psychologically and continued to work efficiently. He even looked the same as he had back on earth: dark brown hair slicked back with water and a neatly trimmed mustache. After sucking down dinner, we often shared pictures of our infant sons with each other. I would remind him of what a great reunion he would be in for when he got back home. His eyes would light up and sparkle with the pride of a father.

Sasha Kaleri knew how to be helpful and unobtrusive at the same time. The more I watched him, the more impressed I became. I decided to pattern my space routine after his, since he seemed so unchanged and unaffected by the isolation and workload.

I observed that he kept to a strict routine. He would follow the daily schedule sent up from mission control in Moscow, but not blindly and not without altering the sequence of events to fit his style of working. He was flexible enough not to become a slave to the schedule as I had seen others do. For example, if a repair took longer than expected, he would stay on the job until it was complete rather than rush off to a different scheduled chore, only to waste time reorganizing the first worksite upon his return.

Regardless of the demands on his time, he was fastidious about his two scheduled daily exercise sessions; nothing got in the way. He maintained his biological clock—sixteen sunrises daily in space can wreak havoc on biorhythms—by going to bed at the same time each night and getting up when the morning alarm sounded. He knew that pulling all-nighters would only set him up for failure in the long run; he understood that after one repair was made, another would be waiting. He realized that six months in space is a long haul, and that one must pace oneself in order to optimize overall productivity.

Kaleri looked good nearing the end of his tour of duty. I wanted to look that good, to work that efficiently, to be that psychologically stable at the end of my stay. If he could do it, so could I. It was all a matter of self-discipline, and self-discipline was something that the naval academy had pounded into me in good measure. I patterned my approach to life on *Mir* after Sasha Kaleri, and probably looked like his clone.

I wanted to complete all mission goals—no exceptions—and to go beyond the stated objectives whenever possible. People were depending on me, vast sums of money were invested on getting me up here, and if I had to become something of a robot, so be it. I make no apologies when saying that getting the mission accomplished was my primary focus.

AWAKENED by the master alarm, which doubled as the morning alarm clock, I would immediately check my watch to assure that it was indeed a wake up call and not a warning signal. Unstrapping myself from the wall I was sleeping on and twisting to an upright position—I always slept upside down on the wall—I would fly off to the restroom. Not wanting to waste forty-five minutes shaving each day, I would simply squirt some water onto my face, rub it around with my hands, and then dry my hands by dabbing them on my uncut hair. After slicking my hair back with my fingers, I would head for a breakfast of dehydrated soup, a can of chicken, and some fruit drink sucked through a straw.

Breakfast finished, I would then fly to the message board and read the plan of the day. Mission control in Moscow would send up the plan using an ancient, clackety Teletype machine that printed out the schedule on a long roll of paper. The plan listed, minute by minute, the tasks that needed to be done that day. I would translate the applicable portions into English and write them on my kneeboard.

A typical morning might read: 0800–0820: morning hygiene and toilet; 0820–0950: activate space acceleration measurement system, section 2.2, 2.3, 2.4; 0950–1040: day two exercise—treadmill; 1040–1050: personal hygiene; 1050–1300: spacesuit preparation; 1300–1400: lunch.

The afternoon was likewise planned to the minute, my day completely filled until 7 P.M. In the late evenings I would catch up on all the tasks that I was unable to accomplish during the day. Time permitting, I would also try to load data files onto the telemetry system for downlink to earth, unload spent film and reload fresh film into the Hasselblad camera using a darkbag, and take some photographs of the earth.

Although the plan was to have Sundays free, there was so much to do that rarely would I find more than an hour or two free on any day of the week. In fact, because I was doing a sleep study and was wired as I slept—with eye sensors to record my rapid-eye-movement sleep, and scalp electrodes to record the brain-wave pattern—I can honestly say that I worked twenty-four hours a day, seven days a week, for five months. Later in the flight, as we suffered major system failures and near-disasters, even the free hour or two each week disappeared. But my first month with Korzun and Kaleri on *Mir* was rather pleasant: busy but not overwhelming. Experiments ended with a satisfying sense of accomplishment, and living in space was gradually beginning to feel almost normal. Life was pretty much as I expected it to be, the way that I had heard it described by American astronauts Shannon Lucid and John Blaha before me. I was glad to be onboard.

11

The Arrival of Vasily
and Sasha

As VALERI KORZUN and Sasha Kaleri were nearing the end of their stay and the *Mir-22* mission reaching its conclusion, our attention turned toward getting the station ready for the arrival of the incoming *Mir-23* crew. Two cosmonaut replacements, *Mir-23* crew members Vasily Tsibliev and Sasha Lazutkin, would soon be arriving in a three-seat Soyuz spacecraft. The new crew was also bringing with them a third person, German researcher Reinhold Ewald. He would stay onboard *Mir* only during the twenty-day changeover period, perform his experiments, and then fly back with the two departing cosmonauts, Valeri Korzun and Sasha Kaleri. They would use the old Soyuz, the one that Valeri and Sasha had used five months ago to get to the space station, for their return vehicle.

The space station has three places where incoming vehicles can attach themselves. One port is reserved for shuttle dockings. The other two ports, identical in configuration, are located at either end of the longitudinal axis of the station—one at the end of Kvant I, the other at the base block node. While these ports are designed to accept either the manned Russian Soyuz spacecraft or the unmanned Russian resupply Progress spacecraft, the preference is to park the Soyuz at the base block node. Docking is achieved when either of the incoming Russian spacecraft gently slams (yes, *gently* slams, not too hard, but not too gingerly, either) their attached probe (the "male" part) into the waiting drogue (the "female," conically-shaped receiving part) at the docking port.

BEFORE the docking of the arriving Soyuz could take place, we had to move the old Soyuz from the node docking port to the Kvant I docking port. For a multitude of reasons—including the desirable sun-shading of the space station by the parked Soyuz, which maximized the light striking the solar panels located both on the station and on the Soyuz and protected the aged docking ring by having a vehicle attached—it was desirable to park the new Soyuz, which would remain in position for months, at the node docking ring.

The Soyuz spacecraft is made up of two compartments: the spherical living compartment and the conical command module, connected to each other by a centrally located, internal hatch.

The living compartment looks like a large ball sitting atop the command module and contains the docking mechanism. While cramped, the living compartment is roomier than the command module, allowing enough space for three contortionist cosmonauts to get into their launch and entry spacesuits, with no room to spare. The volume is used during launch to pack cargo heading to *Mir* along with food and water to be used during the transit. The compartment also contains a rudimentary urine collection hose and solid-waste bags. During reentry, the living compartment is jettisoned; only the command module makes it back to earth.

The command module contains three seats, survival gear, instruments, and controls. If a person is claustrophobic, the command module is definitely a place to avoid.

On *Mir* we powered down all the nonessential equipment in the space station and shimmied our way into the Soyuz living compartment. Powering down the station was essential, because if we experienced difficulty redocking, our only option might be to return to planet. Although the *Mir* space station at this stage of its life can no longer stay alive for prolonged periods of time without a crew onboard tending to its needs, the station might survive unmanned for a week or two. Since the replacement crew was due to arrive in less than a week, shutting down power-guzzling equipment might make the resurrection of the station possible if we were unable to redock.

We then got into our custom-made Russian Sokol launch-and-entry suits. The suit consists of a one-piece body assembly with the feet, arms, visor, and hood built in—only the gloves are separate. There is a zipper in front, and one enters the suit through this small opening.

Unfortunately I had grown, or, more correctly, my spine, free of the pull of gravity, had stretched out, making me about two inches taller than when I was fitted for the suit. Only by jamming my chin into my chest and by having Valeri and Sasha cram me into the suit could I pull the hood over my head. I was fortunate not to sprain my neck.

After the three of us were fully suited, we squeezed our way from the Soyuz living compartment into the command module. Valeri Korzun got in last, because once he was sitting in the center seat it was impossible to squeeze past him to either of the side seats. The command module was so cramped that we sat shoulder to shoulder and I had to scrunch my knees nearly up to my chin in order to not bump on the instrument panel. We were stuffed in the capsule like sardines in a can.

We then began methodically powering up the spacecraft. It had been five months since the Soyuz had flown. We needed to thoroughly preflight all of the systems before undocking. From my position in the right seat, I handled the communication system, control of a forward-looking television camera, and most of the life-support system and pressure valves. Sasha Kaleri, in the left seat, was activating thrusters, monitoring the guidance system, and keeping track of our electrical power usage. Valeri Korzun was sitting between us and took care of the onboard computer as well as having the actual spacecraft controls.

Through terrible static—all of our antennas were blocked by the space station—Valeri claimed that he heard the ground tell us that we were "go for undocking." Via telemetry, the ground can look at parameters—for example, the pressure in the fuel tank—that we cannot see from any indicator onboard. Because of this, it was imperative that the ground gave us a "go" before we undocked. After we remotely released the hooks, springs built into the docking ring pushed us away. Valeri then fired thrusters to increase the separation between the vehicles. He did not have a window to look out of. Only Sasha and I had four-inch diameter side portholes—nearly useless because of their size and location. Valeri instead peered through a small periscope between his legs that gave him an indirect view of where we were heading. Once at a safe distance from the space station, we then began circling *Mir*.

After fifteen minutes or so, the Kvant I docking port appeared on the periscope. Valeri centered the docking port on the crosshairs and drove our Soyuz probe into the awaiting drogue on *Mir*.

Contact was firm, but not frightfully so. The docking mechanism functioned correctly to secure us to the station. We then verified that the seal between the station and our vehicle was airtight. After powering down the spacecraft, we got out of our spacesuits and opened the hatches. The smell of space—a distinct burnt-dry smell that I can't describe any other way—wafted in from the small vestibule between the vehicles. Looking into the station I could see a lone ray of light shining through the port window and outlining the dining table. We had left some food out for dinner. It was the only time during my stay in space that *Mir* looked warm, inviting, and *spacious*. It reminded me of opening the door to a summer cottage that had been boarded up for the winter, looking inside, and seeing familiar surroundings.

It had felt good to go for a Sunday ride and to escape *Mir*'s confining clutches. But at the same time, it was good to be back again. *Mir* no longer seemed just a mechanical object designed to keep us alive, but home.

WITH our Soyuz now parked in its proper position, we were ready to receive the incoming capsule.

I was the first to catch a glimpse of the incoming spacecraft carrying the replacement cosmonaut crew. It was a few hundred miles away, but its two solar panels reflected the rays of the sun brightly. As it came nearer, I could distinguish its parts more clearly: the black, spherical living compartment on top, a conical command capsule below, and two solar panels sticking out of the sides. It looked like a stout, winged insect.

As best as I could ascertain, all was going well for the crew of the inbound Soyuz. I had positioned myself at a large window at the end of the Kvant II module, which offered a clear view of the approach. Following standard procedure, the Soyuz was flying toward our space station in a fully automatic mode—the crew merely monitoring the systems, ready to act should a failure occur. It came closer and closer, until it was so near that it ducked behind an appendage sticking out of *Mir*. I stayed perfectly still and held my breath, concentrating on the stillness, wanting to feel the docking with all my senses. Seconds ticked by and I felt nothing. I saw no movement of loose, floating objects. Something must have happened.

I rushed back to the window, looked out again, and saw the tail end of the Soyuz coming *back* into view—the spaceship was backing away! I quickly assessed the condition of the craft—I could detect no stuck-on thruster or other problem that might cause the spaceship to lose control—and then watched as the Soyuz stopped moving, stabilized, and then began to approach the *Mir* space station once again.

Valeri Korzun, who had been observing the docking indirectly by watching the camera view as relayed from the Soyuz to the *Mir,* could essentially see the same view that the incoming crew was seeing on their periscope inside the Soyuz. He came flying in frantically, screaming: "Jerry, they are backing away! What did you see?"

His face was red with rage. He looked helpless, almost tearful. His reaction was, of course, understandable: he had a huge stake in that Soyuz docking. He had already spent five months on the station and these were his replacements arriving. If the docking were unsuccessful, he would have to extend his stay onboard until a different Soyuz could be launched—in all likelihood months down the road.

To me personally, the docking was less critical. I was slated to remain onboard for four more months regardless of which two cosmonauts I spent the time with. My departure was not linked to the Soyuz arrival, but to that of the space shuttle. This was not my ticket home. I was much calmer and told Valeri that, yes, I had seen it back away, but that I could not detect any instability in the way that it was flying, and that it had reversed direction again and was heading back for an apparent second docking attempt.

At that moment, we both felt the impact. It felt solid, and although I was now sitting on the *Mir* side and not the Soyuz side of the docking, very similar to the impact that I had felt during our own docking a few days earlier. Korzun, almost in a panic, flew quickly back to the base block module to look at the monitor.

It was indeed a successful dock. Korzun looked as crazily happy as he had only moments before looked forlorn. Kaleri also was smiling broadly. It was obvious that both of them had been repressing their very heartfelt I-want-to-go-home emotion until this moment.

Now that the replacement crew had arrived, they pushed their coast buttons, saw the light at the end of the tunnel, and allowed themselves to let down their guard. The major obstacle blocking their return to earth had been removed. They were soon to go home.

Hatches were opened. We stuck cameras in the newly arriving faces and greeted our guests in the traditional Russian manner, offering them bread and salt. They reciprocated by offering us a special treat of fresh bananas, apples, lemons, and oranges. While the fresh fruit, to be sure, tasted delicious, the aroma of the citrus was what made the gift so wonderful—the aroma of the good earth.

Two of the three new arrivees expressed no interest in eating the bread, or, for that matter, anything else. Their faces looked pale; they flew tentatively, trying to move as little as possible and always with their feet down. Vasily Tsibliev, the oncoming commander, did do a vigorous barrel roll for the camera, but after the camera was turned off, he too preferred stability to floating. The threesome had been crammed into the Soyuz spacecraft for nearly two days. Since there was so little room to move, it was difficult to get adapted to space under such circumstances. Furthermore, not only was the spacecraft cramped, but it also does a continuous barbecue roll. The slow roll is necessary to keep all sides equally heated and thereby avoid expansion-contraction strain on the structure of the vehicle. While good for the metal, this rotation about the longitudinal axis of the vehicle was not pleasant for the occupants inside. Reinhold Ewald, the arriving short-stay German researcher, later told me that on top of the roll, the Soyuz was also unbearably cold inside during their entire journey. So cold, in fact, that no one could sleep without shivering regardless of how much clothing they wrapped themselves up in. It was obvious that they were all relieved and glad to get out of that capsule; but it was also obvious that the voluminous *Mir* nauseated them. The freedom of motion came with a price—space motion sickness. While everyone was able to smile during the press conference, the newcomers were glad when the cameras were turned off and they could remain still and feel miserable alone.

Vasily Tsibliev, who had guided the Soyuz into the *Mir*, related what had happened during the docking. The automatic approach sensors seemed to be working fine until the Soyuz was very close to the *Mir*. Then he noticed that the alignment was out of limits—his spacecraft's probe was about to miss hitting the awaiting drogue on

Mir—so he took over manually and backed out. He flew out the error, and then steered the craft back in for the docking.

This unexpected problem may have been an omen of things to come for Tsibliev. During his tenure on *Mir*, nothing would go according to plan.

12

"Fire!"

I KNEW FROM THE START that I would enjoy working with Vasily. Vasily Vasilievich Tsibliev, forty years old and making his second flight, was like a kid let loose on a playground. As soon as he began feeling normal, he reverted to his military test pilot days and flew from module to module doing barrel rolls. He liked being a cosmonaut. He smiled a lot, always had a story to tell about his teenage son and daughter, and was confident enough in his role as *Mir* commander and in my role as an already-experienced onboard engineer and scientist that he did not try to prove anything or interfere with my work.

Alexander "Sasha" Lazutkin was harder to figure out. He wore a droopy mustache that matched the way he felt for his first two weeks on *Mir*. He was a former world-class gymnast, slightly younger than Vasily and I, and was married, with two school-age daughters. He appeared languid and detached, not at all the stereotypical hard-driven, high-performing cosmonaut. I tried to be sympathetic toward him not feeling so well, frequently offering medical help and the assurance that he would adjust to microgravity soon.

Knowing that the three of us would get along fine, I was becoming anxious for the old crew and the German researcher to depart. *Mir* was too crowded with six people onboard, its life support systems pushed too hard. It would be nice to complete the twenty-day crew overlap and get back into the routine.

THE TWO overlapping *Mir* crews—one crew a week away from returning to earth, the other crew two weeks into their planned six-month stay, and me bridging the gap between them—were gathered around the table for dinner after a busy but fairly routine day. Most of us had already finished sucking down the jellied piked-perch and borscht, and were sitting, idly shooting the breeze. I excused myself and flew into the Spektr module to begin cueing some experiment data results on the telemetry system.

Because we had six people onboard, we had to supplement the oxygen supply by using backup solid-fueled oxygen canisters. The small wastebasket-sized cylindrical canisters were filled with a chemical slurry that, when activated, would release oxygen. Sasha Lazutkin, the newly arrived Russian onboard engineer, headed off to activate the canister just as I was leaving the dinner table. The canister was located on the other side of a three-foot diameter tunnel that connected the base block module to the Kvant I module, about ten feet from where I had been sitting. The rest of the gang continued to linger around the table and talk.

Blaang! Blaang! Blaang!

The blaring of the master alarm was nothing unusual. In fact, it was an almost daily occurrence during the five weeks that I had been on *Mir*. I began to treat the sound of the alarm with a certain nonchalance.

The sound, however, was deafening since the speaker was positioned on the bulkhead only two feet from my ear. I reached over my right shoulder and grabbed my earplugs, and inserted them.

My computer was still working, so at least, I reasoned, the electrical power was not down. Perhaps the carbon dioxide scrubber had failed again.

As the spongy material in the earplugs expanded to fill the contours of my external ear canal, the clamor of the alarm lessened. I proceeded to move the cursor on my IBM Thinkpad to the save portion of the computer screen and clicked. If the electrical power was teetering again and was about to fail, at least I had not wasted the last five minutes of data entry.

I had been typing in a horizontal position as if lying on an imaginary bed. The computer was attached by Velcro to the "ceiling." To prevent my body from drifting away from my workstation, I had wiggled my toes under a footloop on the wall. To determine why the alarm was ringing *this* time, I uncurled my toes from the footloop and straightened out my body from its simianlike hunch—the natural posture astronauts typically adopt in the weightlessness of space.

I gently pushed off the wall with my feet and I did a barrel roll, centering myself on the longitudinal axis of the module. Floating swiftly down the length of the bus-sized module, I approached the space station's node—the connecting terminal for five of *Mir*'s modules. From the node I could bank ninety degrees to the left and enter the space station's base block module, where the caution-and-warning panel was located.

Vasily Tsibliev and I narrowly avoided a mid-air collision as he came frantically, and rather clumsily, charging out of the place I was headed.

"*Seriosney?* [Serious?]," I asked of the soon-to-be commander of the space station.

Before Tsibliev could respond, I had my answer. I saw a tentacle of smoke snaking its way behind him.

"*Ochin! Poshar!* [Very! Fire!]," he spat out, sharply and breathlessly. He swung his head and darted his eyes in the direction of the base block module.

I turned toward the left and peered down the length of the cylindrical module. I saw a roaring fire burning in the attached Kvant I module. We were in big trouble.

"Not good," I mumbled to myself.

I glanced down at the caution-and-warning panel. It looked like a Christmas tree, with fire and smoke warning lights flashing everywhere. I could see the fire was wildly out of control. Smoke was billowing out of the connecting passageway and into the base block module.

Squinting against the brightness of the flame, my eyes already stinging from the smoke, I studied the play of the fire in order to determine just what we were up against. A full foot in diameter at its base, the flame shot out two to three feet across the diameter of the cylindrical module. As the fire spewed with angry intensity, sparks—resembling an entire box of sparklers ignited simultaneously—extended a foot or so beyond the flame's farthest edge. Beyond the sparks, I saw what appeared to be melting wax splattering on the bulkhead opposite the blaze. But it was not melting wax. It was molten metal. The fire was so hot that it was melting metal.

Another cosmonaut—I could not tell for sure who it was through the ever-thickening smoke—yelled out to be prepared for decompression. He recognized that this fire could swiftly torch its way through the thin aluminum hull of the space station. Penetrate the hull, and the air onboard the station would whoosh into the vacuum of space. We would all suffocate. Our lives depended on stopping that fire.

By now, smoke was rapidly filling up the entire space station. It was so invasive that, in the few seconds that I peered down the tunnel, visibility was reduced within the base block module to near zero. Shadowy, ghostlike figures were scrambling about. One of the cosmonauts came flying out of this haze toward me, clutching a dirty rag over his nose and mouth.

"Not good," I repeated aloud to no one in particular. Then I tried to hold my breath.

The smoke became so thick so fast that I needed to put on an oxygen respirator. Flying recklessly in the reduced visibility, I banged the back of my hand on the control panel at the entrance to the node. Turning right, I reentered the U.S. science module.

The smoke quickly enveloped my body. I knew I could no longer gulp the tainted air into my lungs. Darting toward a personal respirator hanging on the bulkhead, I cautioned myself, "Stay calm, Jerry. Panic and it is all over."

The respirator casing was attached to the bulkhead by two C-clamps, each clamp held together by a quick-release fastener. Still holding my breath, I released the clamps and grabbed the blue plastic case containing my lifeline—the oxygen-producing respirator. Opening the case, I removed the rubberized full-face respirator and untangled the head straps that were stuffed inside the faceplate. I tried not to panic in spite of my ever-increasing need to breathe.

Smoke burned my eyes. Holding my breath became more painful by the moment.

I instinctively lowered my head toward the floor in an effort to locate a clear area in which to catch a quick breath. Earth instincts did not help. Warm air and smoke do not rise in space. The density of a gas becomes irrelevant in microgravity.

The thought "Open a window" swept across my mind and, in

spite of the desperate circumstance in which I found myself, I could not help but smile at such an absurdity. Open a window to the vacuum of space.

My brain overruled the urging of my oxygen-depleted lungs to breathe. Slipping the respirator over my head, I scrambled to locate the activation toggle on the attached oxygen canister.

I threw the lever full right. I had gone too long without air.

I breathed in deeply, anticipating heaven. I got nothing, just the collapse of the mask around my face.

I quickly double-checked to make sure that the lever was thrown completely. It was.

I sucked in again, harder this time. The rubber mask collapsed further around my face. The respirator was not working!

Unexpectedly, my oxygen-starved mind suddenly revealed to my consciousness that I was about to die. Remarkably, the abrupt realization of this possibility—even probability—did not come as some kind of desperate scream. It came, instead, as a surprisingly rational, sober awareness.

I never thought that my life would, in such an unexpected moment, just abruptly end. Well, I thought to myself, I guess this is how it happens. At some point we all die. I just never expected it to be now.

These reflections on life were occurring involuntarily, almost subconsciously. My rational brain was still functioning and screaming at me to *find another respirator!*

I was moving at a frenetic pace. I yanked the defective respirator off my head and began blindly feeling my way along the bulkhead to locate another.

The smoke swallowed up everything. My drink bag, the science module control panel, my heart-shaped photo of Kathryn and John taped to the wall—all vanished from sight, my eyes blinded by the dense smoke.

Still my mind processed in microseconds vast amounts of information and concerns simultaneously. As if Kathryn could hear me, I said my goodbyes.

"Kathryn, take care of John and of our newborn to come. I love you all. God, I am so sorry, John. I let you down. I won't be there for you. I hope you understand that I tried my best to get back to you all. Raise him well, dear. I will be watching over you always."

I felt as if I had been swimming underwater for fifty meters; the unfound respirator representing the side of the pool just ahead, representing my only hope. My head hurt, my mind felt dull, and everything was getting dark.

I finally felt the bulge of the protruding respirator case. I grabbed the case, ripped off the cover, and yanked out the mask from the case. With my lungs about to burst, I thrust the mask to my face, this time not bothering to untangle the head straps.

"Lord, make it work."

I flung the lever on the canister to the "on" position.

I gasped for air.

The oxygen flowed.

Breathing deeply and with reckless abandon, I hyperventilated. Oxygen, blessed oxygen! After thirty seconds I began to slow my rate; and after a minute I held my breath, closed my eyes, and took off the mask. I reached in and pulled the mashed straps out of the faceplate, moved them to the rear, and donned the mask properly. Tightening the straps, I made sure that the mask seal was airtight.

"Okay, I am alive. Now, we have to fight this fire. We have to do everything right. No mistakes." Then I added with absolute unwavering conviction: *"We will get this fire out, we will survive."*

IN SPITE of the circumstance, I was calm; pulse around sixty. My past life experience—parachuting, landing on aircraft carriers, launching in rockets, trying to save the lives of gunshot victims in emergency rooms—had taught me that panic only kills, either yourself or the patient. I was in my unemotional, rational survivor mode. I headed toward the node again, this time trying to locate my cosmonaut crewmates to ensure that they were under respirators.

We congregated at the intersection of the modules. I counted six— we had all made it thus far.

Like scuba divers incapable of speaking under water, we gave each other hand signals indicating that we were okay, that we were getting oxygen. Although we could talk to each other, our words were muffled because of the masks. Hand signals proved universally understandable, and eliminated the need to mentally translate from Russian to German or English.

Valeri Korzun, who maintained his position as the *Mir* commander during the crew changeover period, took charge and ordered the newly arrived crew of Tsibliev, Lazutkin, and Ewald to prepare one of the two Soyuz escape vehicles for evacuation. Sasha Kaleri, the second member of the seasoned crew, would shut down equipment on the space station—especially the fans—as well as act as an overall coordinator of our actions. I would assist Korzun in fighting the fire, as well as help anyone needing medical attention.

Unfortunately, of the two docked Soyuz capsules, only one was accessible. The second vehicle was parked on the far side of the impassable fire. Since each capsule could only hold three people, only three of us could evacuate. Quite a dilemma, since the three cosmonauts leaving would essentially be deserting the remaining three to fight the fire alone.

Sasha Kaleri showed the right stuff. In the middle of this crisis, he remained remarkably cool-headed and methodically worked through the checklists as if this actual emergency were nothing more than a drill. Kaleri somehow kept the individually frantic activities coordinated, always maintaining a clear image in his mind of what actions needed to be completed in order to increase our chances of survival.

Korzun and I were right next to the inferno. I wedged my legs into the three-foot diameter connecting tunnel leading to the Kvant I module. Vasily "stood" just inside the module. Because the fire extinguisher acts almost as a thruster in space, I grabbed Korzun around the waist to stabilize him. I would also periodically shake him, he would shake back—a signal indicating that we were both still conscious. The flame was five feet in front of my face, the smoke so dense that I could not count the fingers in front of my face, let alone see Korzun's face.

I relayed information between the firefighting team and the evacuation team. I made sure that no one was overcome by smoke. To Sasha Kaleri I might yell: "Valeri is okay! Grab me another fire extinguisher. And then again to Sasha, "Is the Soyuz activated and ready to depart? Is everyone okay?"

The first fire extinguisher did not put a dent in the fire. If anything, we merely reduced the heat load and perhaps prevented secondary fires from erupting. When one extinguisher would run out, I would leave Valeri to get another.

I left to get a third fire extinguisher. Flying blindly through the smoke, more by familiarity than by sight, I accidentally bumped into

a platform holding a laptop computer. Grabbing the platform to help
stabilize myself and correct my flight path, I noticed that the computer was still working and was displaying the program World Map.
The map traced our flight path and blinked a marker showing our
present location. We were above Boston. That meant that we would
be out of communication range with mission control in Moscow for
at least half an hour.

I considered using the ham radio that we had onboard to make a
distress call, along the lines of: "This is Astronaut Linenger aboard
Space Station *Mir*, broadcasting in the blind. We have an emergency,
a fire. We are preparing to abandon the space station. Please contact
the Johnson Space Center, Houston. Inform them of our situation
and ask them to contact mission control in Moscow. This is an
emergency. Out."

Such a call would give the Russian ground controller's time to call
in their Soyuz control team in the event that we were forced to abandoned ship. Evacuation was a very real possibility. In fact, even if we
were able to extinguish the fire, we might still be forced to return to
earth. Because of the fire, *Mir*'s environmental control systems could
become so saturated with smoke that the air would never clear.
Unable to clear the smoke, all six of us would be forced to abandon
ship as soon as the oxygen in our respirators was spent. That meant
that the Russian controllers would have two Soyuz capsules undocking from the station simultaneously. The call would also allow them
time to get recovery teams into place in Kazakhstan for the unexpected landing of two capsules.

I never made the ham radio call. It dawned on me that it was more
important to get the fire extinguisher back to Korzun than to take
the time to bark out a distress call. People on the ground could not
help us in the near term. Our survival rested upon our own shoulders. I pushed off the platform and back toward the fire.

In spite of the fresh fire extinguisher—the third used—the charac-
ter of the fire remained unchanged. Smoke continued to billow
through the tunnel and the flame continued to roar.

I continued to hold tight to Korzun's waist. After not feeling any
motion from him for thirty seconds or so, I moved my way up to his
chest and then face in order to be sure that he was still conscious.
Two inches from his face, I was still unable to see distinctly whether

his eyes were open and alert. I shouted at him. "Yes, I am okay, Jerry" he replied. "How are the others?" I assured him everyone was still okay.

The flame looked no different than it had from the start. Molten metal was still spewing from the far edges of the flame and splattering on the far bulkhead. That particular bulkhead was charred coal-black, but was not actively burning. I realized that we were lucky that we had stuffed much of the garbage that normally floats in the module into the Progress garbage truck two weeks earlier, or else secondary fires would surely have started.

I noticed that behind the flame, the immense heat generated by the fire had melted the valve covers of the carbon-dioxide scrubber equipment. And then, after raging for fourteen uncontrollable minutes, the fire consumed itself and went out.

KORZUN announced joyously, "The fire is out!" and we all breathed a momentary sigh of relief. But after quickly reassessing our situation, the outlook still appeared bleak. Thick smoke was everywhere. The air was not breathable. We all realized that the oxygen respirators we were using had finite life spans—one to two hours at most.

We immediately shifted gears. We went from a flurry of activity to deliberate inactivity. All we had left were the respirators on our faces and a spare one for each of us. The aftereffects of the fire could still defeat us. I suggested to Valeri that everyone do as little as possible to keep our metabolic rates to a minimum.

I was the only one who kept working, though slowly and methodically, being careful to expend minimal energy. I had to be prepared should one of the crew begin to have respiratory problems. Inhalation injury to lungs often manifests itself well after the exposure to smoke. If one of the crew began gasping for air, I needed to be ready immediately.

I grabbed my emergency medical kits and moved them to the airlock. It was always damp in the airlock—free water actually accumulated pints at a time on its cold aluminum hull—and this condensation would help to clear the smoke from the air. In fact, although Energia, the state-run company that built the modules for the space station, would later claim that the air-filtering system on *Mir* worked superbly to remove smoke and contaminants from the air after the fire, we were convinced that simple condensation of the smoke and water mist—the fire extinguishers were water based—on the cold hull was the most effective filter.

I used bungee-cord straps to hold my mini-emergency room instruments—tracheotomy tubes, laryngoscope, ambulatory-breathing bag, oxygen tank, scalpel, stethoscope, and blood oximeter—in place. I then mentally rehearsed what I would do should someone go into respiratory distress, which included such weightlessness-related complications as how to secure the patient to the floor before I would attempt to intubate him or slit his cricothyroid membrane. Looking at the makeshift emergency room, I hoped that no one would need my services.

We were growing concerned. The smoke remained thick even after forty-five minutes. Until that moment, I had never really paid much attention to my every single inhalation and exhalation. We waited, hoping that the air would clear before the oxygen in our masks stopped flowing.

Each personal respirator ran out of oxygen at different times. Korzun's respirator ran out first, after about an hour, probably because he had been breathing the hardest while firing the extinguishers so close to the flames. He sniffed the air in the airlock and declared it breathable. We were all relieved. We would not have to abandon the station.

I went into a damage-control mode. Relatively certain that we had avoided any life-threatening acute medical effects of the fire, I focused my attention on trying to minimize any long-term health problems that we might suffer. I recommended that anyone with a less-than-depleted respirator continue to use it until the last breath of the oxygen was used. Although the air was breathable, it was still smoky and was surely contaminated by metal fumes and other by-products of the fire.

I found some 3-M filter masks and gave one to each of the crew. As our respirators ran dry of oxygen, we replaced the full-faced rubber mask with a filter mask. Although not ideal, the filter masks would at least block out some of the larger floating particles.

I made a number of preventive health recommendations to Korzun, all of which he accepted. Any contaminant in a closed ecosystem like *Mir* would inevitably end up back in the air. Anything in the air would eventually end up in our lungs. We bagged what remained of the burnt canister in an airtight rubberized bag. We washed down all the bulkheads and sopped up the soot-laden condensate from the hull. Everyone removed his smoke-contaminated clothing and washed down from head to toe. Consequently, the scene onboard *Mir* a few hours after the fire was almost laughable: six floating men, scrubbing away, all naked but for a filter mask over their faces.

I did medical exams on everyone. A few members of the crew had minor decreases in their blood-oxygen saturation, but nothing severe. Everyone's lungs were clear. I treated the skin burns—most minor, but some second degree—by cleaning them as best I could, applying ointment, and then covering them with a gauze dressing. I was asked to not report any of our injuries to the ground. Korzun was fearful that they might order him to stay onboard *Mir* longer in order for the burns to heal and not return to earth as scheduled in a few days. I complied with the request, and when later asked by the Russian flight surgeons in Moscow, I feigned misunderstanding their question—Russian sure is a tough language to comprehend—and simply replied that I had the medical situation onboard under control.

I did an exam on myself last. I had good oxygen saturation in my blood: 98 percent. No wheezes or rales in my chest. I had a few scrapes and bruises—too much fast flying in poor visibility—but no severe burns. I also noted that I was unshaken, mentally and psychologically I felt fine. I made a note to myself to keep a close eye on the rest of the crew's mental health.

It dawned on me that the extreme density of the smoke had been, in some ways, a blessing. The suffocating smoke forced each of us to put on a respirator immediately, thus protecting our lungs from being damaged. Nonetheless, over the next forty-eight hours, I repeated the medical exams on everyone and requested that the minute anyone felt even the least bit uncomfortable breathing to see me immediately.

I also grabbed every air-sampling device we had onboard and began taking air samples. Most of the sampling devices that I borrowed from the U.S. science program stash were small metal spheres with an attached valve. Inside each sphere was nothing, a vacuum. Open the valve, and air from the space station goes into a collection device. Close the valve and the sample is preserved.

I took the air samples from several different locations at thirty-minute intervals. By later analyzing these samples, environmental engineers in Russia and the U.S. would be able to evaluate the effectiveness of the air-cleaning systems onboard *Mir*. Furthermore, toxicologists would be able to tell us what contaminants we were exposed to, at what level, and for how long. Because the fire was the most severe ever to occur in an orbiting spacecraft, I figured that we needed to learn everything possible from our experience.

AFTER nearly forty-eight hours without sleep, I climbed onto my sleeping wall and wrapped a bungee cord around my chest. I thought for a moment about our crew.

No one had panicked. All did their part, and had acted heroically. I felt my level of confidence in the crew and in myself rise. I knew that if another emergency arose that was humanly survivable, we would survive.

I adjusted my filter mask, closed my eyes, and, without the slightest feeling of anxiety, fell asleep.

13

An Attempted Coverup

IN THE DAYS FOLLOWING the fire we got back to the business at hand aboard *Mir*. With the exception of doing some wound dressing changes and further cleaning up of the station, we settled into a frenzied, but normal routine.

While not dwelling on the fire, the subject did become the primary topic of conversation among the crew. In addition to our discussions around the dinner table, individually, I think, we all reflected on how tenuous our existence was here on the frontier, how our lives could be snuffed out in an instant.

We talked about what we might have done differently, given hindsight. During a private conversation between Valeri Korzun and me, we broached the subject of evacuation. He told me that there was no way he was ever going to abandon the space station; he would, essentially, have gone down with the ship. "Jerry, how could I climb into the Soyuz and leave three people behind?"

To be sure, Korzun, the *Mir* commander at the time of the fire, was in a no-win situation. Vasily Tsibliev, the oncoming *Mir* commander, was able to complete all of the steps in the Soyuz activation checklist during the fire and had the only accessible Soyuz escape vehicle ready to depart. But since each of the three seats in the Soyuz is customized to fit only one particular person, which of us could evacuate was predetermined. In the ready-to-evacuate vehicle were the custom-fit spacesuits and custom-fit seat liners of Tsibliev, Lazutkin, and myself. In theory we were the only three that could have left during the fire. In actuality, any three of us could have ridden in the vehicle—risking reentry without a spacesuit or wearing an ill-fitting spacesuit (survivable, as long as the spacecraft maintains pressure integrity*), and risking a landing injury secondary to an ill-fitting impact-absorbing seat liner. But surely these would have been risks worth taking if the only other option was remaining in a space station with a completely out-of-control fire.

Unfortunately, there is no way to squeeze more than three people into a Soyuz capsule. There are only three seats in the spacecraft. Even if one other person, without a seat, sprawled across the sitting crew, the presence of that fourth person would shift the center of gravity of the vehicle, most likely causing the capsule to tumble during reentry. A tumbling vehicle means that the spacecraft's heat shield would not be pointed in the proper direction. Those inside the spacecraft would find themselves inside a fireball and, without the heat shield, the capsule and the crew inside would all burn up.

I pressed the discussion further with Korzun. "Valeri, you are about to leave in less than a week anyway. Why not go? The three of us remaining could do our best and fight the fire. Risking the lives of three is better than risking the lives of six." Despite my theoretical argument, he remained firm; there was no way that he was going to leave.

The way I saw it, there was no way Tsibliev, Lazutkin, and I were going to leave the other three behind either. We would all succeed in getting the fire out or we would all go down with the ship. That was the reality. That reality lends further support to the premise that we should never tolerate unsafe and unreliable equipment because there is "always the option to evacuate." Doing so, at times, goes against the nature of astronaut and cosmonauts to stick together as a team, to be gallant and brave.

Another consideration that cannot be discounted and that might have swayed Korzun's thinking—for that matter, all of our thinking—was that *Mir* can no longer mechanically survive without the

---

*The Russians lost three cosmonauts in 1971 when the pressure equalization valve of Soyuz 11 stuck open during reentry. None of the cosmonauts was wearing a protective spacesuit, and all suffocated.

care and attendance of human beings aboard. A decision to leave *Mir* is essentially a decision to allow *Mir* to die. And there is a lot riding on that decision, a lot of pressure—not spoken directly, but strongly implied—from mission control in Moscow for the crew to hang in there. After all, without *Mir,* the flight controllers in mission control in Moscow have no jobs. And without *Mir,* the Russians have no space program. In a similar vein, from the American viewpoint, without *Mir* there can be no cooperative shuttle-*Mir* program with the Russians. No joint cooperative space program, and the U.S. administration loses one politically justifiable way to funnel money to Russia as part of an American foreign-aid program. These are big stakes.

According to one *New York Times* article, "Washington wants to do all it can to help the shaky Russian economy. . . . When the cooperative [space] program got under way, the United States provided cash incentives, and nowadays when things go awry, they look the other way." Described by the media as a "bargaining chip" of foreign policy, the shuttle-*Mir* program enabled the United States initially to pay "several hundred million dollars to train its astronauts onboard the *Mir,* and in Russia these days, money like that is rare."

That the shuttle-*Mir* program is primarily a political rather than a technical endeavor is obvious to anyone working on it or familiar with it.

And there is yet another aspect to this situation. Had we abandoned the space station, we would have to live the rest of our lives under the yoke of being labeled the crew that bailed out of *Mir.* Perhaps there would be whispers that our crew did not have the courage needed, the mettle required. But misplaced courage could have left six of us dead.

OUR CONVERSATIONS were not always so serious. We would all roar with laughter after embellishing, yet further in each retelling, what we had seen the competent off-going flight engineer Sasha Kaleri doing during the fire.

With the fire raging five feet in front of my face, and as I looked back over my shoulder, I noticed the shadowy figure of Sasha Kaleri typing on a laptop computer. I squinted, looked again, and confirmed that yes, indeed, Sasha was typing away on the laptop.

"Man, this guy is *really* cool," I thought. "In the middle of all of this mess, the guy is floating there casually typing a letter!"

In fact, Sasha was not typing a letter, and we knew it. He was printing out the reentry profile data for that particular day, one printout
for each of the Soyuz capsules. The printout listed vital information
that we would need to fly the Soyuz back to the planet and to reenter
earth's atmosphere without input from the ground. Without the
information, should our radios in the Soyuz fail and render us pow-
erless to communicate with the ground, we would not be able to
accurately pilot the spacecraft back through the atmosphere.

To be sure, that information should have been printed out first
thing each and every morning, but it had not been. The fire experience reawakened us to the possibility of a sudden and life-threatening emergency on the aging *Mir*. Thereafter, we printed out reentry
profiles each day. We were no longer cavalier about the safety of our
space station and always prepared for the worst.

Resurrecting his own memory of watching Sasha calmly typing in
the midst of the space station's angry fire, Vasily Tsibliev, wearing his
patented smirk, could not resist teasing Kaleri about his apparent
composure, even serenity. "Here we are, Sasha . . . everyone scrambling . . . smoke so thick that we couldn't see anything clearly . . .
the fire is raging. And you are over there, typing a letter on the computer and printing out messages. You are a crazy man, Sasha."

WHILE I was never forewarned about any previous fires onboard *Mir*
before my flight, I have since been told, privately, by another cosmonaut, that during his flight two years prior to my *Mir* flight the
same type of canister caught on fire. Fortunately, in that instance, the
canister burned for only a few seconds and with a small, easily extinguished flame. But were lessons learned from this incident? Was the
design improved? Not at all.

About three weeks after the fire, I indirectly received word from
the small NASA team at mission control in Moscow that the
Russians maintained that the fire was most likely caused by operator error. They maintained that Lazutkin had opened the seal of the
canister, let it sit for hours in the damp Kvant I module, and that,
somehow, water had seeped into the canister's chemical mixture. The
Russians suggested that when Lazutkin finally got around to activating the device, a damp plug of chemical somehow caused the canister to burst into flames.

Although perhaps a well-orchestrated theory, it did not fit the facts. As I recalled it, Lazutkin finished eating dinner, flew into the Kvant I module, and, without delay, removed the canister seal and activated the device. To confirm my recollection, I asked Sasha about his memory of the event, and he said that, yes, he had immediately activated the device. "That cannot be the reason for the fire," he told me.

I told the NASA group in Moscow via radio that somebody on the ground had better start looking seriously into what caused the fire. I also suggested that future theories about what caused the fire should be communicated to the crew to check their viability, before they were officially accepted by the ground. After all, as the only ones present when the fire occurred, we could accurately account for its circumstances.

Unfortunately, it became clear to us that by seeking to propound such rationalizations and theories, the Russians were implementing a strategy concerned less about crew safety than space station publicity. As long as the crew was said to have made an error and could be used as a scapegoat, and as long as the actual cause of the fire remained unknown, then the real cause of the fire—apparently an innate problem with the system—need not be reported to the world. As a corollary, the crew could be told to continue using the canisters since they were "safe" if operated properly, and the *Mir* could continue flying.

Frankly, it was clear to all of us onboard that the Russian space officials were doing their best to try to minimize any bad publicity concerning the *Mir* fire by not being forthright about the fire's severity. The original Russian press release stated that there was a minor fire on *Mir* that burned for a few seconds. The cosmonauts easily extinguished the fire, and no one was hurt. NASA public affairs officials followed suit and even praised the Russians for being "very informative and forthright as to what happened." A NASA press release, titled "Small Fire Extinguished on *Mir*," and published the day after the fire, reported that "a problem with an oxygen-generating device on the *Mir* space station . . . caused minor damage to some hardware when . . . a small fire burned for about ninety seconds . . . and was easily extinguished by the crew."

By crew consensus, we concluded that the fire had burned for *fourteen* minutes. It was a big fire. The fire extinguishers did little to extinguish the fire.

WITH primary oxygen-system failures occurring frequently over the next few months, we were constantly activating more supplemental oxygen canisters, as many as three canisters a day. We were told by mission control in Moscow that the canisters, the same type from which the fire had originated, were now safe to use. They were deemed safe not because anything had been changed in their design nor because the cause of the fire had been determined, but rather because mission control in Moscow now introduced the requirement that whenever we activated one of the canisters, we stand by with a fire extinguisher.

This added requirement was no confidence-builder to us on *Mir.*

We did what we were told to do. What option did we have? We needed to breathe; we needed to replenish our oxygen onboard. When the primary oxygen-generating system failed, which, unfortunately, was an almost-every-other-day occurrence, we had to resort to using the canisters to produce oxygen. Even when the primary system was working, electrical power-system failures often resulted in inadequate power to run the primary oxygen generator. During these power outages, we were once again forced to use the canisters to produce oxygen.

To be sure, Lazutkin, Tsibliev, and I never really believed that a fire extinguisher would effectively put out a canister fire. We had already seen the ineffectiveness of the fire extinguishers in putting out such a fire. In spite of our best efforts, and in spite of emptying the contents of three fire extinguishers on the fire, it had burned out of control for fourteen minutes. In our judgment, the fire was extinguished only by consuming itself; that is, it ceased to burn only when most of the chemical in the canister was used up. To stand by with a fire extinguisher when activating future canisters in hopes of putting a fire out quickly was ludicrous. We all knew that we had gotten lucky during the fire. We barely survived.

IN RETROSPECT, I am amazed at the amount of information that passed through my mind during the fire. Time expanded. The intellect refused to blend each split second of reality and perceptions and feeling into a fluid, chronological movie. The memory of those mental gymnastics will stay with me forever.

In a strange way, the *Mir* fire experience has become a defining moment in my life. From what was a jarring encounter with my own mortality came insights I would not have otherwise had about human nature and about myself. About our ability to remain calm in the face of a terrifying circumstance. About our capacity to care about others in times of greatest personal danger. And about our ability to put past troubles behind us and to press on.

14

Cosmonauts, *Da!* Mission Control, *Nyet!*

DURING TRAINING SESSIONS in Russia, a Russian psychologist would sometimes tag along in order to observe the interactions among the crew. He was a jolly fellow, irritatingly so, always smiling and upbeat regardless of the circumstance. I was thankful that my life was not as sugar-coated and sweet as his must have been. I did not mind being serious now and then. Trying to be inconspicuous and covertly observe our behavior, he was always the center of attention, and loved to tell stories in his big, booming voice. Over time, we began to regard him as part of the crew.

In fact, and I might be mistaken since I am not a psychologist, I think that the two Russian cosmonauts I was training with began to prefer him over me, and probably would have liked to have him as their crewmate instead of me. We all felt badly for him that the Soyuz only had three seats and that he could not come with us on the mission.

From his inconspicuous position—standing right in the middle of us—he would, without disrupting what we were engaged in doing, pull one of us out of the training and provide some suggestions as to how to better handle certain situations or more smoothly engage in interpersonal interactions. The more he interrupted, the less we talked among ourselves, fearful that we might say the wrong thing and be singled out for another lecture on "how to get along, how not to offend." My favorite moments with him would occur when he would urgently pull me aside, hand me a deck of ten colored cards, and ask me to arrange them in the order that I "felt" at that moment.

I always tried to cooperate, in spite of the fact that the game got old after the fifth or sixth time. On one occasion, we were doing Soyuz water survival training on the Black Sea aboard a Russian Navy trawler. Should the Soyuz miss the thousand-mile-wide desert and end up parachuting into the drink, we had to be ready. I was in a particularly good mood that day, since, being a U.S. naval officer, it felt good to be back at sea with saltwater splashing in my face. The sailors onboard were fun to be around.

When the Russian sailors learned that I was a navy man, they could not resist taking me up to the signal bridge. There, stenciled to the bulkhead, was the silhouette of all U.S. fighter, attack, and patrol jets. "Are these accurate?" they asked me, smiling. I told them that they could scratch off the S2 anti-submarine warfare plane; it had long ago been replaced by the S3 *Viking,* which was pictured accurately next to the S2.

I told them that I had once flown in the S2 with some navy special forces SEALs who were using the operationally retired plane for parachute training. I further explained that on that particular flight my friends, the SEALs, pulled me to within one foot of the door and almost pushed me out without a parachute. Well, the Russian sailors laughed almost as loudly as the cosmonauts laughed at the psychologist's stories. Armed with this new firsthand naval intelligence, a sailor then took a marker pen out of his pocket and scratched through the S2, bringing their display up to date.

Returning from the signal bridge and the engine room and all other parts of the rusting ship that the sailors insisted that I see (no U.S. Navy ship that I was ever on was in such a state of disrepair), we got down to the task at hand. Entering the bridge where the cosmonauts were sitting at a table captivated by yet another story told by the ever-present psychologist, I could tell that my absence was duly noted with yet another black mark. I was off on my own, not bonding as I should have been. My punishment was having to do the card trick once again, the result of which I am sure indicated that I was too free-spirited, too independent, to make a very good crewmate.

The cosmonauts and I got into our spacesuits and were lowered into a bobbing Soyuz capsule on the surface of the sea. Crawling inside the cramped and stuffy capsule, we closed the hatch and began to gather our survival gear. The gear was stuffed behind the seats in any available crevice, seemingly placed only in the hardest to reach places. After all gear was located and unpacked, it was time to get out of our spacesuits and into the survival gear. Unfortunately, we were so crammed in the capsule that only one of us could maneuver at a time to get undressed. That struggle complete, and after bobbing around sweaty and naked trying to cool off, we would then reverse course and struggle to get dressed in the rubberized cold-water survival gear. The rubber suit was hot, the capsule stuffy and unstable, and the waves nauseatingly high.

Once everyone was fully suited, we thankfully opened the hatch, tossed out our life rafts, and then, after climbing atop a precarious perch on the hatch-opening ring, we back-flopped into the icy water. My waterproof suit had numerous leaks, and I quickly climbed into the raft before the suit, rapidly filling with water, pulled me under. I then bobbed around for too long in the life raft—activating flares, tossing dye markers and shark repellent into the water, and bailing water from the raft, proving to the instructors that I could stay afloat. A safety diver was clinging to my raft trying not to drown. I asked him whether the shark repellent actually works.

"No, it does not do a bit of good," he replied in short gasps, as the saltwater sprayed into his face. "In fact, the sharks might even be attracted to the color for all we know."

The important thing, he then explained, was not whether the repellent worked or not, but that the cosmonauts *thought* that it worked. The repellent helps to reduce not shark attacks but anxiety attacks caused by the ordeal of being stuck in the middle of the ocean alone thinking that sharks might attack. I wished that I had not asked the question. I wished that he had not replied truthfully. I decided to forget his answer immediately.

A crane reached over the gunwale of the ship and swooped me back onto the deck. Standing dripping wet, shivering, and on the verge of getting sick on the shoes that I saw squarely planted in front of my stooped head, I tried unsuccessfully to straighten up. The hood of my survival suit was yanking my head down so that I could not stand upright. "Who is that standing in front of me?" I wondered.

I next saw a deck of colored cards coming into sight. Ah, the shoes must be those of our friend the psychologist. He must have astutely ascertained, tipped off no doubt by my body language—head drooped downward in a sullen gaze—that my mood had changed, that I was no longer smiling. It was a perfect time to play cards and perhaps capture a mood shift.

But I defied all anticipated odds and put the brighter colored cards at the beginning and black colored cards at the very end, as I always did. I figured that the color black must represent a "dark mood," something that I thought might be held against me in the psychologist's mind. I always put black last.

The fact is, I like the color black. I even own a black sweater. The fact is, sometimes I "felt" more black than indigo. But I did not want him to know that. He might find me "not psychologically adapted for long duration spaceflight" based on the black card being placed in any position but last.

I will admit that after being interrupted a number of times throughout training sessions to do this card trick, I would sometimes intentionally put the cards down in some oddball order just to give the doctor something to analyze later in the day. The exception being, of course, the black card, which I placed last consistently, whether I felt like vomiting or not. Inkblot tests would surely follow; did they really think that I was crazy?

I later found out that based on the card "feel" test and other highly scientific tests originally designed to detect overt schizophrenia, I was labeled as having the egocentric personality type and that I would be a difficult person to get along with for months on end. Who would not be difficult to get along with trapped on a school bus with nowhere to go for five months? That I was labeled egocentric was the biggest surprise of all, not because it was an incorrect diagnosis, but because it was a correct diagnosis. His methodology worked!

All astronauts are high achievers or they would not be astronauts. Pilot-astronauts are so off-scale high on the ego scale of pen-and-paper personality tests that the tracing blip goes off the top of the paper. As a flight surgeon, I knew that egocentricity, as defined by personality testing scores, is a positive and highly desired trait for aviators. All military pilots worth their salt must feel extremely confident in their abilities and must prefer to do it themselves rather than have someone else do it for them.

In fact, a naval aviation applicant who scores high on the ego scale of personality tests is predicted to be a more successful fighter pilot or attack pilot than the applicant who scores low on that particular scale. Being egocentric is a desirable characteristic for aviators, explorers, and adventurers. It does not mean that the person goes around all day declaring how great they are, but rather indicates that the person with that personality trait possesses the self-confidence to survive some trying times.

I learned, only after my flight, that the inconspicuous Russian psychologist expressed "grave concerns" that I would not fit in well with the other two cosmonauts. I can only say that he was lucky that I was not the typical astronaut, or he would have been shocked. I am only mildly egocentric, not off-scale high egocentric like many of my talented, well-liked, and extremely capable astronaut colleagues.

WHILE I felt extremely well prepared technically, I could never fully prepare for the human and psychological aspects of the flight because of the uncertainty about who I would be flying with. Even while I was training on the ground for *Mir,* I recognized that it was critical that I should get along with my two cosmonaut crewmates, whomever they turned out to be. Interactions with visitors to *Mir* were of no concern. The five days that the shuttle spent docked to the *Mir,* at both the beginning and the end of my long-duration stay, would be insignificant in comparison to the months of time involved with only two other people on *Mir.*

Besides, these few days of crew-overlap during the shuttle-*Mir* docked phase are dramatically different in spirit and protocol from a routine shuttle or *Mir* workday. In fact, the atmosphere aboard *Mir* during the shuttle docking is almost festive. If they were to exist at all, conflicts between the crew members always seem irrelevant at this time. Who cannot tolerate even his worst enemy for five days? Even if a serious conflict arose, with nine people onboard the combined complex, it was quite easy to avoid the person with whom there are tensions and mingle, instead, with the other members of the crew.

But I was going to be spending more than a few days with, as it turned out, the Russian *Mir*-22 and *Mir*-23 crew. I would be looking at the same two faces of the *Mir*-22 crew for a month followed by the faces of the two cosmonauts of the *Mir*-23 crew for almost four months. These were the people with whom I had to work, eat meals, overcome obstacles, and live, day after day after unchanging day. It meant that I had to put aside any cultural or political differences; we had to be able to work together as a team for months on end. While I hoped that we could put our differences aside, I knew that it would not be an easy task.

I WAS the replacement for U.S. astronaut John Blaha, who had spent the last four months on the space station. When I arrived on *Mir,* and during the five-day shuttle docking period with the space station, John did his best to acquaint me with the U.S. science hardware on the space station as well as the general lay of the land. He showed me how he did the daily housekeeping and personal grooming tasks associated with living on the space station. He instructed me in the use of the treadmill, the toilet, his technique for bathing, and even such mundane activities as where to find a clean towel. All this information was very important because, to be honest, much of the housekeeping and science equipment on the then eleven-year-old space station had been modified or jury-rigged over time, so much so that the ground training I had received in Russia was outdated at best, and in many cases, no longer usable.

One of the two treadmills on *Mir,* for example, did not operate in a programmed mode and did not run at three speeds, as I had been taught it would when I was training in Russia. Instead, as John carefully explained to me, only the fast speed still worked on this piece of old exercise equipment. If I turned the treadmill on, I had to be ready to sprint. Without his warning, I surely would have been thrown from the treadmill, for the treadmill abruptly accelerated to full speed in a matter of seconds. So fast, in fact, that I was the only person in the new crew who could use this particular treadmill, for the pace it demanded was too fast for my crewmates to maintain for any length of time.

John Blaha stuck with me. He crammed into five days useful information that might have taken me two months to acquire back in Star City. More important, the information he conveyed was both relevant and correct.

Furthermore, John's unalloyed frankness about his own experience on *Mir*—the good and the bad—proved invaluable to me. John's uncensored remarks allowed me to fine-tune my mind-set, to anticipate the obstacles, including the not-often-discussed mental and psychological hurdles that I would face. Knowing what to expect, I could keep my guard up.

John told me that living on *Mir* was an endurance test. There was nowhere to go; you were trapped. And no matter how bad things became, no matter how uncooperative the Russians were or how poor the ground support was, there was nothing that you could do about it. He insisted that it was important for me to accept my circumstances early on. Whether I liked it or not, I was stuck onboard for the duration. Since the only person you can truly depend upon is yourself, when an uncomfortable situation arises, face it, do something about it, overcome it. Do not let problems linger, because they never go away by themselves.

The one subject that John could not talk about without his neck veins bulging was the *Mir* communication system. The *Mir* air-to-ground communications system onboard was "atrocious." He warned me to expect no reliable communications, or "comm," with the ground, despite what I had been told by the Russians. Contrary to any expectations that I might have, there would be limited conversations with members of my family or with the NASA support team in Moscow. Even if the notoriously unreliable comm system was working technically, the Russian ground controllers would, without apology, interrupt and use the U.S. scheduled time slots to conduct their own business.

"You are an inconvenience, a nuisance to them; your work deemed unimportant," John warned me. "Jerry, you will be cut off and isolated to a degree that is hard to imagine. Coping with the isolation will be your greatest challenge. And no one on the NASA side seems to care one bit; no one seems willing to take a stand." John spoke with such emotion that he was very close to choking. He was a wounded soul, a person who felt abandoned. He was trying to hang in there for a few more days on this cursed outpost. He felt that he had been betrayed, not supported, forgotten both by the Russians, which he could accept, and by our side, which to him was inexcusable.

During private conversations with John, it became apparent to me that he had not only become frustrated by the technically poor and often rudely interrupted comm, but more so by the fact that he was unable to correct the situation. Try as he might, he was unable to get anyone on the ground to fix the problem. John's disillusionment and obvious frustration about the lack of response to his pleading made such an impression on me that I decided that I would use the comm for only the first month. If after the trial period it became clear to me that the Russians were still not delivering on their promise to give the American onboard adequate comm time, then I would just stop using the system. I vowed, for the sake of my own mental health, that I would not allow myself to become as frustrated about the poor communications as John had obviously and justifiably become.

Disturbingly, John also told me that the supposed "equal" partnership between the Russians and the Americans on *Mir* was anything but equal. The *Mir* commander and the Russian ground-control team in Moscow had treated him like a second-class citizen during his entire stay on the space station. It was a Russian space station; all communications were conducted in Russian, and only with mission control in Moscow. Houston was involved only during the five-day shuttle-docking period. Although the *Mir* mission would be John's fifth trip into space, and even though he had previously commanded shuttle missions, the Russians did not regard John as the professional, highly trained, and experienced astronaut that he was. Instead, he was relegated to guest cosmonaut status, which was the same job given to former Eastern bloc one-time fliers who had, years before, been put on *Mir* for short stays, mainly to satisfy Soviet propaganda goals.

These one-time flyers of the past were typically selected from a Soviet-bloc country to be on the space station, not for months at a time, but rather for days. During this brief visit to the station, the guest cosmonaut, who had only limited scientific responsibilities and virtually no space station system responsibilities, was expected to follow strictly the orders of the ground and of the other Russians onboard. If the guest cosmonaut touched a switch, his hand was slapped. John felt that he, too, had been regarded as a guest flyer and not as an equal. That his NASA ground-support team in Moscow, and even more so, the shuttle-*Mir* management team back in Houston, did nothing to try to change that situation, bothered John deeply.

Interestingly, the United States was funding *Mir*'s continued existence. In fact, without NASA participation and financial support, *Mir* would have collapsed long ago. Yet John clearly felt that NASA, despite the leverage that it should wield, had done little to improve his situation on *Mir*. John was not whining or complaining, he was being honest. We were friends. I respected John; he respected me. He knew me to be a competent astronaut who had worked very hard to prepare for the mission and planned on accomplishing all of the mission goals. He wanted me to know of the barriers and pitfalls that I would face, obstacles that might imperil my chances of success.

ALSO contributing to John's problems was the often tense relationship John had with the *Mir* commander, Valeri Korzun. Worried about the possibility that Korzun would treat me as he had treated him, John advised me not to take Korzun's behavior toward me too personally.

According to John, Korzun would drive his crew crazy with his insistent micromanagement of their assigned tasks. Korzun constantly looked over John's shoulder and never showed confidence in John's competence. John believed that Korzun obsessively worried that one of the crew might do something that would get the commander in trouble with Russian ground control, thereby ruining Korzun's report card at mission control in Moscow.

Historically, management at mission control in Moscow grades each *Mir* mission task by task. The pay that the Russian cosmonauts receive upon landing is determined by their performance grade. Make a mistake, lose money. Miss doing a planned spacewalk and your pay is docked.

In reality, a *Mir* commander's report card was in large measure a reflection of a commander's compliance with mission control in Moscow. The implied threat: Do what you are told, don't rock the boat, keep quiet about any trouble on board, and you will receive your full pay. High marks reflected compliance with Moscow's wishes. Low marks might reflect poor performance, but on the other hand, they might be more indicative of a crew that openly discussed needed improvements and safety concerns and acknowledged problems brewing onboard.

Korzun understood that the ground's impression of a mission was only as good as what he reported to them. The only people in the world who actually knew what was happening onboard the space station were, of course, the people on the space station. Everyone else had secondhand information. Opinions were formed only by what they heard over the radio. Korzun adopted the strategy of "tell them what they want to hear," and thus ensured that he would be regarded as a very good *Mir* commander in the eyes of the ground controllers. While I do not believe that his actions were dictated entirely by considerations to maximize his pay and to enhance his image with the ground, the carrot-and-stick pay system was one Korzun obviously accepted.

John told me that the situation between him and Korzun had improved over time, but only after John and the *Mir* commander had many heated discussions. Blaha suspected that I would not have the strained relationship with Korzun that he had had, mainly because he believed that Korzun, in the end, recognized that his overweening approach toward John was counterproductive. John also suspected that Sasha Kaleri had spoken privately with Korzun concerning the matter, warning him that his tactics were a threat to crew unity.

Armed with the insights I had gained from John's experiences, a strategy of forthrightness and taking responsibility for myself enabled me to remain on a very even keel throughout my entire stay on *Mir.* Despite the many tense moments, and often overwhelming frustrations and dangers that I faced on the Russian space station, I remained emotionally, psychologically, and mentally healthy throughout my entire stay. By remaining healthy, I stayed efficient to the end and was able to accomplish 100 percent of the U.S. mission goals despite the circumstances we faced.

If the Russian controllers found me difficult to work with and labeled me "not a team player" and as a rebel, so be it. While they were sitting smug and comfortable in their armchairs getting second- and thirdhand information, we cosmonauts were facing real danger and trying to get the job done. How could they understand? What right did they have to guess at how well any of us were doing in space, especially in light of a communication system that hardly worked? If feathers were ruffled on the ground, they needed to be ruffled. The only objective report card, the one that reflects whether the crew was able to keep a crumbling space station alive and still accomplish the mission goals, is a report card that I am proud of, a report card of success.

AFTER Korzun, Kaleri, and I spent a cordial and productive month together on the space station, their time aboard *Mir* came to an end.

Sasha Kaleri and I shook hands. I told him that I was very happy for him, and that I would love to see the look on his face when he was reunited with his wife and infant son. He told me that he would send my love to Kathryn and take John a toy. He then flew into the Soyuz and began powering up the spaceship for departure.

Valeri Korzun was much more sentimental. While he was glad to be going back to the planet, he was going to miss being in space. He had to swallow hard a few times in order to keep his emotions in check. After assuring me that he would smuggle my handwritten letter to Kathryn—he had stuffed it inside his spacesuit—he said a final good-bye, shook my hand, bear-hugged Vasily, and reluctantly departed.

IMAGINE living on a couple of school buses with two strangers for five months. The school buses are not traveling down a familiar road, but are flying through space at twenty-five times the speed of sound. The buses are crammed with science gear and equipment. The decor is not warm and soothing, but rather more closely resembles the furnishings of a factory. They are old and in constant need of repair, smell like a musty cellar, and are filled with the irritating noise of valves opening and closing and of fans constantly whirring. The walls creak and groan every forty-five minutes as day turns to night, night to day.

The strangers talk only in Russian. No English. They know nothing about the New York Yankees or Babe Ruth. Small talk is limited, and the phone is, more often than not, broken.

Change the equation. Handpick any two people whom you care to choose. Now imagine five months with them, constantly in their presence, never getting away from them. Would conflict arise? How well would you hold up psychologically? Would claustrophobia haunt you?

It was anticipated that conflict in such an environment was inevitable, and that isolation off the planet would place an unnatural psychological strain on a human being, so a group of experts was formed to help support us psychologically while we were in space. The cosmonaut psychological support group consisted of Russian and American psychologists, social scientists, and flight surgeons. Their task was to attempt to keep the crew mentally and psychologically sound and motivated throughout the long space flight. This group of experts would also intervene from afar if they sensed that a member of the crew was not handling the isolation and stress well or was not getting along with the other cosmonauts on the space station.

To evaluate the crew's psychological status from their position on the ground at mission control in Moscow, the psychological support group would monitor the crew during selected communication passes. Voice inflection, apparent moods, and even how many times each of the crew laughed were factors taken into consideration. On the basis of this very subjective approach, the psychological support group made their judgments and planned their form of intervention.

Because our comm passes with the ground were characterized by approximately five minutes of static-filled and generally garbled shouting, the attempt to clinically diagnose crew moods and interactions by such indirect methodology proved to be a very inexact science.

I learned from John Blaha and from my own experience that the U.S.-designated comm sessions would either be so static-filled as to be totally incomprehensible, or, if clear, the Russians would interrupt and use the time for their own purposes. After a month of trying to remedy the situation with no success, I asked the NASA team in Moscow to start trying to fix the problem for the subsequent American flight. In the meantime I was going "off comm." I did not want to participate in a farce. Nor did I want to become as frustrated as John had become during his continual attempts to fix the system.

My silence was, of course, misinterpreted by the psychologists as some extreme measure to totally isolate myself. I was losing it. They probably figured that if given the colored deck of cards, I would put, God forbid, the black card *first!*

According to Tom Marshburn, the U.S. flight surgeon who worked at mission control in Moscow, the Russian members of the psychological support group also misinterpreted the relationship between Vasily Tsibliev and myself. They were convinced that we hated each other and were battling constantly. "Cats and dogs," Tom told me after the flight. Because Tsibliev and I were scheduled to do a spacewalk together near the end of my stay on *Mir*, the members met in a closed-door session to decide whether or not it was safe to pair us for the walk.

So convinced were they of this interpretation that they had even imagined a scenario in which one of us might deliberately push the other one off the station during the walk. They had visualized the victim of this scenario subsequently running out of air and suffocating, his remains orbiting the planet for ten or a hundred years before colliding with enough atomic oxygen and cosmic dust to slow down the spacesuited body and cause it to reenter the earth's atmosphere. Whatever remained of Vasily Tsibliev or me would then slam into the dense upper part of the atmosphere, where the friction created would result in a fireball. Ashes to ashes, dust to dust.

Despite these grave concerns, fed, I think, by overactive imaginations and by a reluctance to ask the crew directly about our relationship for whatever reason, the committee decided to proceed with the space walk. But they warned the flight director to proceed cautiously.

When I returned to earth and learned that the psychological experts had conjured up the scenario of Tsibliev and I as nearly homicidal enemies, my mouth, quite literally, fell wide-open in disbelief. I even heard that someone claimed that we had a fistfight during the spacewalk! This is too absurd to even address, but the writer said that although Vasily and I denied the allegation, some thought that it had occurred. Who else was there besides Vasily and me? Incredible.

The truth was that Tsibliev and I, almost miraculously when one considers the circumstances under which we were placed, had no major disagreements in the four months that we spent together on *Mir*. We got along wonderfully. Vasily was a great guy, under a lot of strain, no doubt, but that never affected our personal relationship. In fact, over the same period of time I would disagree more with my wife, whom I love deeply and whom I have chosen as my mate for life, than I ever did with Tsibliev.

Russian Air Force colonel Tsibliev used to fly combat air-patrol missions from his base in East Germany, in direct confrontation with American pilots doing the same over West German skies. On many occasions, I have flown in the backseat of American navy warplanes escorting Russian Bear bombers away from our carrier task force over the Indian Ocean and Persian Gulf. For a career U.S. Navy officer to live in harmony with a Russian Mig fighter pilot cooped up on a space station for four months seems almost unbelievable. So unbelievable, in fact, that it seems that no one on the ground did believe it.

The Russian experts saw me as egocentric, independent, a rebel—in short, a typical American. They heard Vasily's temper flare on numerous occasions when he disagreed with the actions that the ground advised and, especially near the end of our flight together, they heard him rant and rave about how messed up things were on *Mir* and how it was never this bad during his first tour of duty on the space station. Vasily privately attributed the *Mir*'s problems to the economic decline in Russia. There was no money to make the necessary repairs, to pay the flight controllers, and to do the necessary upgrades. As a result *Mir* was, in Vasily's words, "falling apart." Not wanting to indict themselves, the people on the ground concluded that the American onboard caused Vasily's anger.

WHILE my interactions with both *Mir* crews were almost unbelievably positive, the relationship between the *Mir*-23 crew (Tsibliev, Lazutkin, and me) and the Russian flight controllers at mission control in Moscow was unexpectedly dismal and extremely tense.

Given my medical background in the study of human psychology, in which I specialized to some extent on the problems and adaptive strategies of people living in isolation, I was both astonished and appalled at how poorly the Russians, who had more than eleven years of *Mir* experience, handled the psychological aspects of long-duration flight. Mission control in Moscow became our enemy rather than our friend, our nemesis rather than our support structure. During our time aboard *Mir*, mission control in Moscow repeatedly offered us calculated misrepresentations of facts. In serious situations, they deliberately omitted information until, by the end of the mission, we had no confidence in them. Nor did we feel that we could trust anything that they told us.

Crew-ground confrontation is nothing new to the history of space flight. In 1973, aboard the United States' first space station, *Skylab*, the crew decided that they had had enough of the ground constantly "hawking them" and trying to plan every second of their workday. Apparently, the crew was very much overworked and never allowed to make their own decisions. In an act of frustration, they announced to mission control in Houston one morning that they would not be talking to the ground that day. They told Houston to not bother calling because they were going to turn off the radio and take the day off.

This gesture, of course, got the attention of the ground. The following day, the crew and the ground had some serious discussions. The ground wisely modified the way that they were doing business with the crew. Instead of sending up a detailed timeline indicating how the crew must spend each minute of their day, mission control sent a list of tasks that needed to be accomplished during the course of the day. The crew would decide upon the most efficient and effective sequence for accomplishing those tasks.

Micromanaging a crew in orbit from a remote location (the ground) makes no sense. Such micromanagement also becomes psychologically frustrating to competent professionals. Obviously, the *Skylab* crew needed to exercise a certain amount of autonomy in their work aboard the space station. They needed to decide upon the most efficient way to work, when to take a break, when to return to work, and when to use the toilet!

Yet despite years of experience with *Mir* and with their previous space stations, and despite many serious incidents, the Russians had never modified their approach to tasking the crew. Instead, mission control in Moscow sent us a detailed timeline that would make any person feel like a robot. And these timelines were not broken down into hourly blocks, but sliced to the minute.

Valeri Korzun, who played everything by the book, actually wanted us to adhere strictly to the time line. If the schedule said to begin running on the treadmill at 1105 hours, then he expected to see me running at 1105, not 1100, and not starting at 1110. I followed the schedule, roughly, during my time with Korzun as *Mir* commander, but quickly shifted gears with the arrival of the new *Mir* crew. The way that I saw it, I had one of two choices before me. I could continue being a slave to the clock, work inefficiently and, in the process, become exasperatingly frustrated. Or I could look at the content of what had to be done on a given day, rearrange the schedule to efficiently get the work done, and in the process preserve my sanity. After I took control of my life, my efficiency improved dramatically, as did my sense of well-being.

I knew that I could not tolerate being controlled, minute-by-minute, for five months. I had observed in some of my crewmates the toll that blind adherence to the schedule had on their psychological health. I was determined not to slide down the slope that led to a wounded cosmonaut, a cosmonaut worn out and beaten by the supposed support system that undermined the basic human need of self-determination. If I needed to be a bit of a rebel in order to remedy a bad situation, and if I needed to exercise a certain amount of good judgment and independence to remain intact as a person, I decided, "So be it." While I could have continued to modify my own schedule covertly without the ground knowing, I chose to try to formally correct the situation so that we could improve the way that we operate in space in the future.

I always proceeded cautiously when deviating from the planned schedule. I was careful to check operational parameters, such as the electrical power margins, to insure that the experiment that I was conducting did not cause any conflicts with other activities on the station. As a courtesy, I would inform the *Mir* commander of my planned actions. For example, I might tell Vasily that the metal alloy sample needed another twenty minutes of processing to complete the melt, and that the furnace consumed 400 watts of electrical power. I would then ask whether there were any other power-hungry activities taking place that might create a problem. If I had to wait to consult with the ground I would waste half a day. As professional astronauts and cosmonauts, we were well aware of things such as electrical power constraints. That we were not given the authority to make such decisions made no sense.

To assure that I could achieve my assigned mission responsibilities, I essentially followed in the footsteps of the *Skylab* crew. I told the NASA group in Russia that I strongly preferred to design my own daily schedule of activities from the universal list of tasks that they wanted me to accomplish on a given day. Along with those tasks, I asked the NASA group to include a look ahead to the following two days of work so that, should I have a problem with the planned tasks of a particular day, I could substitute other required activities. My experience to date onboard *Mir* had taught me that by organizing my day in this manner, I would not waste a second of valuable time.

As was my habit, I consulted with my crewmates about my proposal before I sent it to the ground. Vasily and Sasha concurred that this approach would be a far more effective way to work, a definite improvement over how things were currently being done. While reluctant to speak directly to the Russian ground controllers, they were happy that I felt comfortable talking openly about the proposition with the American contingent on the ground. Vasily and Sasha hoped that if I could get the ground to change its approach for me, the American, then, perhaps, down the road the ground would also modify their approach toward my *Mir* crewmates, as well as future Russian crews.

After a lot of struggle and digging my heels in for what was right, a modified schedule was finally sent up to me daily. My crewmates continued to be scheduled in the traditional way and suffered because of it. There is no doubt that the change helped me to improve my work efficiency. Without my taking a stand, we would never have completed the U.S. science mission objectives, nor would I have had time to help repair broken-down *Mir* equipment. The Americans who followed me on *Mir* continued to benefit from the change.

WHILE I found the degree of harmony among the crew onboard *Mir* to be one of the most surprising and uplifting aspects of my flight, I was profoundly disappointed with the manner in which the ground interacted with the crew. Using a carrot-and-stick system—threatening a pay cut for poor performance or trying to entice with bonus pay—is not the way to motivate professionals. Yelling at a crew is not the way to create good relations or to get an honest assessment of the situation onboard. Placing blame on a crew for mishaps before the crew returned to earth to give their side of the story and a full accounting of the facts is inexcusable.

Hopefully, we have now learned these lessons. But I am not so sure.

Triathlon training in San Diego.

Afloat in the Black Sea, undergoing recovery training for emergency splashdowns. (Courtesy NASA)

Left　Star City, Russia, (left to right) Sasha Lazutkin, Vasily Tsibliev, and I standing in front of a Soyuz capsule simulator. (Courtesy NASA/RSA)

Below　Final spacesuit checkout in the white room just prior to entering Space Shuttle *Atlantis* for the trip to Space Station *Mir.* (Courtesy NASA)

Opposite　*Atlantis* transforms the early morning darkness into near-daylight as seven million pounds of rocket thrust propels the shuttle from Launch Pad 39B at 04:27:23 A.M. E.S.T. on January 12, 1997. (Courtesy NASA)

Above   *Mir* as seen from *Atlantis*. Note the numerous winglike arrays of solar panels projecting from the modules. (Courtesy NASA)

Left   *Atlantis* docked to *Mir* as the complex soars at twenty-five times the speed of sound over the coast of the Carolinas. (Courtesy NASA)

Opposite   *Atlantis* pulling away and returning to earth after leaving me on *Mir*. The open payload bay doors reveal the aft-located boxlike Spacehab module and the cylindrical tunnel connecting it to the middeck of *Atlantis*. (Courtesy NASA)

Above   Floating a transfer package through the connecting tunnel into the Spacehab module of *Atlantis*.   (Courtesy NASA)

Opposite   Cramped quarters: exercising aboard Mir. This photo was taken by me using a camera timer, as were the most of the photos of myself on *Mir*.   (Courtesy NASA)

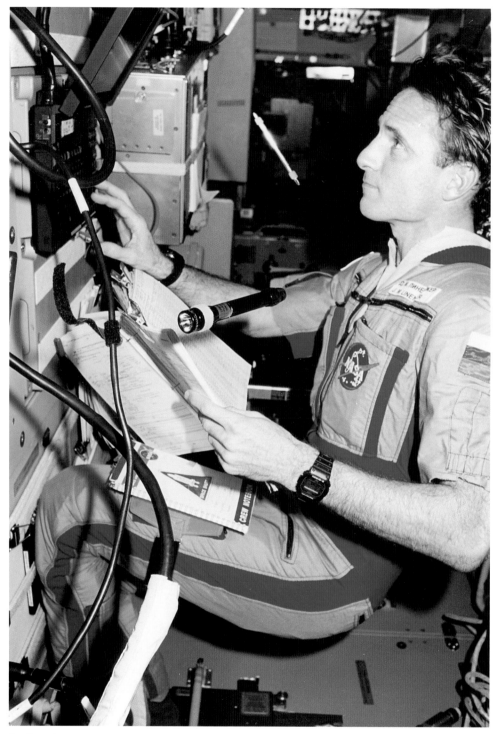

Performing an experiment with flashlight and pen conveniently floating. (Courtesy NASA)

15

The Glories of Earth Gazing

As PART OF THE American science program on *Mir,* I was required to photograph the earth. Demanding and time-consuming, earth-observation studies were, nevertheless, my favorite work.

Along with my other experiments, I had transferred from *Atlantis* bags full of film and cameras. For the most part, I used slow-speed and color-positive film. Earlier testing of film on *Mir,* by astronauts who had preceded me, had shown that high-speed film was highly susceptible to damage from radiation exposure and that negative film became cloudy. I also brought over fruitcake-tin-sized canisters filled with various other brands and speeds of film.

In what had to be the least challenging of the experiments I performed on *Mir,* I simply stored these canisters of film for the duration of my mission, and then returned all this previously stored film with me to earth after my five months on the space station. This film would then be analyzed on the ground to determine which film type survived the prolonged trip to space with the least degradation of quality. Based on the results of the evaluation we would be able to determine the best types of film to use on future missions.

For all earth-observation studies, I used 70-mm film. To compliment the standard ASA 100, 70-mm color-positive film—over 10,000 frames worth—I also brought along 70-mm infrared (IR) film. From earth orbit, infrared film is especially useful for penetrating haziness over jungle areas, thus showing the extent and progression of rain-forest clear-cutting and devegetation.

For most in-cabin shots, visual 35-mm film was used. I also carried special films to meet the requirements of certain scientific experiments. For example, to film the flame propagation experiments in the low-light conditions of the space station, I used a faster speed film in spite of the fact that we fully expected the film to degrade somewhat while in orbit. Rounding out my photo supplies were two video cameras and plenty of Hi-8 film to record action shots where required.

Given this enormous quantity of film and not wanting to come up short on film toward the end of the flight, I began tracking my film usage from the start of my mission. For example, I knew I would want to film the space shuttle as it approached *Mir* to pick me up at the end of my mission. In addition to its sheer beauty, such a picture would be operationally important to engineers on the ground. After studying the photos and comparing them to what was found on inspection of the shuttle after landing, the experts could determine whether any unexplained discrepancy occurred prior to or during re-entry. For example, if delicate tiles on the undersurface of the wings of the shuttle were found to be damaged, experts could pinpoint the time frame in which the damage occurred by examining the photos. Armed with this additional information, steps could be taken to prevent such an occurrence on future flights.

While it was important to me not to run out of film during the flight, I did not want to finish the mission with extra film on hand. Storage space is valuable on *Atlantis*. Scientists on the ground deserve to have the photographs they requested. I was determined to shoot every last bit of film. By tracking film usage from the beginning of the flight, I realized early on that ten thousand photographs are a lot of photos, and that I would have to work diligently to take not only ten thousand pictures, but also ten thousand valuable photographs.

Therefore, I was not merely a sightseer armed with a camera and a great view. Fortunately, since I was a kid in Michigan, I never could put a map down. During our family vacations, usually three-week road trips where we would travel to California and back with seven of us jammed in Dad's Ford LTD, I was the designated navigator. *National Geographic* magazines line my bookshelf at home. Looking out the window and capturing some of the majesty of the earth was something that I considered a rare privilege.

In fact, after I had been assigned to fly on *Mir*, I set a personal goal to become a world-class geographer. I wanted to take advantage of the opportunity afforded me—a view from atop the world. On the ground before flight, I worked hard studying maps and reviewing previously-taken shuttle photography. I mingled whenever possible with geologists, oceanographers, and other earth-science specialists in order to be up to date on their latest research endeavors. I examined scatter-plot maps that indicated with dots where past space photographs had already been taken.

The scatter plots proved revealing. The United States stood out as almost a black blob—so concentrated were the number of dots. While it was not surprising that shuttle crews—made up primarily of American astronauts—would tend to take more photos of the United States than other parts of the world, the extent of favoritism shown that region of the world was vast. I know from personal experience that it is difficult . . . no, impossible . . . not to photograph your state and hometown from space. Home is home. Resist as I might, I was partial to the Great Lakes. Michigan's Lower Peninsula does, indeed, appear to have been formed by a giant who, with a mitten on his hand, pushed down on that section of the planet. I unabashedly proclaim that I have taken some of the best space photography ever of my home state of Michigan—Upper and Lower peninsulas included.

Furthermore, most of us know the geography of the United States, but are lucky if we have even heard of Alma-Ata, let alone be able to point it out on a map. Likewise, the Mediterranean region is known geographically to most and, as the scatter-plot map shows, is also a favorite shuttle photographic target. Also to its advantage in tempting astronauts to snap photos, the Mediterranean generally has cloud-free weather, making sites consistently clear to viewing. The boot of Italy looks like, well, a boot. And the historical significance of the entire Mediterranean area to Westerners is substantial. Yes, I, too, could not resist photographing the Nile delta, the Greek islands, and the Holy Land. How could one not do so?

While the density of dots on the scatter-plot maps of past shuttle photography was high over the United States and the Mediterranean, sections in the interior of Asia look almost white, with only a scattered dot here and there. In fact all hinterlands, the interior regions of the continents, are underrepresented, while coastlines are overly photographed.

To be sure, if one were to remove the underlying map outlines on the scatter plot, little would be lost. The continents would be defined by the concentration of dots along their coasts. In daylight the contrast between the blue ocean and tan land areas are both visually attractive from orbit and provide easily distinguishable landmarks. San Francisco Bay can be picked out in a glance, while it becomes much more difficult to spot Des Moines, Iowa, located in the heartland. Since San Francisco is more readily identified, astronauts aim their cameras at the Bay Area with greater frequency.

One look at Japan from space at nighttime and it is obvious that human civilizations are concentrated next to water. The Japanese island shapes are well defined by their perimeter of lights. Tokyo Bay is so lit up that I could even spot, with the naked eye, shipping docks jutting out into the water when viewed at night. Mount Fuji, mystical, sacred and, therefore, undeveloped, stood out as a dark circle surrounded by a sea of lights. The Great Lakes are rimmed with Canadian and Midwestern city lights. The U.S. Eastern Seaboard glows, with the subsection from Baltimore to New York City to Boston glowing at an even brighter intensity. The settlements along the Mississippi River appear as a band of pearls stringing their way through the center of the United States and surrounded by hinterland darkness.

UNLIKE the Apollo astronauts, who could see the earth's globe in its entirety on their way to and from the moon, I was limited to viewing only segments of the planet at any given time. As the altitude of *Mir*'s orbit changed within the range of two hundred to three hundred miles above the earth, the visual landscape changed. When we were flying down low and closer to the surface of the earth, I could see more detail, but less scope; flying up high, less detail, but more of the globe's curvature. But in all cases, I was always directly on top of only one point of the earth at any given moment.

Typically, I could see clearly a chunk of the planet about half the size of the U.S. mainland. For example, on one particularly cloud-free night, when the orbit of *Mir* put me directly above Boston, I could look north to Newfoundland and south to Florida and see the entire Florida peninsula outlined in lights. Toronto, Cleveland, Detroit, Milwaukee, and Chicago showed clearly on the Great Lakes' shores. Minneapolis, St. Louis, Memphis, and New Orleans glowed along the mighty Mississippi, while Corpus Christi, Houston, Mobile, and Pensacola defined the Gulf of Mexico. At that viewing moment, however, I could not yet see the lights of London. To see Europe, I would have to wait another ten minutes or so.

But even with so sweeping a view, I could still see minute details: the mighty Mackinac Bridge, spanning the strait between the Upper and Lower peninsulas of Michigan, the Suez Canal, the Pyramids, ship wakes across the English Channel. I never saw the Great Wall of China because, sadly, China was always covered with a sort of haze. The haze occurred because of the terrible pollution produced in its overcrowded cities coupled with its unfortunate location downwind from Mongolia. In Mongolia, for months on end, I spotted hundreds of fires as the people burned down forests in order to convert the timberland into farms. The smoke pall, covering hundreds if not thousands of miles, swept eastward toward the China Sea. I suspect that even if the air were clear, because the color contrast of the wall is so minimal compared to the surrounding areas (it was built, for the most part, of indigenous materials), the Great Wall would be tough to distinguish from its surroundings.

When peering through a 250-mm camera lens, I could actually see interstate freeways, appearing as dark bands winding their way through the white, snow-covered surroundings. I was able to retrace the route I used to drive from Michigan to Florida along I-75 by panning the camera north to south. Incredible!

BESIDES the altitude of the orbit, another factor critical to how much of the earth can be seen from space has to do with the spacecraft's orbital inclination, or tilt of its flight-path ring relative to the equator. The inclination is determined at launch. Launch due east from Florida, and the spacecraft's inclination is twenty-eight degrees. A twenty-eight-degree inclination translates to covering a swath of the earth's surface from twenty-eight degrees north latitude to twenty-eight degrees south latitude. A spacecraft launched on such an inclination would never fly directly over any point on the earth at latitudes beyond this narrow band—nothing north of Egypt, nothing south of Brazil. Although the inclination can be raised by launching in a more northerly direction, this comes at a cost: extra thrust needed to achieve orbital velocities.

Initial velocity can be improved by positioning a rocket's launch site as close to the equator as possible and then launching due east. By so doing, the rocket gains some free velocity, derived from the spin of the earth itself. That is to say, the spinning planet helps to throw the rocket into space. Because points on the equator of any spinning sphere move the fastest, and thus generate more free velocity than points farther north or south, it is no coincidence that NASA chose as its launch site a location in Florida and not in Maine. Similarly, it is also no coincidence that the Russian launch site is located in Kazakhstan, and not in Russia proper. This free initial velocity thereby decreases the demands on the rocket engine to produce all of the needed velocity by itself.

For comparative purposes, it is interesting to note that the first American in space, Alan Shepard, in 1961, was launched on top of a rocket which did not have enough thrust to generate the velocity needed to achieve orbit. Instead, he was lofted up and came down, less than fifteen minutes later, unceremoniously as a big splash in the Atlantic. Shepard never circled the planet on that first flight. To get into orbit, a lot of speed is needed to overcome the counteracting force of earth's gravity. Without adequate speed, gravity prevails, and orbit—a complete circling of the earth—is not achieved.

By 1962, John Glenn's improved rocket had just enough oomph to put him into orbit for four hours, fifty-five minutes—a very flat but velocity-enhancing twenty-eight-degree inclination orbit. Of course, for a modern mission that might be designed to study the earth itself, such a narrow purview around the waist of the earth would be inadequate. During his historic mission Glenn never flew over a point of land north of Florida, and never came close to flying directly over his home state of Ohio. Only during his second flight, aboard the space shuttle thirty-six years later, would he fly over all points of the United States (with the exception of Alaska).

The capability to launch in a more northerly direction came as rocket engine performance improved. No longer restricted to the velocity-enhancing, due-east launch, the shuttle now routinely flies to inclinations of fifty-seven-degrees north and south latitude. But still, if the precise location of the spacecraft's orbit is not of operational significance, and especially if the weight of the payload is close to the rocket's performance capability, a due-east launch may be the only way to get the rocket into orbit.

The fifty-seven-degree limit exists today not because of rocket-engine performance restrictions, but for safety reasons. NASA has decided that, during the critical period from launch to main engine cutoff, the space shuttle will not fly directly over cities located on the East Coast of the United States. Staying just off the East Coast, the shuttle is able to settle into an orbit inclined to the equator at fifty-seven degrees. Such an orbit essentially covers most of the inhabited parts of the earth—from the southern tip of Africa in the south to mid–Hudson Bay in the north.

Space station *Mir* flies in an orbit inclined to the equator at fifty-two degrees. *Mir*'s orbital path likewise offers good coverage over much of the surface of the earth—from the southern tip of Hudson Bay in the north, to just north of the island of Tierra del Fuego at the tip of South America.

Once established, the inclination of any space vehicle's orbit does not change. But although the spacecraft's orbital path around the earth remains fixed in the same relative position in space, that is, flying around the same loop through space time and time again, the earth below is constantly turning. Therefore, after a spacecraft completes one orbit (at the orbital velocity of 17,500 mph, this takes about ninety minutes) the earth has already rotated approximately fifteen degrees of longitude. So after liftoff from Florida the spacecraft will fly roughly directly overhead of Houston ninety minutes later, the subsequent orbit tracks over Phoenix, and the orbit after that over the U.S. West Coast. The spacecraft continues to fly through the same points in space, but the earth below continually shifts toward the east, and the relative position of the spacecraft over points located directly below changes with each orbit.

That meant I could not simply grab a camera, head to the window, and photograph, say, a direct overhead view of Perth, Australia, at any given moment. Instead, I had to wait until the *Mir* orbit was centered over Western Australia. Moreover, I had to wait until the *Mir* orbit was centered over this region when it was daytime in Perth. Even with such careful planning, I would still have to hope for clear weather at the site or the quality photograph that I was attempting to take would be impossible.

ALTHOUGH armed with plenty of film and irresistibly beautiful locations, early on I disciplined myself to resist the temptation to look through the camera, and instead spent time just recording the images in my brain, becoming familiar with the subtleties of the planet, and picking out landmarks; in short, becoming a skilled geographer. Under a self-imposed, one-month moratorium on taking any photos at all with the exception of timely events, such as volcanoes actively erupting, I would sit by the window, with map in hand, and just study the earth. I did not want to waste valuable film until I knew the features of the planet well enough to make every photo count. Only when I could identify with certainty inland locations, such as Kiev or the Himalayan peak K2 or Krakow, did I consider myself prepared to take good photographs.

Beyond knowing the geography of the earth and having a working knowledge of the relevant earth sciences—oceanography, geology, limnology, meteorology—doing a good job with my assigned earth-observation studies required the proper tools: cameras and film, a darkbag to unload the exposed film, a variety of lenses, spotmeters, binoculars, maps with special highlights to emphasize the areas of particular interest to researchers, and computer-generated moving maps, which allowed me at a glance to ascertain the location of *Mir* over the earth at any given time.

NASA supplied me with the NASA/*Mir* Earth-Observations Project Physiographic Atlas. Containing forty-eight pages of maps, including one map of the major world-ocean currents, the atlas highlighted, on each page and in bold black-shaded lines, those areas, all numbered sequentially, which earth-science researchers especially wanted me to observe and photograph from space.

The numbers on the maps corresponded to written descriptions of why the area was of importance to the researchers. These written descriptions could be pulled up on a laptop computer that I had set up to be used strictly for earth-observation photography. Recommended lens selection, viewing angle, and most-desired film type were also indicated on the computer.

Accompanying this information was a software program called World Map. World Map would display a Mercator projection map on the computer screen. The map was overlaid with the present ground track of *Mir* along with a flashing dot indicating our present position over the earth. The dot would move along the projected groundtrack as the *Mir* moved over different parts of the earth. The map also showed the delineation between the lighted side of the earth and the dark side so that I could easily determine whether at any site of interest it was day or night. By locating the *Mir* blip on the computer screen, and then by mentally extrapolating further down the projected groundtrack, I could determine whether we would be passing over any sites of interest in the next ninety minutes. If so, I would set my wristwatch alarm as a reminder to head to the window with my camera, time permitting.

World Map did not have any sensor input to actually look out and determine where we were located at any given time. Instead, it depended on me to supply it with some initial information as to our location at a given moment, and then, using its own algorithm, it would propagate that position to the present and generate the flashing blip to indicate present position. With time, the blip would become less and less accurate as errors compounded. Once the errors became too great—every three days—I would have to enter new data to update the map.

I ran World Map continually. By doing so, I could glance up at any time—even from within the windowless modules where I conducted most of my experiments—and see whether we were about to fly over an interesting site. If the computer program was working properly, and if the area below was of interest, I would grab a camera and the atlas and head to a window.

What kinds of information would the earth scientists glean from my photography?

For oceanographers and limnologists I was, for example, able to document unusual plankton blooms off the western coast of Africa. Near the point where Canada's St. Lawrence Seaway opens into the Atlantic Ocean, I photographed hundreds of two- to three-mile-diameter ice chunks floating out into the Gulf Stream. The ice chunks defined the current, visually marking the otherwise unnoticed movement of the ocean waters. Eddies and fast-moving sheers became apparent, especially near the edges of the current. The whirling white ice chunks spread out over the dynamic, deep-blue Atlantic for hundreds of miles. The display was not only magnificent for me to view, but the photography priceless to any oceanographer studying the macrodynamics of ocean currents.

While I was in orbit, the American Midwest was experiencing flooding along the Illinois River. From space, I was able to photograph the river as it overflowed its banks—not as a one-time event, but actually follow the progression of the flooding. I could track the oversized bolus of water as it made its way down the Illinois to the Mississippi, and then follow its path of destruction as it traveled one day through St. Louis, another day through Memphis, and the next day to New Orleans—documenting the entire event from my unique perch in space.

Taking good photos of the flood as it progressed was not easy. The floods were caused by a stalled weather front. Weather fronts produce massive cloud cover. I would have to position and reposition the camera and look for openings in the clouds in order to record glimpses of the tragedy unfolding below. Maneuvering the camera and eye-sighting the prospective study target sites through occasional breaks in the clouds was something that an automatic camera simply could not do.

Geologists are particularly interested in earth studies from space. Positioned tangentially to an earth-local sunset, I was able to observe volcanoes as they exploded into the delicate band of atmosphere ringing the earth, their ash-filled plumes billowing higher than the outline of even the most massive weather clouds.

From space, I could see the entire lengths of fault lines formed by earthquakes. I could also observe the results of geological plate-tectonic movement where, floating on the crust of the planet, huge land masses, millions of years past, slammed into one another and formed the mountains and topography of the earth we see today.

Seeing the Himalaya Mountains, I could almost imagine how they were formed when the Indian tectonic plate burrowed beneath the leading edge of the Asian landmass, thrusting it upward. And yes, even today, from the vantage of space, the Himalayas look massive and predominant, more rugged than the Rockies or the Alps. The Rocky Mountains, in turn, jut out of the earth at a much more acute angle than the weathered, green, and relatively low-rising Appalachians.

I was also able to document, for the meteorologists on the ground, the global movement of clouds and the massive power of a swirling typhoon in the Pacific. These types of studies repeatedly highlighted and emphasized the dynamism of changing weather conditions on earth. And while I cannot express what the order of things are in these dynamic systems, I can say that I was left with the impression that there is, indeed, order to these weather systems, that what occurs in one area of the earth somehow influences what happens in another region.

For example, although lightning storms at night were incredibly variable in their complexity, order existed, though I could not formulate a theory to either fit the behavior or predict where the sinewy bolts of lightning would spread. I am convinced that electrical storms are not a local phenomenon and are not completely random occurrences. Excitation in one place would trigger a chain reaction and the discharge of energy and light over thousands of miles. The lightning storms reminded me of watching a slow-motion film of a pane of glass breaking: spiderweb-like cracks moving outward in a not entirely predictable or uniform pattern, but the propagation of each subsequent crack being somehow determined by what had already broken.

Equally dynamic, and intriguing, were the Northern Lights. The deep purples and brilliant blues of these lights, fluidly oscillating in tone and hue, were vibrantly beautiful whenever our flight path took us over the southern edge of Hudson Bay, Canada. The lights were mesmerizing and, in pure awe of nature's grand power and lack of predictability, I would find myself cheering and shouting as the Northern Lights danced.

I could always count on comet Hale-Bopp to shine like a flashlight in the sky. The comet accompanied me throughout my entire five months in space. As a fellow space voyager, I came to regard the comet as a friend, perhaps in part because of its reliability.

Interestingly, my acquaintance with the comet Hale-Bopp came at the suggestion of a ham radio operator. During our brief, thirty-second conversation as *Mir* whizzed over Newfoundland, a Canadian ham operator told me that it would be a sin to not look out the window from my vantage point in space to see the comet. I apologetically explained that I had been extremely busy, and that during any free moment I had on *Mir*, I would photograph places on the earth in daylight. During the journey on the dark side of the earth, I would busy myself with other assigned scientific chores. He replied sternly that that was no excuse. Now even more apologetic, I closed by assuring him that I would look for the comet. I also let him know that I could see a huge snowstorm moving his way from the west, and that he had better start a fire in his fireplace.

I followed through with my promise to look for Hale-Bopp. From space, I could see far more stars—the sky was almost cluttered—than I would ever have been able to see from the best observation point on earth. Frankly, I had believed that, without knowing the declination of the comet, or at least the quadrant of the sky in which the comet was located, the chances of my seeing the comet by just casually looking out the window would be slim.

My mouth dropped wide open the first time I saw Hale-Bopp. I actually remember thinking, "That can't be it! It is too bright, too . . . obvious. Maybe it is some space debris being lit up by the last rays of sunlight?"

But that space debris had the classic tear-shape of a comet. I grabbed my binoculars. My night-adapted eyes were nearly blinded by the brightness of what I saw. I floated dumbfounded, overwhelmed, and filled with wonder.

SPENDING five months in space made me a pretty good geographer. When the space shuttle crew arrived to pick me up from *Mir*, I quickly became their reference source for geographical sightings out the overhead window of *Atlantis*. "Jerry, is that Athens or is Athens located up the next bay?" my newly arrived crewmates would ask. Usually, I knew the answer.

On the other hand I had decided early on that, in general, I would not worry about knowing the names of the stars and the constellations. I would just gaze out into the heavens and, with an uncluttered mind, enjoy the shapes and arrangements of the stars until, with time, they became familiar to me. Consequently, I cannot point out the star Sirius to you, but I can point out that "exceptionally bright star in the southern sky." Stargazing, just looking out and appreciating the beauty, became my predominant form of relaxation before falling asleep on the wall at night.

Astronomer Carl Sagan once said that there are "billions and billions" of stars out there. From space, with the naked eye, I could see about four times the number of stars that one sees from even the best viewing spot on earth. But this enormous number of stars is nowhere near billions. It seemed Sagan was exaggerating.

Two years after Sagan's death, astronomers aimed the space-based

Hubble telescope at a dark part of the sky and during the next one hundred orbits kept peering into this same dark spot. The closer they looked at this dot in the sky, the more galaxies the astronomers saw. Based on this look, and extrapolating to the entire sky, the astronomers concluded that there are not billions and billions of stars, but rather one hundred trillion galaxies, with each galaxy averaging a billion stars. It seems that Sagan had *under*estimated the size of our universe!

This number boggles the mind. I am humbled. The earth is a special speck in the universe. Just thinking about one hundred trillion galaxies makes me feel more precarious than when I last stood one foot away from the edge of the Grand Canyon's north rim and gazed down at the magnitude of that hole. The thought of one hundred trillion galaxies is so overwhelming that I try not to think about it before going to bed, because I become so excited or agitated or something that I cannot sleep with such an enormous size in my mind. I am quite sure mine was the proper approach to looking at the stars, just taking them in and not trying to categorize or name them.

MEETING the demand for the earth-observation studies requested, I had taken all ten thousand photographs with about two days to spare. When *Atlantis* docked with *Mir,* I lugged six cases full of film over to the space shuttle for return to earth. Frankly, I considered this film my prize possession.

After I had returned to the planet, I waited anxiously to see the results of my labor. I had worked very hard to take those photos and I knew that within the ten thousand were some of the first-ever photographs of sites and phenomena from around the world. In flight, I was unable to develop any of the film. I was thereby unable to receive any feedback whatsoever as to the quality of the photos. Did I load the film correctly in the darkbag, or had I made other technical mistakes along the way? Was the focus correct? Did I meter properly? What about the composition? And most troubling, because it was out of my control, had five months' worth of radiation damaged my film? When I received a call from the NASA film specialists who were responsible for developing, classifying, and archiving my film, my anxiety level rose.

The conversation was rather humorous. The film specialist

informed me that they had counted and recounted my film, and that I had somehow returned with more film than I had taken up to *Mir!*

To these baffled NASA film specialists, I first teased that some alien kept knocking on the door and dropping off new rolls of film as needed. I then explained that while I was cleaning filter intakes behind the panels in the interior of *Mir,* I would occasionally find an unused roll of film that had, in all probability, drifted away from one of the earlier American occupants of the space station. I figured that, if nothing else, the film could be studied to determine the extent to which it degrades over time in space. At best, I might get some decent exposures.

That mystery solved, I waited impatiently for the verdict on the film quality.

"The film looks great! Very little, if any, radiation damage. Good focus, good exposures. Great job, Jerry!"

My work had paid off. Mission more than 100 percent accomplished, considering the extra film that I had found and shot. Someday, I could put together one tremendous photo album.

16

Profound Isolation

ON NEW YEAR'S DAY, 1996, a year before my flight to *Mir*, instead of making a New Year's resolution, I decided that while I trained in Russia I would try to be sensitive to the passage of time equivalent to my anticipated stay aboard *Mir*. I wanted to "feel" how long I would be on *Mir* the following year.

January. The month crept by ever so slowly. The sun was so low in the Moscow sky that, for most of January's shadowy days, I could watch the sunrise and sunset in less than an hour. February was equally drab and gray. My vitamin D level dropped to an all-time low. The days dragged as I continued to study both *Mir* technical manuals and the Russian language. By March I had had enough of winter, but winter remained stubbornly persistent in Russia. In April, I put away my well-worn cross-country skis for the year. And by the end of May, I was convinced that yes, indeed, the ground would thaw out long enough for the Russians to plant potatoes and beets in the plots of land adjacent to their summer dachas.

From the dim, nocturnal days of January to the onset of a May thaw, this would be the length of time during which I would be confined within the boundaries of a small orbiting space station called *Mir*.

January, February, March, April, May. During this same period of time, I watched my infant son, John, grow miraculously from a helpless, totally dependent, and often screaming baby, who woke up too many times during the night, to a crawling, smiling, eager adventurer, whose coos reflected a real personality, and who still awakened too many times during the night. I would miss him. There was so much more rapid change ahead for my boy, so much more growing and developing. Yet I would not be there for him.

And then there was Kathryn, who was expecting with our second little Linenger. During much of her pregnancy she would be without me. I thought of the doctor appointments that she would keep alone, the ultrasounds that she would take without me by her side. I would not be there to tease her about her expanding waistline and sudden food fetishes. I would miss feeling the baby's first kicks.

It would be a difficult, long haul living off the planet without them.

ISOLATION and confinement was not an entirely new experience to me. I had served for nearly twenty years in the U.S. Navy. During that time, I had been aboard ships at sea, albeit mainly on city-sized aircraft carriers. But I had also sliced through the water aboard sleek guided-missile destroyers in the Mediterranean, bobbed aboard flat-bottomed landing-dock ships, complete with nauseous but ready-to-fight U.S. Marines in the Pacific, and even moved silently under the sea on a nuclear ballistic-missile "boomer" submarine off the Connecticut coast. I once practiced medicine as the lone physician on three-mile horseshoe-shaped chunk of coral in the middle of the Indian Ocean—Diego Garcia. The island had an airstrip, some hootches and huts to live in, and a small clinic. The lagoon was infested with big Indian Ocean sharks, but otherwise the snorkeling was wonderful. Banana and coconut trees grew everywhere, and I often felt like a shipwrecked sailor.

I had also studied the psychological problems associated with living for prolonged periods of time in isolation. At the Naval Health Research Center in San Diego, I had an office adjacent to one of the world's leading experts on living in isolation—Dr. E. K. E. Gunderson. Semiretired and looking the part of the wise professor that he was, Dr. Gunderson had spent his lifetime studying the psychological reactions of scientists and naval support personnel who wintered at research outposts in Antarctica. Many did not tolerate the isolation well. Many broke down, some became schizophrenic.

His seminal work provided insights to help anticipate and possibly prevent similar problems from occurring among astronauts during long-duration space flights.

Based on psychological testing and substantiated by data collected over many years in Antarctica, Dr. Gunderson had devised a method to predict who would do well in isolated environments. During one of our many conversations, he related to me that past performance in similarly isolated circumstances, not unlike the ones I had already endured, was the best predictor of future performance in other isolated environments. When I was selected to be an astronaut he told me that, with my scientific background, past life experiences, and psychological disposition, I was the right kind of person for the job. Of course, at that time, neither of us envisioned my being off the planet for anything longer than the standard ten-day shuttle mission. Nevertheless, I remembered his comments and took them as a good sign that I could endure the isolation on *Mir.*

I also considered the experiences of explorers of old, who were separated from familiar territory for far longer periods of time than I would be separated from the earth. Confronting the dangers of primitive seafaring and always fearing that they might fall off the edge of the earth, they, nevertheless, bravely sailed the seas in search of new lands. If they could do it, I could do it.

MISSIONS to space require the expenditure of a tremendous amount of resources, both technical and human. They are extremely expensive undertakings. If the rocket to *Mir* had to perform flawlessly under some very demanding conditions, so too, did the human being riding that rocket.

Technicians on the ground at mission control in Moscow were constantly scouring temperatures, pressures, and the status of components on *Mir* to try to detect any performance degradation in equipment before the system actually broke down. Similarly, a group of medical experts—flight surgeons, psychiatrists, and psychologists—continually monitored from afar the cosmonaut-astronauts on *Mir,* trying to avert a failure of the human component.

While I felt prepared to live and work totally isolated from other human beings save my two crewmates, I was astounded at how much I had underestimated the strain of living cut off from the world in an unworldly environment. The isolation was extreme in every way. Living on a hunk of coral or inside a submarine did not compare. Intellectual wondering about how sailors of old tolerated being alone at sea or of what coping strategies I might employ imagining the experiences of wintering-over personnel in Antarctica proved an inadequate defense.

We were cut off. All responsibility fell on our shoulders. Scientists, who had spent years designing their experiments, were depending on me to execute them properly. There was no further help, no advice, and no quick answers to questions that arose in the course of conducting the research. Decisions were mine to make in real time. The experiments and critical repair work were intolerant of any lapse of concentration.

I looked at the same two faces for months on end. After a while, our conversations grew stale. We found that we did not have a lot to add to what had already been said. There was no new news. Family and friends existed only in some far-away place that we could see, but not physically touch. We were sucking down the same dehydrated food, day after day.

Mir life support systems, designed to sustain a habitable environment, worked sporadically. Repairmen or repair parts could not be summoned or brought in; our combined human ingenuity had to suffice. Among the three of us, one of us had to have the skill and know-how to do every job, period.

Making a mistake was intolerable. In the pressure-cooker environment of *Mir*, where mechanical breakdowns were occurring almost daily, the human being, subjected to such stresses and bearing the tremendous burden of ultimate responsibility, was also highly vulnerable to breakdown.

Early on I realized that it was important to pace myself if I wanted to make it to the end of the mission intact and effective. I often recalled John Blaha's parting advice to me, "Jerry, you are stuck. The sooner you accept that fact, the better. And remember, it will all eventually come to an end."

That there would be an end, that someday I would be able to relax with my family again and be carefree, helped me time and again to tolerate life off the planet. I found that I could generate the intellectual and emotional stamina required to get the job done because I knew that there would be an end to it all, even if that end was months away.

I also knew, to some extent, what to expect psychologically. On scientific missions to Antarctica or on expeditions to the North Pole, those involved generally experienced a natural dip in motivation as the mission neared midterm. According to these accounts, there was, however, a resurgence of motivation and drive as the mission neared its end.

Armed with this knowledge, I tried to avoid the midterm slump. I knew that I had to resist these natural tendencies because there was simply too much to be done. I worked very deliberately to avoid any slack in performance or efficiency. To maintain my physical stamina and emotional stability, I exercised twice a day whether I felt like it or not. When running, strapped to the treadmill, I would often close my eyes and escape *Mir*, visualizing a favorite scene on earth. Whenever possible, I tried to go to bed on time. If I wanted to perform as well in the fifth month as in the first, I knew that I had to maintain my internal clock and natural biorhythm as best as I could in a place where the sun rose and set fifteen times a day. I could not afford to become an insomniac and lose my edge—my work demanded a high level of alertness during the day. I was adamant about maintaining my health—physical, mental, and psychological. I could not afford a breakdown, a lull in performance. To guard against such degradation, I would not allow personal frustrations to linger too long before making a change. If something was wrong, I spoke up.

As self-serving and contradictory as it might sound, for the mission to be successful and for our crew to function optimally as a team, I had to look out for myself. I had to stay on an even keel.

GETTING the job done and the sense of accomplishment derived from my work kept me going. During a particularly trying time on *Mir* when everything seemed to be failing at the same time, mission control in Moscow called and told me to discontinue doing any of the U.S. science program work and spend all of my time helping with repairs. My response, I knew, was sure to fuel the speculation that the crew was not getting along and that I was off doing my own thing—but it was the right response. I told the NASA team in Moscow that such a plan was not acceptable. I had been working too hard to accomplish our mission goals to just give up because of continuing tough times. I told them to keep scheduling science work and I would work around the repairs to get as much of it done as possible.

Besides, I was already helping with repairs and general space station maintenance. We all chipped in and helped each other. By getting up at 5 A.M., I was able to get some metal samples into the furnace—they took from three to six hours to process—before the morning alarm rang, waking up my crewmates. I could then work with them until the sample had to be removed and the next sample processed. Vasily already knew that I was more than willing to lend a hand when needed, and he was not reluctant to ask me to assist. What the ground did not understand was that in order to work efficiently tasks needed to be segregated—each member of the crew doing what he was most skilled at doing.

I had already volunteered and was doing much of the scut work—vacuuming filters, packing garbage, flattening metal food containers in order to reduce their bulk before packing them into the Progress garbage truck. This enabled Vasily and Sasha to have more time for other tasks. It made no sense for me to begin working on, for example, the oxygen generator, since Sasha had been working on that particular piece of gear for the past three months and was by now the onboard expert. And besides, only one head at a time could be squeezed far enough behind the panel to get to the bulky piece of equipment—it was not a two-person job.

Moscow controllers also did not understand that the entire crew derived a sense of accomplishment from knowing that we were not merely spending our time trying to survive, but were doing worthwhile, productive work. No matter how difficult the day, I could usually cheer Vasily up a bit by telling him—with mock formality, as if I were making a report to an admiral—"Commander Tsibliev, we are still alive and I have processed three more valuable metal samples!" He would usually respond by saying "Ah, another fine day in space," before wishing me *"Spekoni nochi,"* peaceful night.

THE ARRIVAL of care packages in April aboard the much-delayed Progress resupply vehicle—three months into my journey and the only resupply ship I would see during my stay, even though the original plan called for two—proved to be a morale booster. Our families were allowed to send us each a shoebox-sized package stuffed with goodies. When the Progress resupply vehicle arrived, we quickly unloaded equipment and repair parts in search of the packages. Once found, and munching on fresh apples that had also arrived in the Progress, we individually retreated from our work and sneaked off to private sections of the space station, eager to peruse the box's contents.

Kathryn had worked with NASA psychologists to select the items. Knowing that I would want to see how much John was growing and changing, she included a lot of photographs. He looked bigger and just as happy and mischievous as ever. There is nothing like our own flesh and blood, I thought, feeling joyous one moment and longingly sad the next. A pang of loneliness and guilt—for not being there for him—shot through me.

It was already April, but Valentine candy hearts came floating out everywhere. I love U. Be Mine. Birthday cards also arrived. "Happy forty-second birthday, old man," was the general theme. I had already celebrated my birthday back on January 16, when the shuttle was still docked. The crew sang happy birthday and we blew up an inflatable plastic birthday cake that Marsha Ivins had thoughtfully remembered to bring along.

Someone had obviously forced each member of the new astronaut candidate class, nicknamed the Sardines, to write me a letter. They introduced themselves and enclosed individual pictures so that I could get to know them. The thoughtfulness of my friends and family, and of the astronauts of the future, warmed my heart.

Kathryn also included the first pictures of our child-to-be. Delighted, I anxiously held up the ultrasound films to the overhead light and scrupulously searched for the distinguishing features of a male. I saw the head, the feet, the hands. But the torso photos were not there. Kathryn once again did not want to know whether the baby would be a boy or a girl. Consequently, she must have instructed the obstetrician to include, for her doctor-husband, only nonrevealing photographs.

I rummaged further through the package and discovered a pack of twenty postcards depicting sites from around my home state of Michigan. I moved, in my imagination, from my hometown of Eastpointe to eating chicken dinners in Frankenmuth to building snowmen in Marquette. I found myself reading not only the newspaper clippings from the launch of *Atlantis* back in January, but also whatever remained readable on the backside of those clippings.

Starved for any information from earth, I read the weather report in Florida four months ago along with the classified ads. I almost ordered a pizza on a two-for-one deal.

In response to a question asked during an interview from space, I said that the one food that I was craving was pretzels. Perhaps because of the headward shifting of fluid in space and the relative (compared to earth standards) dehydration of my body, I craved salty food. In any case, I longed for pretzels; and sure enough, stuffed into the packet was a bag of them.

Unfortunately, the pretzels had not endured the journey to *Mir* well. Crumbled almost beyond recognition, I was nonetheless determined to eat what was left of them. But if I opened the bag, hundreds of broken pretzel pieces, crumbs, and salt grains would float into the cabin. Not to be denied, I put the pretzel bag into an outer Ziploc bag. I could carefully squeeze out a few broken sticks from the inner pretzel bag into the outer Ziploc, and then, staying close to the intake filter of a fan, open the Ziploc slightly and gulp down the floating pretzel piece like a fish. The few stray crumbs and salt were captured by the filter. It was a lot of work for a couple of hunks of pretzels, but the stale pretzels were worth the effort. Earth food at last!

Also enclosed in the bag of riches were some items that I had specifically asked for: additional geological maps of the world, a calendar, and some marking pens. I used the calendar and pens to boldly mark off the days remaining until the shuttle, my ride home, would arrive.

The package also included some celebrity items. Knowing that I was a big University of Michigan football fan, the former Wolverine coach Bo Schembechler autographed a maize and blue U of M ball cap for me and sent it special delivery. And although sent by NASA to Russia for inclusion in my package, some Russian hockey fan must have lifted a hockey puck signed by the captain of the Detroit Red Wings, Steve Yzerman. I tried not to feel too badly about the missing puck, rationalizing that, after all, most of the Red Wings were, in fact, former Russian players who had defected to America. I figured that whoever snatched the puck was probably a big hockey fan who was only trying to get even. After my return to earth, Yzerman signed a Red Wing ball cap and gave it to me as a substitute for the missing hockey puck.

I am not normally overly sentimental. But I can tell you that after months in isolation emotions become raw and nearer the surface. As I read hundreds of notes written on 3 x 5 cards by friends and family that were at my launch back in January, I was choked up the entire time. The common theme was that the launch was awesome to behold, they were proud of me, and they were all pulling for me and praying for me. I am quite certain that when they were scribbling their words they could not imagine what impact those simple messages would have for me. But I drew strength from them. I was not going to let them, or my U.S. Navy, or my country down.

Along with the photographs of John and the 3 x 5 cards, the letters written and enclosed by Kathryn were what I enjoyed most in the care package. Like a sixteen-year-old in love for the first time, I read and reread those letters everyday until the flight ended.

NASA psychologists planned ahead and provided us with some diversions. For example, they sent ten full-length movies up with me on the shuttle. The movies were recorded on 8mm tapes and could be watched on the screen of a laptop computer rigged with a special adapter. While the movies were a good idea, I never found the time to watch any of them. After my work was complete at the end of the day, I was too exhausted and my eyes were too tired to sit in front of a computer screen for two hours.

I did read a couple of books, a few pages a night just before dozing off to sleep on my wall. The book *Endurance* described the experiences of a group of explorers who were attempting to cross Antarctica. Their ship was crushed in the ice just as winter set in. They survived by eating seal meat and by living inside snow shelters for months.

Reading that book while in space made me appreciate the wisdom of the sayings Misery loves company and All is relative. The unchanging diet of dehydrated food, month-long ninety-degree temperatures, and wearing the same clothing for two weeks did not seem quite so bad when compared to lying day after day in a cold and dark snow cave. I could float. I could look out of the window. And I was certain that someone would at least attempt to pick me up and take me back home. Their circumstances put mine into proper perspective, and I closed my eyes each night counting my blessings.

The psychological support group also packed a variety of compact discs that I could run on my computer. One was titled *Great Speeches,* and included excerpts from inspirational talks given by educators, statesmen, and military leaders. It became my favorite disc, in part, because it was refreshing to hear human beings talking about something besides valves and widgets and wiring. The orators spoke of the greatness of man, of human achievement, of the call to higher ideals. The inspiration helped me to step back from the daily grind and appreciate what I was doing: colonizing space.

Infrequently, mission control in Moscow also set up communication passes with Russian dignitaries. I spoke via radio with His Holiness Alexis II, patriarch of the Russian Orthodox church. He seemed to have a great interest in space and asked numerous questions about our "grand view from the heavens." He was surprised that I spoke Russian. I was surprised at his down-to-earth friendliness. I enjoyed our conversation, and figured that we could use all the prayers and help that he might summon for us.

At the other extreme of diversion was our "special medicine" aboard *Mir.* The *Mir* had a well-stocked liquor cabinet. When checking out my newly arrived spacewalking suit, I found a bottle of cognac and a bottle of whiskey secretly placed in each arm of the suit. While Vasily and Sasha were always cordial in offering a drink, I politely declined. While I respected the right of the Russians to do what they please on their own space station, I complied strictly with the NASA policy of no alcohol consumption on duty.

To be honest, regardless of NASA policy, not being 100-percent ready at all times for any contingency made no sense to me. Vasily and Sasha took no offense when I did not join them since our supplies were limited. This was unlike the situation back in Star City where, if I refused multiple toasts of vodka, whether it be at ten in the morning or in the sauna or at a social gathering, I was more or less ostracized. A Russian who obviously did not care for my nonconformity gave me what he interpreted to be the ultimate insult when he told the press that "Linenger never went along with the group. He did not seem to fit in. He was the worst toaster that I ever saw!"

More important than the actual movies and books and other diversions was that someone at NASA was concerned about us, empathized with us, and understood, at least as well as someone who is not there can understand, the profound nature of our isolation. They had made an effort to make our lives more pleasant. Just knowing that meant a lot.

I ALSO made my own diversions. Looking out the window and gazing at the stars and at the earth was my favorite. But I also enjoyed playing the space version of "sneaking up."

Mir was a dark and noisy ship. The fluorescent lighting was inadequate, with many burned-out bulbs, and the electrical power supply was insufficient to keep all of the functioning lights on. Turning fans and the buzz of machinery created a background hum that never ceased. There were no creaking floors, no shuffling feet.

Flying silently down the length of a module, I would approach one of my crewmates and, still undetected by him, move very close. I would then hover patiently until he turned around. I knew that I had gotten him whenever he would gasp and flail his arms backward.

I would appear utterly innocent of any roguish intent, pose a feigned question, gratefully acknowledge the response, and fly away. Only then would I allow myself a grin.

In retrospect, maybe the isolation had gotten to me and I was not that psychologically intact after all . . .

17

Escaping a Near-Death Collision

AFTER THE PROGRESS resupply vehicle arrived in April, we spent two weeks unpacking the provisions and repair parts that were stuffed into it. Unpacking was a particularly arduous task because of the vessel's internal latticework of steel frames to which had been bolted everything from food canisters to refrigerator-sized mechanical equipment. The latticework assured that all of the items would stay secure during launch and would not shift within the vehicle. Should heavy items move, the center of gravity of the vehicle would also shift. The spacecraft in turn would not react to thruster firings in the predicted manner.

We used an adjustable wrench to remove the bolts. After marking the retrieved item off on an inventory sheet, we floated the gear to wherever we could find room to store it. For want of any other available space on *Mir,* we often strapped the arriving gear to the floor of the base block module, directly in front of the oft-used control panels. If *Mir* were a rowboat, the space station would have sunk long ago from overloading.

Once we had emptied the Progress, we reversed the process and began to load broken equipment and garbage into the spacecraft. Empty metal food containers were stuffed with garbage and placed back on Progress in the same locations that we had days earlier retrieved containers full of dehydrated food. The Progress had become our garbage truck.

We tried to load the Progress spacecraft with *Mir*'s excess junk according to instructions from the ground. Especially important was the placement of heavy items within the Progress, since the ground would need to estimate the new center of gravity of the vehicle. We bolted the larger-mass items into the latticework whenever possible to prevent the load from shifting during thruster firings. Packing in the prescribed manner was difficult. The latticework had been laid out to specifically fit items that were on their way to the space station, and not to accept odd-shaped items that were returning from space. Furthermore, since everything floats in space, packing the items tightly in the limited space became an almost impossible task.

To further complicate the work, the controllers in Moscow were constantly changing their minds about what should come back. They often second-guessed themselves, deciding that an old, worn-out piece of gear might be cannibalized for parts someday and should remain onboard. Inevitably, the part that the experts on the ground wanted unpacked was already bolted down and behind five other bolted-down pieces of junk. We began to dread calls from the ground. Their inability to plan properly wasted our time. We thought that we would never get out of the cold, damp, and malodorous vehicle and move on to more important work.

We eventually crammed in the last morsel of trash and closed the hatch. Satisfied that the seal around the hatch was airtight, we loosened the bolts that had held the Progress doubly secure to the docking ring of *Mir*. The ground controllers then commanded—via radio signal to the spacecraft—the final latches to spring open. Progress sprang away from the space station.

Inside *Mir*, we could feel the push-off force as the spacecraft began its spring-assisted break away from the station. I watched through a tiny porthole near the docking ring as Progress flew away from us, its thrusters firing in short, sporadic spurts. I continued watching until the spacecraft resembled nothing more than a dot of reflected light in the blackness of space.

Normally, the controllers would send further radio commands to the Progress, instructing the spacecraft to fire its braking thrusters and slow down. Traveling slightly slower, but still at tremendous speeds, the Progress would reenter the atmosphere and become sub-jected to tremendous friction as the spacecraft plunged further through the thick atmosphere. The friction would create an enor-mous amount of heat, and the Progress, not equipped with any heat-protective tiles or insulation, would be obliterated inside the plasma fireball. I bade the ship good riddance.

For anyone located on the darkened side of the earth, the Progress reentry would look like a meteorite streaking through the sky. But to us in space, and assuming that we were in an orbital location that allowed us to see the disintegrating spacecraft, the fireball would resemble a shooting star moving not above us, but below us—between the space station and the earth below.

MUCH to our surprise, a week after I had watched the Progress dis-appear into the blackness of space, the Russian ground controllers informed us that we would be redocking this same Progress to the *Mir.* We had all assumed that standard procedures had been followed and that our Progress garbage truck no longer existed. Evidently, we were wrong. The Progress had been flying independently and had not been ordered back to earth.

The reason for redocking a used Progress eluded us. The contents of the spent Progress—decomposing garbage and broken-down equipment—were of no use to us. The spacecraft would surely reek inside. We almost dreaded its return, fearing that the ground might want us to rearrange its contents yet again. Eventually, controllers assured us that we would not have to open the hatch, and that the reason for the redocking was to test a new method of docking.

NORMALLY, the Russian Progress resupply spacecraft is launched unmanned and full of supplies from the Baikanur Cosmodrome in Kazakhstan. Externally the vehicle resembles the manned Soyuz spacecraft, but inside the three cosmonaut couches and accompany-ing life support systems are removed to make room for more gear. The launch is timed so that the vehicle is put into a proper trajectory to intercept the *Mir* space station. All commands are sent to the Progress onboard computers from mission control in Moscow, the ship itself being completely automated. In the final stages of the Progress's approach to *Mir,* rendezvous and docking equipment mounted to the front-end of the Progress zeros in on a target that is permanently mounted to the space station near the *Mir*'s docking port. In its final stage of docking, the Progress essentially flies itself into the station.

As the Progress begins rendezvous and docking, the ground monitors the spacecraft's systems to assure that all parts are functioning properly. The docking system, *kurs* (course), is a completely automated system and responds to the commands sent to it via radio from the ground. The controllers stand by and are ready to interrupt the docking sequence should something go awry with Progress. If a malfunction were to occur, a manual backup system is in place. But since the Progress is unmanned, someone outside the spacecraft has to do the flying. The designated driver is a cosmonaut located inside the space station *Mir* who can remotely drive the Progress into the docking port.

In order to do this successfully, the cosmonaut must have visual information. A black-and-white portable monitor mounted inside *Mir* supplies the visual cues. The image appearing on screen is relayed from cameras mounted on the front of the approaching Progress spacecraft. In other words, the cosmonaut, although physically located inside the space station, sees a view on the monitor that reflects what he would see were he sitting in the approaching spacecraft.

In addition to this video image, the cosmonaut stands in front of a portable Progress control panel. The control panel reflects the status of the systems onboard Progress, such as fuel tank pressures and thruster status. Control sticks that resemble the joystick found in a jet fighter are also mounted to the panel. Two sticks are required because unlike in a jet, a spacecraft can fly in virtually any orientation—frontward, backward, or even cocked off to the side. The second joystick allows the cosmonaut to fly the vehicle multidirectionally.

By pushing and twisting these joysticks, commands are generated and sent, via radio, from *Mir* to Progress's computers. The spacecraft responds to these remote inputs in the same manner that it would respond if the cosmonaut were onboard steering. In fact, Vasily Tsibliev had used a similar onboard backup system when he had been forced to back the Soyuz away from *Mir* because of misalignment during his arrival at the space station.

But in what represented a significant departure from standard procedure, the ground was asking us to use this backup system as the primary method for docking the Progress to the space station. The rationale for this unorthodox approach was as follows.

Although the *kurs* automatic docking system has proven to be reliable, it adds both weight and expense to every Progress resupply vehicle built. Because of this, the Russians wanted to do without the system on future launches. In order to be confident in doing so, it was thought prudent to first test the effectiveness of the manual backup system during a noncritical docking. Since the used Progress was already full of garbage, if we could not dock it there would be little lost, whereas if a new Progress could not be docked, vital equipment would not be delivered to the space station, perhaps jeopardizing the station's survival.

The rationale made sense, to a point. If the *kurs* docking system were removed, an equivalent mass of cargo could be added. Since it is very expensive to lift anything into earth orbit because of the tremendous thrust required of the rocket, each pound saved could be replaced with a pound of useful cargo. But the real reason behind the sudden interest in not using a docking system that had proven itself capable over the past ten years was economic. The *kurs* was expensive. It was being manufactured not in Russia, but in the Ukraine. Since the breakup of the Soviet Union, the Ukrainian space program was no longer a partner, but rather a competitor to the Russian space program. The Ukrainians, tired of not being paid on time or of being handed bad checks, demanded hard currency for each new *kurs* system. The Russian space program was nearly bankrupt. Simply put, if the Russians could do without the *kurs* system, money could be saved.

While improving efficiency and decreasing costs are worthy goals, what the people on the ground failed to appreciate, or chose to ignore, was that docking two spacecraft, both of which are traveling at 17,500 mph, is a dangerous operation. Unfortunately, the manually-controlled-from-*Mir* docking system, while a good backup system, was never designed to serve as a primary docking system.

Risky operations demand proven, reliable systems. When designing a system that is critical to operations and whose failure can endanger the lives of the crew onboard, spacecraft engineers normally require that all components be built not only reliably, but also redundantly. Should a component fail, a backup component that can be brought on-line quickly must be available. While no mechanical system can ever be deemed completely reliable, the old and worn *Mir* systems could not by any stretch of the imagination be considered so. Built-in redundancy under such circumstances is essential toward assuring safe operations. The manual backup system was, in fact, the original *redundant* system—brought on-line in the case of a primary *kurs* system failure. No redundancy existed beyond the manual system.

On the space shuttle, for instance, most critical systems are built triply redundant to ensure an even greater margin of safety. If one part fails, another part takes over, and should it fail, another part takes over. The backup manual-docking system aboard *Mir*, on the other hand, was a totally nonredundant system. We would be a single failure away from a catastrophe.

Further complicating matters, there was no way to accurately determine the center of gravity of a space-filled Progress, especially one packed by edict of an ever-changing loading plan. While we had bolted the equipment in as best we could, the latticework did not fit the odd-shaped equipment in many cases. Items could shift as thrusters fired.

Finally, the backup docking system was designed to provide to the cosmonaut on *Mir* only enough sensory data to successfully tweak the trajectory of the Progress should the primary system fail near the end stage of docking—with the vehicle near the space station. That is, it was designed to be a close proximity backup system and was never intended to be used to drive the Progress in from great distances. To do this task safely, better sensor information, especially concerning range and range rate is desirable, if not essential. We did not have such equipment onboard *Mir*.

When docking the shuttle to the *Mir*, for example, the shuttle commander is provided both measures, range and range rate, from three different, independent sources—again using the principle of redundancy to improve safety. The shuttle commander uses this information to better assess the relative position between the vehicles and can quickly ascertain whether the vehicles are closing in on each other at the planned rate. If something appears to be out of kilter, the approach is arrested until things can be sorted out.

But, no range-rate information was provided at all to the *Mir* commander attempting a manual docking of the Progress and using the backup system. Instead, the cosmonaut attempting to control the

Progress's approach and docking was forced to estimate how fast the Progress spacecraft was approaching *Mir* by looking at the relative size of the *Mir* on the video screen. If the image of *Mir* is getting larger, the spacecraft is approaching. If the image is getting larger more quickly than it was the previous minute, the rate of closure must be increasing. In effect, the cosmonaut would be forced to eyeball the approach without any objective confirming information.

This combination of factors made the surprise docking of the garbage-laden Progress using only the manual system failure-prone and, to be frank, downright dangerous. As a crew, we had never trained together before the flight to perform this complicated task. We would essentially be winging it, and in order to be successful, luck would have to be on our side.

ON THE MORNING of the planned docking, Vasily Tsibliev, already weary from the travails to date aboard *Mir,* looked like a different person. He had arisen early, shaved, neatly combed his hair, and had even put on clean coveralls. He looked the part of a *Mir* commander, confident, weariness suppressed—a military pilot who would be exercising his flying skills today. As I was sucking down hot borscht for breakfast, I saw him at the newly erected, portable Progress control panel, checking and rechecking the controls, one last time, to make sure that everything was in order. I could detect that Vasily savored the moment and was trying his best to rise to the occasion. This was going to be his day and, if we had been on earth at that moment, I suspect that he would have walked with a livelier-than-usual step.

In place of our typical, friendly morning bantering, he simply told me that I would be posted at the window of the Krystall module. I would be wearing a radio headset and was to keep him informed of anything I saw that was unusual about the movement of the incoming spacecraft. I gave him the equivalent of a U.S. Navy "Aye-aye, sir" and, although uncharacteristic of our normally friendly relationship, I could see that he appreciated my recognition of him as the leader of the upcoming operation.

I decided that this was probably a good day for me to shave and put on my cleanest elastic penguin suit as well. After many chaotic days on the station, I savored the new orderliness, the military crispness, imposed on this particular day. After shaving and patting down

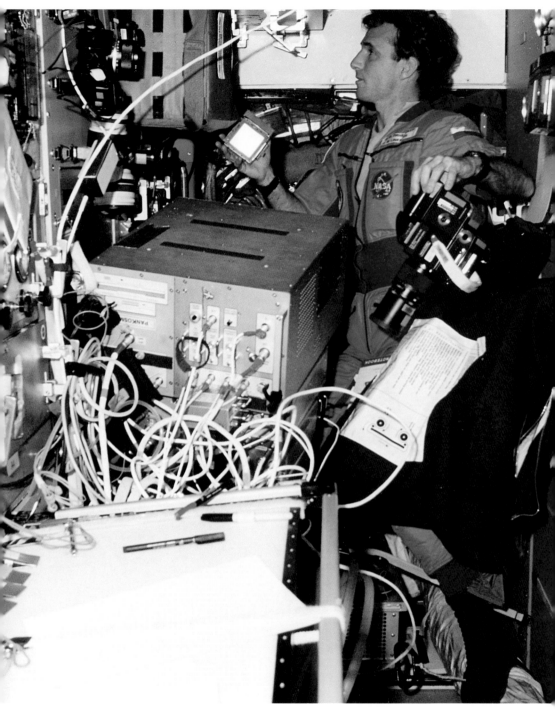

Inside the *Mir* module Spektr, preparing the camera for an earth-observation session. (Courtesy NASA)

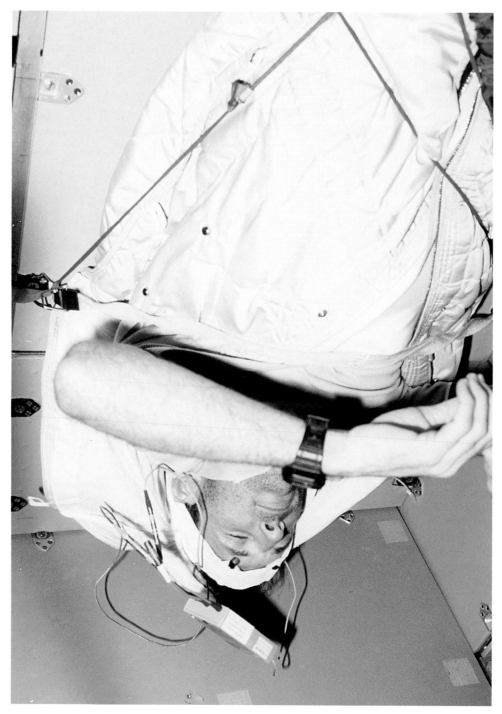

Asleep aboard *Mir*, inverted and strapped to the bulkhead. Sleep-study sensors are attached and floating. (Courtesy NASA)

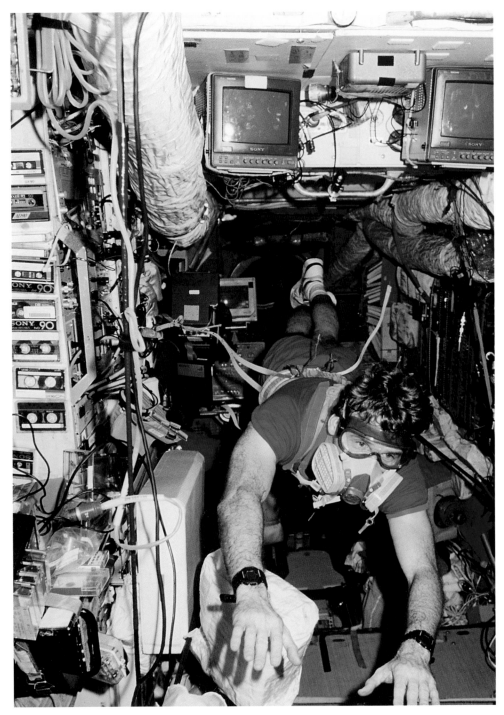

Typical garb worn on *Mir* during the month of antifreeze leaks, floating metal shavings, and ninety-degree temperatures. I am entering the base block module wearing a treadmill harness and tennis shoes, about to begin an hour-long training session on the treadmill. (Courtesy NASA)

The *Mir*-23 crew gathered in the base block module of the space station, (left to right) Cosmonauts Vasily Tsibliev, myself, and Sasha Lazutkin. (Courtesy NASA)

Right Kathryn and I, pictured here on our wedding day, were married in Chicago on March 24, 1991.

Above Six years later, I send a message to my wife from space. (Courtesy NASA)

A sweeping view of the Great Lakes, with my home state of Michigan clearly defined by Lake Huron and Lake Michigan. (Courtesy NASA)

Above Boston and the hook of Cape Cod. (Courtesy NASA)

Right Fifteen minutes after my return to earth, ready to greet my family with a NASA teddy bear for John, a rattle for our baby-to-be, and tulips for Kathryn. (Courtesy NASA)

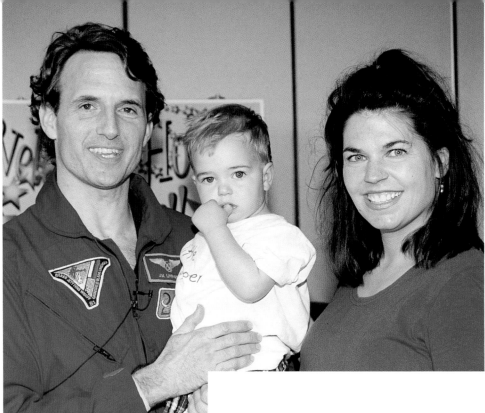

Above   Less than an hour after landing, reunited with John and Kathryn at the Kennedy Space Center. (Courtesy NASA)

Right   Relaxing "back on the planet" with my family in the Cayman Islands. Kathryn is holding Jeffrey, I am holding John. (Photo credit: Scott L. Holman)

my long-ago-out-of-regulation-length hair, I reported sharply to Vasily that I was going to my post, and then took up my lookout position at the far end of the Kristall module.

When I left the other member of the crew, Sasha Lazutkin, was already in his assigned position. Serving as the second set of eyes, he was nearer to Vasily and would be moving between windows in the base block module and the adjoining Kvant I module. He would pick his spot according to where he could best see the incoming Progress—something that none of us could predict with any confidence.

Vasily himself was hunched over in front of the television monitor at the nerve center of the base block module. While the usual *Mir* caution-and-warning panels surrounded him, he was singularly concentrating on the newly erected Progress docking panel. In either hand he was fingering the joysticks. It was obvious that he felt good being back in the cockpit, ensconced in his Mig fighter getting prepared for a sortie. He was in his environment and, probably most significantly, back in control.

I reflected momentarily on how we had all been reduced to an almost slave status—always at the beck and call of the ground. In order to protect my sanity, I had early on in my flight resisted having my day scheduled minute-by-minute by the ground. Vasily and Sasha, perhaps because they had grown up Russian, learning since childhood to go with the flow even if it made no sense, had not resisted. They were being wagged by the ground, working in a constant frenzy, and not in control of their lives. Although they had spent less time on station than I, they were both generally looking frayed and tired.

For the first time in months Vasily looked more like his old, confident self. He had regained some control over his life. Not only was he responsible for the operation, but since we would be out of the zone of communication with the ground during the approach and docking, he had the authority to carry out the operation as he saw fit. I could sense that he relished the thought of driving the spacecraft in himself. For once it would be his operation and, for a short time at least, he would not be subjected to the whims of the ground controllers.

The Russian ground controllers hurled the Progress spaceship toward us by sending up commands to the craft by radio. As we passed over Russian ground antenna, within the zone of radio communication, we were informed that all was well on Progress and that it was on its way to rendezvous with us. They wished us good luck.

Once set in motion and toward a collision course with *Mir*, the Progress spacecraft moved beyond the zone of radio control from the ground and, indeed, was flying on its own. We would try to assume control as the spacecraft moved in closer.

Vasily stood behind his control panel with his toes tucked under toe loops attached to the floor in order to stabilize himself. From his position, he could not see out *any* space station window, and, therefore, would be relying solely on the television picture before him and any visual sightings of Progress that Sasha or I might report to him. The nearest window to Vasily was eight feet away—a small porthole in the floor of the base block.

As lookouts Sasha and I began to survey the heavens, looking for the approaching spacecraft. Although I saw some fantastic views of the Himalayas on the planet below, I had not yet spotted the Progress. Sasha also reported no sighting. By this time, Vasily was expecting to see the *Mir* station view from the Progress cameras on the video screen. Contrary to his expectation, the screen remained static-filled and blank. Becoming more concerned with each passing minute, Vasily, talking into his headset over the intercom system, asked Sasha and me whether we saw anything. He told us to keep a sharp eye out since the Progress must "surely be getting close," and reported to us that his monitor was still showing only static. Though I was moving from one *Mir* window to another, I could still not see the approaching spacecraft. We all began to worry.

More time passed. For some reason, I was no longer hearing either Vasily or Sasha over my headset. Since the internal-communication system on *Mir* was notoriously prone to failure, and since silence did not seem to fit the tense circumstance that enveloped us, I suspected that my radio headset had failed. After not hearing from either Vasily or Sasha for quite some time, and still not being able to sight the incoming Progress, I floated back to the base block module to see what was happening. What I saw was alarming.

Vasily was flying frantically back and forth between his control station and the nearest porthole-sized window on the floor. Sasha was crouched down at this same window, and shouting to Vasily, "It [the Progress] looks like it is coming right at us! It's coming way too fast, more braking, Vasily!" Having dashed from the window to return to his control station, Vasily grabbed the joysticks. His face was covered with sweat as he yanked on the sticks. One could almost sense his uncertainty and what must have been running through his mind: "I can't see what I am doing, I can't see the reaction that the vehicle will have to my action, *but I must do something*. I must fire the braking thrusters or surely we will get hit!"

Vasily moved the control sticks, guessing as he blindly fired thrusters on the fast-approaching spacecraft. He then yelled to Sasha, "Did that help? Is it slowing? Is it veering away?"

Seeing me for the first time, Vasily yelled, "Prepare to abandon ship and get into the Soyuz!" before he flew back to the porthole to see what effect his last action had had on the essentially out-of-control vehicle.

I flew to a window that faced the same general direction as the window Sasha and Vasily were using, and did so just in time to see the Progress go screaming by us. Fearing the very real possibility of collision, instinct told me to brace for impact. I gritted my teeth, held my breath, and hoped for a miss. Although the Progress had disappeared from view under the edge of the window, I quickly calculated that, having felt nothing, the Progress must have missed hitting the base block.

Fractions of seconds ticked by ever so slowly. One second, no impact. I imagined where the spacecraft must be—heading directly for one of the science modules. The next second seemed to last forever as I continued to hold my breath. No grinding of metal, no rush of escaping air nor the accompanying popping of my ears, no resultant tumbling of the space station. With each passing fraction of a second—time was being felt in tenths if not in hundredths of a second in my mind—I sensed that the Progress had somehow miraculously threaded its way past the modules and the protruding solar panels, and was now racing away from us through the void at 17,500 miles per hour. I breathed out again, feeling spared.

Like me, Vasily and Sasha watched the Progress cannonball by our space station. Apparently, they also expected the Progress to hit *Mir*. When it was certain that the spacecraft was safely beyond the *Mir*, I watched as Vasily finally released the breath that he had been holding for too long. He slumped, thoroughly drained.

I felt as if I had been on some kind of cosmic highway with a rocketing car trying to merge onto a crowded freeway in heavy traffic. Meanwhile, a different rocketing car, the one that I was sitting in, was already traveling at a high rate of speed and trying to exit the freeway to the right. The cars nearly collided. In the end, the entering car was forced to exit and the car already on the freeway was forced to continue down the road. The drivers no longer cared where they were on this cosmic highway. They were simply grateful to be alive.

Reconstructing what had happened, Vasily told me that the video screen upon which he was forced to rely for visual information was filled with static during the entire flyby of the Progress spacecraft. Vasily never once saw the view from Progress of *Mir* on the screen. Without any visual assistance, even eyeballing to determine range, range rate, and then the final mating of the two spaceships was impossible. Sensing that the Progress must be approaching very near to the *Mir,* Vasily resorted to leaving his control post and flying to a window eight feet away in order to provide another set of eyes. At this window located on the floor of the station, he desperately tried to locate the incoming Progress. Eventually, what he saw was a vehicle closing in on the *Mir* at excessive speed and in what appeared to be a direct collision course with us. Vasily flew back to the controls and using his best guess in the face of limited input blindly started firing the Progress's braking thrusters.

The only way Vasily could determine whether he had done the right thing was by yelling to Sasha Lazutkin. He queried Lazutkin as to how the Progress was responding to his latest move. For Lazutkin, accurate description was an impossible task. Describing an object that was flying, with lightning speed, in three-dimensional space, and calculating the closing speed of that object without a relative reference point, cannot be done impromptu. Without a reference point, "right," "left," "up," or "down" are words without meaning.

As a consequence, and with no other options available to him, Vasily was forced to rush back and forth to the window at which Lazutkin was posted in order to try to see for himself what was actually happening with the Progress. Based on what he saw during these quick glances, Vasily was compelled to quickly assess what effect his thruster inputs had made and then to plan his next action. He would fly back to the control sticks and, giving it his best shot, fire the thrusters once again. Without continuous visual feedback, Vasily was forced to fly back and forth between the window and the controls—a terrible predicament.

Disaster averted, Vasily, still drenched in sweat and not looking at all the part of the crisply adorned fighter pilot that he had appeared to be earlier in the day, seemed as though he were ready to collapse. Shaking our heads in disbelief, we remained for the most part silent while we recovered from spent adrenaline. After thanking God for our survival and reflecting on the absolutely dreadful position in which he had been placed, Vasily emerged animated and livid.

"What was I supposed to do?" he shouted. "I never got a picture on the video monitor! It was coming at us way too fast. There was no way that I could stop it! We were lucky that it didn't hit us!" He was screaming in understandable rage, his arms waving wildly. Looking toward me, I sensed that he needed some reassurance, or was it my confidence in him that he was seeking? I assured him that it was, indeed, an impossible situation, and the fault was not his. I even thanked him for keeping the craft from striking the space station, even though I was not entirely sure that that was the case.

When we came into radio contact with Moscow, Vasily could not be restrained. With his neck veins bulging even more than fluid-to-the-head, space-induced bulging of neck veins warranted, he let loose on the Russian ground controllers. For the full seven minutes of communications time, he ranted. Justifiably seething, and without a scrap of diplomacy, he told them exactly what he thought about their idea to dock the Progress. He repeatedly asked, and almost pleaded with the ground, "What did you expect me to do?" and "How can anyone dock a spacecraft when he can't even see the thing!" at least a dozen times. Wisely, the controllers on the ground remained quiet and let Vasily do exactly what any psychologist would recommend that a person who was cut off, isolated, and had just undergone a life-threatening debacle do: vent.

After the radio communication pass ended, I stayed by Vasily and offered a sympathetic ear as he let off steam. I knew that our journey had not ended, that other challenges would surely face us before returning to earth, and that we all needed, every one of us, to stay on as even a keel as possible. Justifiably so, but ominous nonetheless, Vasily was coming apart. Stuck within the confines of a cramped and failing space station, we could ill afford any one of the three of us becoming incapacitated.

I began to not only listen, but to wear my doctor hat. To an out-side observer, the session might have appeared to be one conducted between psychotherapist and patient. I stayed professionally detached, because I knew that, although myself stable, the pressure cooker environment of *Mir* could rattle anyone's nerves, mine included.

AFTER this near collision of the Progress, none of us onboard *Mir* thought much of the idea of attempting another docking of the worthless, garbage-filled cargo ship to the space station. On the other hand, Vasily was still at heart a Russian fighter pilot, with the personality traits that make up good fighter pilots everywhere: off-scale high egos, a strong sense of self-sufficiency, and a need for peer approval. In short, he had the right stuff, but such characteris-tics, while vital components to being a good pilot, do not necessarily serve one well when confined on a space station, for months on end, following the orders of others who are themselves far removed from the inherent dangers.

His personality characteristics made it especially difficult for him to directly tell the people on the ground that "I refuse to try to dock a Progress in that fashion ever again," even though that is what he believed. Knowing this, I suggested that I might help by sending down a message to the NASA contingent at mission control in Moscow. I would tell them that we, as a crew, were not at all pleased with the last attempted docking and that unless the people on the ground looked very hard at the procedures and came up with a much improved method of docking, that we did not feel comfortable doing such a docking in the future.

Vasily and Sasha both liked this approach. And given Vasily's state of mind, and in my role as onboard physician and friend, this tack made good sense. I could protect Vasily from any additional strain created by the internal psychological dissonance he was already struggling to mend.

Curiously, none of us onboard knew exactly what had happened. Too much of the docking sequence was out of our control and out of sight. Was the initial trajectory too juiced? Was the Progress com-ing at us with so much speed that no matter how hard we fired the braking thrusters, we would never be able to arrest the motion and stop the vehicle in time? Why had we seen only static on the monitor; had the camera on Progress failed, or the radio transmitter that was to relay the signal to us, or was the problem with the monitor itself? While we did not have insight into this onboard *Mir*, the ground, by looking at telemetry data sent down from the spacecraft, might have enough data to make such a determination.

When days had passed and we had yet to receive any further information from the ground concerning the possible cause of our near-collision, I queried the NASA representatives in Russia. I echoed Vasily's request—and it was a request, not a demand—that we not repeat a similar docking attempt until some very knowledgeable people, perhaps a joint U.S.-Russian safety team, looked very hard at the whole procedure and deemed it safe. I told them that, from the best that I could ascertain from my glimpse of the Progress speeding by us, we had come very close to colliding with a spacecraft that was rocketing toward us at a high rate of closure. Tongue in cheek, I assured my NASA team that we needed no more challenging operations on *Mir* merely to spice up our lives.

I was dumbfounded by my NASA team's response.

Roughly stated, they responded with a fairly nonchalant, "Oh, we heard that there was some problem with the attempted docking, but we weren't given any details. Do you want us to look into it?" Astonished, I strongly urged my support team to look into the matter, and told them that I would like to be informed immediately if it were ever decided to repeat that attempted docking procedure again because I would like to give my input before such a decision was carried out.

After my return to the planet, I would learn just how much in the dark the Russians had kept their NASA "partners" about this incident. A few weeks after landing, I gave a debrief of my *Mir* mission to a group of rendezvous specialists at the Johnson Space Center, Houston. After hearing my debrief, three engineers approached me and told me that, during the near-miss Progress docking, they had been tied in to mission control in Moscow. Their task was to try to track the docking by using ground-based sensors.

While the rendezvous and docking between Progress and the *Mir* was being attempted, these engineers received a telephone call from their Russian counterparts at mission control in Moscow, who told them that the docking had been postponed, probably until the next orbit. Ninety minutes after the first telephone exchange between these Houston-based engineers and their Moscow-based counterparts, the Russians again called their NASA counterparts and, without further explanation, told them that the docking had been canceled. They never informed them that the docking had indeed been attempted and resulted in a near collision. It was not until I told them what had happened that these engineers first learned that the attempted docking had even taken place. They were aghast when for the first time they heard the details during my debriefing.

FOR MOST of this century, Russians have been living in a closed society in which failure of agriculture to meet crop quotas, of the space program to reach the moon, or of industry to provide adequate goods without causing environmental catastrophes, were always suppressed for fear of exposing the shortcomings of Soviet-style communism. Historically, the international press was kept in the dark. The formerly Communist-run newspaper *Pravda,* meaning *truth* in Russian (a misnomer indeed), would usually alter any disparaging story or just not report the bad news.

Today, that tradition of news suppression continues and apparently even extends to Russia's American partners in space. Space Station *Mir* is all that remains of the "crowning glory of communism"—the Russian space program. Trips to the station, now almost entirely financed by other countries, provide the hard cash necessary for Russia to try to keep its space program going. Failures do not sell well. When the Progress near-collision with *Mir* occurred, the Russians, as they had done after the *Mir* fire, once again tried, through misrepresentation and dissimulation, to keep NASA and the press unaware of the event. Unfortunately, when the safety concerns and violations associated with such incidents are not brought to the forefront, these incidents, and others like them, have a tendency to be repeated.

WISELY, or because the Progress no longer had enough fuel to attempt another redocking, the Russian flight controllers decided not to try docking that particular spacecraft to *Mir* again. Perhaps, in part, the decision was influenced by the fact that I had already told my NASA team in Russia that I had very strong reservations, based on safety concerns, regarding the procedure. I would guess that they knew that I would raise objections to any further docking attempt until the near-collision of the previous attempt was thoroughly investigated. In any case, the Progress spacecraft was deorbited and destroyed in the fireball of reentry. Vasily was especially glad—I could sense his relief—when the spacecraft was no longer chasing us and was gone for good.

AMERICAN astronaut Michael Foale arrived in late May as my replacement on *Mir* to join Vasily and Sasha as the new crew member. Less than a month after Mike's arrival and my return to the planet, the Russians once again decided to dock a spent Progress vehicle to *Mir* using the same manually-controlled backup system. They must have felt that the nonredundant video screen would work this time and that the trajectory was okay after all. Maybe they reckoned that with me now back on earth, no one in the remaining crew would question their orders. NASA must not have been asking the right questions and, if necessary, pressuring the Russians to thoroughly review the circumstances and safety implications surrounding the near collision before proceeding with another docking.

I am not sure how Vasily was persuaded by the controllers to attempt such a docking again with all the inevitable dangers and still unanswered questions associated with it. My guess is that they appealed to his manhood, backing him into a corner by telling him what a great pilot he was in the eyes of his peers, and assuring him of redemption for his earlier "failure." The *Mir* video glitch was apparently fixed so that a visual of *Mir* could now be provided. Basic deficiencies in the system, including no built-in redundancy and inadequate range and range-rate sensing equipment, still existed. NASA raised no official objections to the plan. In fact, up to that time, no joint American-Russian safety investigation had been convened to determine the cause of the near-miss incident.

THE PHONE, or another master alarm, was ringing. *Where am I?* was my first thought, and looking around the room, I determined that I was no longer in space but at home. I then ascertained that I was in a real bed, with my wife at my side, and that it was very early in the morning. I fumbled for the receiver and croaked out a hoarse hello.

"Jerry, there has been a collision on *Mir*," a NASA shuttle-*Mir* program manager from the Johnson Space Center informed me.

Details were sketchy, but it was *thought* that the crew had survived the initial impact and that they were in the process of trying to close off the leaking module before all the air from inside the space station was vented to the vacuum of space. They had lost all electrical power and the space station was tumbling uncontrollably through space. At least as far as they knew at the time, they had not yet evacuated the station. The pressure inside the space station was still falling, but the crew was fighting to survive, at least according to the last message this manager had received. I had been there in similar times; I could feel their plight.

Heart sinking, worried for my former crewmates, and imagining . . . no, knowing . . . exactly what it must be like for them up there, I told the manager that I would be in right away to help in any way that I could. Hanging up the phone, I clenched my fist and angrily blurted out to my still half-asleep wife the terrible news. I felt so helpless. I was mad, fuming. Perhaps feeling guilty, back here safely on earth while my former crewmates were still up there once again fighting for their lives, I wished—was I crazy?—that I was still there with them. "How could this happen again?" I kept repeating to myself as I threw on my NASA-logo polo shirt and headed out the door into the already muggy Houston morning.

Driving to the Johnson Space Center, I thought, *I am really worried.* Worrying was something that I did not do while on *Mir*. I did not become anxious, I did not fret for my life, and I always slept well at night. Up there, I realized early-on that returning to the earth was not an option and that I was stuck with my circumstances. Dangerous situations were something that I had to deal with and, in order to survive, I had to remain unflustered, at my best. I was committed. I had volunteered. I was doing something that I wanted to do. Worrying would only wear me down and make me less effective in dealing with any tense situation. But as I drove through the gate of the Johnson Space Center, my heart was racing, and I was praying that the news would be good, that my former teammates were still alive.

THEY survived. Barely.

After feeling the jolt and hearing metal crushing, everyone's ears began popping. The pressure hull was violated. Vasily's initial calculation showed that the air was rushing out of the space station at a rate that would render the atmosphere incompatible with life in twenty-two minutes. The flight rules—outlining the predetermined plan of action in the face of a decompression emergency—clearly state that if less than forty-five minutes of life-sustaining pressure remains, the proper course of action is to get into the Soyuz capsule *immediately* and evacuate the space station.

It is assumed that any hole in the hull cannot get smaller, only bigger. If a seam is split, the opening might unpredictably split still farther, sucking out the last of the life-sustaining pressure with a sudden whoosh. The crew would instantly suffocate, their blood would boil. Locating a leak takes time. If the leak is found, the hatch between the leaking module and the rest of the station must be shut. Unfortunately, hatches are no longer easily closed on *Mir*. Over the years, extension cables, ventilation tubing, and sundry experiment wires have been added to *Mir* and now wiggle their way through the hatch openings. In order to close a hatch, the obstructions first have to be cleared. Some of the wires are hot—flowing with electricity—and cannot be cut without the danger of electrocution. The forty-five-minute rule makes good sense.

Urged on by mission control in Moscow and the controller's frantic call to find the leak and shut down the hatch leading to the leaking module—contrary, of course, to what they themselves had written to be the proper action, immediate evacuation—the crew further risked their lives for the sake of the station and stayed with the ship. As their ears continued to pop, they were able to clear cables and ventilation tubes from the hatch opening and shut the hatch leading to the leaking module. With the hatch closed, the pressure in the remaining sections of the space station held steady. They had saved themselves and *Mir*.

Space officials at mission control in Moscow immediately blamed my former crewmates for the collision. Russian President Boris Yeltsin issued a press release stating that the collision was caused solely by crew error, and that nothing was innately wrong with the *Mir* space station or the way in which it was being operated.

18

Housekeeping in Space

IT TOOK ME a mere month in space to become a totally adapted spaceman. It felt normal to fly and float, normal to suck dehydrated, puréed food from tubes. Twenty-four-hour time became meaningless—the sun rose fifteen times a day. Clothing became an expendable item—I wore it, then threw it away. I slept inverted on a wall and urinated into tubes. It felt as if I had lived there all my life.

WHILE it was possible to go through the motions of running while floating in space, without the pull of gravity, running was effortless. I could run while floating for hours without tiring and, unfortunately, without doing myself any good. To gain any training effect whatsoever, resistance had to be created. Therefore, before getting on the treadmill, I would put on a harness. The harness closely resembled the type that a windsurfer might wear, and was attached to force plates located on either side of the treadmill. The harness would yank me down into the treadmill with seventy kilograms of force—thus mimicking the pull of gravity.

On the planet I so enjoyed working out that nothing could keep me from running, biking, or swimming—or all three combined—practically every day. But strapped to the treadmill I felt like I was running with someone sitting on my shoulders. The soles of my feet, grown unaccustomed to any load, felt as if pins were being driven into them for the first few minutes of practically every exercise session. As the training session progressed, the bottom of my running shoes would heat up from tread friction to such an extent that, at times, I could smell rubber burning.

Like the Tin Man in *The Wizard of Oz,* I felt as if all my joints needed oiling. The harness, pulling down with over one hundred pounds of force, was only partially successful in distributing the load evenly on my body. My shoulders and hips would painfully revolt under the load of artificial weight. Inevitably I would develop painful hot spots and friction burns over my shoulders and hips. I found myself constantly adjusting the harness in an attempt to alleviate the localized pain, but to no avail. Exercising was unwelcome to my space-adjusted body. It took all the willpower and self-discipline that I could muster—along with Bob Seeger blasting over my floating, portable CD player—to stick to the regimen of one-hour sessions twice daily.

I needed to work out. The human body, while lavishing in the effortless sea of space, weakens dramatically. Bone loses its density, muscles atrophy. If I did not have to become an earthling again at the end of the five months, the deterioration would be less important. But someday soon I would have to walk and lift my twenty-five-pound son. And should there be an emergency during landing, I would need to get myself out of the spacecraft under my own power. Exercise was a countermeasure to stave off the physiological ill effects of weightlessness.

My body would eventually limber up. My pulse would move from the lethargic space-adapted thirty-five or forty beats a minute to one hundred fifty. In spite of the discomfort, exercise still offered respite—a means of release. Once running at a comfortable pace, I would close my eyes and visualize myself jogging along my favorite route back home—the park, children playing baseball, swaying trees. Doing so would make the time pass more quickly.

Sometimes I would think of my deceased father. I felt his presence strongly, perhaps because I was up there in the heavens, nearer to him. I would hold a silent conversation with him, and tell him that I missed him. He seemed happy and content. He was pleased with me. Talking with Dad was somehow okay, even if I would sometimes feel tears welling up in my eyes. Being with him was comforting, and the tears were the kind that make one feel better after being shed.

Sometimes the running turned to pure joy. I felt pumped up and jubilant. Although I have never felt anything near the often-described runner's high while running on the planet, I did reach that euphoria when running in space. On the treadmill of *Mir* I suppose I felt both a runner's high and a runner's low.

I also got into the unofficial record books. During my first shuttle flight, while we were flying over the United States, I set my stopwatch. Then I began to run and continued to run nonstop for the next ninety minutes. One orbit of the earth with the space shuttle traveling at 17,500 miles per hour takes ninety minutes. I had circled the globe. I glanced out the shuttle window and once again saw the United States. *Runner's World* magazine subsequently wrote an article about my nonstop run around the world. Aboard *Mir,* I repeated this feat numerous times. While I do not care to disclose the exact number of my nonstop gallops, let me just say that I have run around the world a time or two.

WHEN not strapped to the treadmill, there was no force pulling me down, nothing to compress my intervertebral discs. I grew.

On launch day I had been a shade less than six feet tall. But by the end of my first day in orbit, I was a solid six-footer. By the end of my second day in orbit, I measured six feet, two inches. "Hmmmm," I thought, "Maybe I can retire when I return to earth and start playing in the NBA. I'm growing every day. Slam dunks would be no problem. As a matter of fact, I could float up into the rafters and shoot *down* at the hoop!"

At the end of day three, my expansion complete, I was still at six feet, two inches tall. I remained at six-two for the next five months in space, only to shrink on my first day back on the planet to what had been my normal height before I left.

So much for my NBA dreams.

OUR CLOTHING consisted of a cotton T-shirt, a pair of cotton shorts, and sweatsocks. No underwear provided. The T-shirt and shorts came in a variety of unappealing colors. One of the nicer looking sets was a nauseating green accented by a neckline trim of bright red. The Russian-made cotton was so thin that the clothing was almost transparent. Furthermore, none of the shorts had a built-in jock. Without being crude, let me just say that the shorts fit loosely and that everything floats in space. Quite an outfit.

Prior to the flight I had been instructed by my Russian trainers to change clothes, for sanitation reasons, no less than every third day in space. Unfortunately, after taking an inventory of clothing packets on *Mir,* we found that there was only enough clothing onboard to allow us to change clothes every two weeks.

Two weeks is a long time to wear the same set of clothes. There were no shower facilities and no laundry. The failure of the *Mir* cooling system caused the temperature on *Mir* to soar to ninety-plus humid degrees continuously for over a month. When running hard on a treadmill in space, I would sweat profusely, with the perspiration clinging to my face in globs.

I tried to accommodate the two-week schedule without becoming too revolting to myself. For one week, I would wear the same clothes, day and night. The following week, those clothes would become my running outfit. I would attempt to dry out the soaked T-shirt between the morning and late afternoon workouts by stuffing the exercise clothes near the outlet fan of the refrigerator-freezer unit. But more often than not, I would put on a still-damp T-shirt before strapping on the treadmill harness for my afternoon workout.

After two weeks of wear, I found the clothes thoroughly offensive. I would squish the damp clothes into a ball and, using duct tape, wrap them up. I would then put the ball of clothing into the Progress garbage truck. The Progress would eventually burn up when reentering the atmosphere, which provided a fitting end for my thoroughly disgusting, malodorous rags.

THERE is no shower or bath on *Mir.* The bathing process in space is tantamount to a sponge bath on earth—with additional difficulties posed by microgravity and a scarce supply of water.

To wash myself, I would begin by shooting water from the water-dispensing unit into a small tin-foil packet that contained a special low-suds soap. Through a leak-proof diaphragm on the packet, I would then insert a straw with a built-in cutoff pincher. Then I would shake the bag, open the pincher, and squeeze a few drops of the soapy water onto my body. If I remained still, the water would cling to my skin in small beads. I then spread the water around using a piece of cloth that resembled a four-by-four-inch gauze pad. Because the cloth became rather dingy during the washing process, I would always bathe my feet, crotch, and armpits last.

On my overgrown hair, I used a no-rinse shampoo. The shampoo required no water. I applied the shampoo directly to my scalp and then scrubbed. I would then wipe away the shampoo with the twice-used piece of cloth. Intellectually, I knew that my hair was not much cleaner than it had been prior to the shampooing—where could the dirt have gone?—but somehow I felt cleaner.

The Russians supplied me with a special tooth-care item in my hygiene kit—a condom-style saturated gauze pad that fit over my little finger. Slip the pad over your finger and rub your teeth and gums. Although not as ingenious, I preferred Crest toothpaste spread on a toothbrush. To keep mouth fluids and foam from floating, I would keep my mouth closed as best I could while brushing. After brushing my teeth, I would spit the excess toothpaste and water into the same cloth that I had used to bathe and to remove the shampoo from my hair.

In space shaving was no easy task and was rather time-consuming. I would squeeze a thimbleful of water onto my face. Surface tension and my stubble made the water cling to my face. To the water, I would add a specially formulated NASA shaving cream called Astro Edge. With each stroke, the shaving cream and whisker mix would stick tentatively to the blade until I deposited them into my week-old dirty towel. With each new deposit, I would roll the towel to retain the discards.

Because of the amount of time involved, I chose to shave only once a week, each Sunday morning. I could not grow a beard because it might interfere with the airtight seal of my full-face respirator should I need to wear it during an emergency. Shaving only once a week became a means of marking time. If a glance into the mirror revealed a rather scruffy face, I knew that it was either Friday or Saturday, and that I had made it through another week.

My bed was a wall in the back of the module Spektr and a ventilation fan was located on the floor opposite. Because warm air does not rise in space, there is no convection current. Fans are the only means of moving air.

When sleeping in an insufficiently ventilated area, it is possible to breathe yourself into an oxygen-depleted and carbon dioxide–rich bubble. Air starvation and hyperventilation result. The person wakes up with a severe headache and gasping for air.

For this reason I slept inverted on the wall, with my head across from the blowing fan. I would use a bungee cord or a piece of Velcro to keep from floating away during the night. I have seen other astronauts who sleep floating freely—they drift around the spacecraft during the night and usually wake up stuck to the suction side of a filter.

AND that is how I lived in space for nearly five months. Despite the inconveniences, I was not bothered by the lack of amenities. Remembering how I used to moan and complain on bath night as a boy, I considered the space station, in some respects, to be a kid's haven. Besides, being unkempt, unshaven, and even a bit grungy seemed to me to fit the space exploration scene quite nicely. We were, after all, adventurers on a frontier. We were too busy to worry about how we looked or even smelled.

After I returned to the planet, *People* magazine voted me one of the "Ten Sexiest Men of 1997." The magazine had selected men from ten different categories. Actor George Clooney won in the celebrity category and graced the cover of *People*. I won in the explorer-and-adventurer category and was buried on the inside pages. When television talk show host Oprah Winfrey did a show featuring "*People*'s Ten Sexiest Men," she asked me if I was surprised to have been selected.

"Yes, definitely," I replied. "After five months of no haircut, no shower, and only an occasional shave—the distinction was indeed, unexpected."

I figured that the static-filled video downlink worked in my favor. After talking about the excitement of launch, of doing a spacewalk, of returning inside a fireball, she asked me what was the single greatest experience in my life.

The answer, I told her, was easy: the birth of my son. There is nothing on the planet or off the planet that can top that.

19

Hurtling Into Nothingness

MIR CIRCLES THE EARTH every ninety minutes. Each time that the space station moves from the dark side to the sunlit portion of the earth, the exterior shell is subjected to tremendous temperature extremes. In the shadow of the earth, and facing the bitter cold of space, *Mir*'s aluminum skin contracts. Forty-five minutes later, as *Mir* emerges out of the earth's shadow and abruptly confronts the blistering rays of the sun, the metal shell rapidly heats up and expands. *Mir* was continually expanding and contracting—straining—as temperature extremes ranged from minus 180 degrees Fahrenheit to plus 200 degrees Fahrenheit; heat, cold, metal fatigue. The cycle was repeated more than four thousand times during my stay aboard and more than one hundred thousand times since *Mir* was first put into orbit.

Inside the space station this strain on the only protective barrier between the vacuum of space and us inside usually went unnoticed. We could not feel or hear *Mir* responding to this intermittent onslaught of heat and cold because of the constant vibration and buzz of turning fans and operating machinery. But when the machinery fell silent during the electrical power failures that we experienced on *Mir*, the hull came alive—groaning, popping, squeaking—battling in an effort to maintain its integrity. The erratic sounds were routine reminders of *Mir*'s vulnerability and, therefore, our own.

WITH the exception of the hull groaning under the thermal stress, the silence invoked by an electrical power failure on *Mir* was more beautiful than any other sound that I had ever heard in my life. My quickened pulse, unconsciously revved up by the constant background noise, would slow as my body soaked in the utterly peaceful stillness. Bathed in quiet, I was overwhelmed by its nothingness, distracted, unable to concentrate for a moment on anything but the strange sound of nothing. I understood for the first time that silence was a blessing that I had always taken for granted. "Don't breathe, just listen," I told myself. "Savor the music. Remember, again, how beautiful silence sounds."

Power system failures were not, unfortunately, our only problem. Antifreeze leaked out of the numerous corroded cooling lines that wormed through the space station, contaminating the internal atmosphere and causing the temperature inside *Mir* to rise. The lack of adequate cooling to vital equipment—oxygen generators, carbon dioxide scrubbers, and condensers—caused those mechanical systems to fail.

Our attitude control computer was also much less than reliable and failed at a rate of six times a year. Like the cooling system failure, the crash of the attitude control computer set off a flurry of other failures.

The attitude control computer's purpose is to keep *Mir* properly oriented in space. The attitude of a spacecraft has nothing to do with its approach to life. It is the technical term used to indicate the spacecraft's three-dimensional orientation in space. By determining our three-dimensional orientation, the computer could keep *Mir* pointed in the right direction. By assuring that we were stable and properly positioned, the attitude control computer could indirectly aid a separate control system that kept the *Mir*'s solar panels pointed perpendicular to the sun's rays. Then the solar panels could capture enough sunlight to recharge our batteries and produce the electricity needed for use throughout *Mir*.

DISTURBING our already harried work pace, the *Mir*'s master alarm again bellowed out its warning. Blaaang! Flying to the caution-and-warning panel in the base block module, Vasily punched off the master alarm tone and, after studying the pattern of lights on the panel, declared that the attitude control computer had failed once again. I almost immediately noticed that the walls of the space station were rotating slowly around me. *Mir* was tumbling out of control.

Looking out of one of the side-facing portholes, I saw the earth below slowly moving by until the planet disappeared from view. Three seconds later, I observed the earth reappear in the porthole located overhead. One-quarter revolution in three seconds, not so very fast, perhaps recoverable, I reasoned. I knew that *Mir*'s solar panels could not track the sun during such uncontrolled movement of the space station. Power would be our next problem.

Blaaang!

The master alarm repeated its screech, warning us of a new threat. Assessing the newly glowing lights on the caution-and-warning panel, Vasily confirmed what I had already guessed at, that the solar panels were no longer producing enough electrical power to keep up with the drain on the batteries even though we were still in orbit on the lighted side of the planet. Sasha and I frantically began to turn off the lights and all noncritical equipment that drew electricity, hoping to lessen the demand on the batteries.

Blaaang!

Too late. The caution-and-warning panel lit up like a Christmas tree once again, this time indicating that the electrical power was so critically low that the gyrodynes, ten-or-so spinning gyroscopes that help to stabilize the station, were failing, starved of electrical energy. Once the gyrodynes are lost, recovery is at best a slow process. At worst, the power-dead space station could be lost forever and we would be forced to evacuate in the Soyuz lifeboat.

We had all the lights turned off as *Mir* entered the night portion of its orbit once again. The space station darkened abruptly. Without sunlight for the next forty-five minutes, there would be no means for us to recharge the batteries. Slowly the batteries discharged the last of their electrical charge to the gyrodynes. Hearing the last gyrodyne wind eerily to a stop, I knew that the space station's batteries were now totally dead, not an electron of electricity left. Unnerving silence joined the utter darkness. We all felt uneasy.

But we knew what to do, for the mechanical misadventures of *Mir* were, by now, quite familiar to us. While this particular failure was new, general principles applied. Stay calm. Remember that panic can kill. Assess the situation. How can we recover? Draw upon our skills and training and the one thing that has kept the space station and us alive up to this point: human ingenuity. Above all, do nothing that will aggravate our already critical situation. *Mir* is fragile and critically ill—not unlike the triple-gunshot patients that I used to treat in the ER at Detroit General Hospital. Make no mistakes, Jerry. Mistakes at this critical juncture might not be reversible.

We reached for our penlights and held them in our teeth. The penlights were equipped with a bite bar and, since the lights are weightless, holding them in ones' teeth is done without strain. With the narrow light beam shining down the length of the module, I methodically began turning off the power switches to everything. We then waited in the quiet darkness until our orbit swung us back to the lighted side of the earth.

The bulkheads were moving around me as we continued to tumble through space but the rate had not increased. We still had a chance to recover if our solar panels could capture enough light during the sunlight portion of the orbit to partially recharge the batteries. With all the equipment now turned off, there would no longer be any drain on the batteries. As long as we could recharge the batteries, if only partially during each sunlit phase of the orbit, we could repeat the tedious process orbit after orbit until we had recaptured enough power to restart the gyrodynes. Once we had saved up enough power to spin a sufficient number of gyrodynes, we could once again stabilize the space station.

The process required patience. Based on a rough calculation determined by looking at volt and amp indicators, probably thirty orbits or so worth of patience—more than two days—all the while knowing that even if we were successful in recovering our batteries and in restarting all of the equipment flawlessly, we would be set back two days in our work.

During the recharging process, almost nothing worked. The urine collection system, a funnel hooked to the end of a hose, uses an electrical fan to create suction. There was no electricity to spare for the fan. We relieved ourselves using rubberized, condom-fitted bags. We all tried to avoid eating solid food.

IF WE were unable to capture enough energy to recharge the batteries, we would be forced to try to stabilize the tumbling space station using a last-ditch effort. We could attempt to use the thrusters on the

Soyuz spacecraft, now docked to the *Mir*. If we were successful in getting the *Mir* at least roughly pointed in the proper direction, the solar panels could capture more of the sun's rays. Using the Soyuz in such a manner, while theoretically possible, was untried.

Questions remained. Where was the center of gravity in the gangly, spiderlike space station? How would the station respond to a force being exerted on the extreme end of the fulcrum? Were the thrusters of the Soyuz strong enough and oriented in such a manner as to affect the pivoting of a structure as large as the 120-ton space station? And finally, how much thruster fuel would be required?

The Soyuz was our lifeboat, our means of returning to the planet. Fuel indicators on all spacecraft are notoriously inaccurate, in part because the fuel is floating in the tank. Only during spacecraft accelerations, when the fuel is thrust back to the rear of the tank, can somewhat accurate readings be assured. By using the Soyuz to rescue the space station, we might use too much fuel and, as a result, leave ourselves with a spacecraft incapable of executing a deorbit burn.

Because the tumble rate was slow, the *Mir*'s solar panels did capture enough sunlight to generate some electricity. Because we had completely powered down the station, the batteries held the slight charge as the space station reentered the shadow of the earth. Forty-five minutes later, emerging into sunlight, we were able to recharge the batteries a little more. We would not, thankfully, have to use valuable Soyuz fuel to recover.

Orbit after orbit, we painstakingly repeated this recharging procedure until the station had enough power to spin up one gyrodyne, then the next gyrodyne, and so forth.

Two days later, with all the gyrodynes spinning again, we rebooted the computer and kept our fingers crossed. There were no spare computer components onboard, so we just hoped that whatever had caused the computer to fail in the first place was not a permanent defect, but rather a temporary insult, caused, perhaps, by radiation. The computer worked, and although we knew that the underlying problem was not fixed, we were relieved.

Based on the history of the computer, one could predict that it would probably fail again. But we could not predict precisely when. This generated a great deal of concern at NASA since, if such an event occurred during a space shuttle docking and the shuttle collided with the tumbling *Mir*, the result could be disastrous. By some hocus-pocus the Russians reassured NASA that the computer would never fail again (although it did, repeatedly, once only days prior to a shuttle launch, almost forcing a launch delay). NASA managers, taking the Russians' word for it, decided that the docking risk was acceptable.

With the computer on-line again, and with the gyrodynes spinning, we were able to reestablish the space station's proper orientation. Once the batteries were fully charged, we then methodically tried to bring the life support systems back on-line. Some of the equipment worked. Other equipment, sputtering like a stubborn old lawn mower engine, choked, gasped, and refused to restart. As our to-do list grew, we tried to catch up on the two days of missed work.

AFTER my return to earth, Sasha Lazutkin, still on the station with Vasily Tsibliev and my replacement, Mike Foale, inadvertently disconnected the wrong cable after being ordered to reroute a number of them. The cable supplied power to the attitude control computer. The station tumbled; two days were once again required to recover. The lead flight director at mission control in Moscow screamed at the crew, insulting his "underlings" by saying, "It is like a kindergarten up there!"

That cable bundles might contain hundreds of wires, many of which are improperly labeled, that a human being cannot perform flawlessly for months on end, and that Sasha did not already feel terrible about the mistake, was not taken into consideration by the flight director. Instead, he insulted the crew. That particular Russian controller has much to learn about human relations.

ALTHOUGH we were able to restore enough power to right the *Mir,* the space station continued to suffer from less-than-adequate electric power supply. Without adequate electrical power, we could no longer collect and recycle the urine. Normally we would purify the urine, converting it into water. The water, H_2O, is then hydrolyzed, splitting the molecules of water into hydrogen and oxygen. Because hydrogen is an explosive gas, obviously unwanted within the confines of a space station, the gas is vented into space via a vacuum-vent valve. This process requires no fan, relying instead upon the free suction of space. The oxygen, however, is good stuff. The urine-derived oxygen percolates into the air. We breathed it, consumed it.

The people on the ground swear by the quality of the urine-derived water. The controllers insist that the water, thus purified, is potable. "Drink it, use it to rehydrate your dehydrated mashed potatoes and borscht," they insist. I can stomach a lot. During navy aviation jungle-survival school in the Philippines I ate many dinners of snake and roots. Always wanting to be an astronaut, I decided that "Yes, I can drink my own urine if necessary." But I could not stomach the idea of drinking someone else's urine. Vasily and Sasha were of a similar mind. We chose to use the purified urine-derived water to make oxygen. We could breathe our urine, but not drink it! Now, without adequate electrical power, we could do neither.

The other source of recycled water, incidentally, was human sweat and spacecraft humidity. Both vapors were extracted from the air of *Mir* by cold condenser coils, in much the same manner as water droplets form on the exterior surface of a glass of iced tea on a hot summer day. After the condensate was purified, we would drink and use this water to rehydrate our food. With the cooling system failure, this water recycling capability was already lost. Eventually our water supply would dwindle, but this was not of immediate concern. Other factors would force an evacuation of the space station long before the well ran dry.

One such item was carbon dioxide (CO_2). With each exhaled breath, carbon dioxide, a waste product of respiration, would build up in the air. The primary carbon dioxide scrubber was an electrically power-hungry piece of gear that, after clearing the air, would expel that carbon dioxide into the vacuum of space. Without adequate electrical power, we were forced to turn the already finicky, primary carbon dioxide scrubber off. We watched as the CO_2 level rose within the cabin daily.

As the levels climbed to toxic proportions, we began to use our backup scrubber, a nonrenewable, chemical-based canister that functioned to bind the carbon dioxide in a chemical bed. The backup scrubber required very little electrical power to function, only enough to turn a fan. The high heat and humidity aboard *Mir*, however, caused the chemical bed to saturate quickly with water, thus decreasing the effectiveness of the system. Furthermore, we had a limited number of these canisters onboard—less than ten days' worth. The CO_2 levels became so critically high that we were

ordered by the ground to stop exercising, since the increased metabolic rate secondary to exercise causes an individual to exhale more
carbon dioxide. We reluctantly stopped.

We knew that exercise was critical to our health. In space, exercise is not a diversion, but necessary for maintaining the density of
bones and muscular strength. "How long do you expect that we will
not be able to exercise?" we asked the ground. In our minds, a day
or two was acceptable, but what about a week, two weeks? How
long would the controllers string us along without exercise, with
ninety-degree temperatures, and without adequate electrical power?
What was the end point? When would mission control in Moscow
declare that things had gone too far, that *Mir* had crossed over that
tough-to-determine line where the risks outweighed the benefits on
the crumbling space station?

We made it clear that we were willing to continue to work under
the present conditions and to continue our efforts to overcome the
dominolike progression of failures onboard. But we asked the questions because we wanted Moscow control to know that we did not
consider ourselves expendable. We felt, by unanimous consensus as
a crew, that an end point should be determined rationally, beyond
which someone would tell us that it was time to get into the Soyuz
and leave the crippled space station behind. The decision was theirs
to make. We would follow orders and give it our best. But we felt
strongly that someone on the ground should at least determine the
boundary, beyond which they would order us to evacuate. We also
felt that consideration of our long-term health should at least enter
into the equation.

WE WERE constantly asked, hounded really, by the Russian ground
controllers to "find the leak" in the ethylene glycol–filled cooling
lines. We told them repeatedly that there was no single leak, that
there were multiple leaks, many of which were located in inaccessi-
ble places. That we could never be totally successful was something
that we could not seem to get through to the people on the ground.

In the course of our discussions with the ground, it became evi-
dent that the controllers did not really know where the pipes were
located, or which valves cut off flow to which lines. We were asked
to describe to them where the lines were throughout *Mir.* That the

experts on the ground did not have an accurate idea of the configuration of the space station that they were supposed to be controlling
was nearly unbelievable to me. Where were the engineering draw-
ings? Probably lost ten years ago, or locked away in someone's safe
at the factory where the station had been built as "proprietary material." In the secretive society of the Soviet Union, paper documents
had never been readily available.

THE PRIRODA module was where about half of the experimental
apparatus for the U.S. science program on *Mir* was located and
where most of the American experiments were conducted. Along
with the similarly equipped U.S. Spektr module, it was the only place
on *Mir* where we were able to get any productive work done. To be
sure, we were working everywhere throughout the space station
doing repair work, but only in these spaces were we doing work that
advanced our presence in space, work that went beyond just trying
to stay alive.

Trying to find cooling-line leaks in the already overstuffed Kvant
I module forced us to move much of the garbage from Kvant I into
Priroda. Priroda took on the look of the rest of the space station—
cluttered from floor to ceiling. No longer the efficient working place
that it had once been, Priroda was instead stuffed with used food
containers, discarded gear, and garbage. The additional items
stacked in Priroda impaired the air circulation. The temperature in
the module began to rise. Water pooled behind the panels along the
cold aluminum hull and settled on sensitive electronic gear no longer
in the stream of freshly circulating air. As the temperature rose, so,
too, did the smell.

The temporary storage in Priroda turned out to be anything but
temporary, since the leaks in Kvant I proved to be far more extensive
than the ground, ignoring what we told them, had reckoned. Weeks
passed. The space station was turned into a chaotic, unorganized
mess. Gear was floating everywhere or was temporarily strapped
down in every available place. Living conditions went from bad to
worse.

We began to lose the sense that we were accomplishing anything
productive. We were just hanging in there, trying to survive. I had to
plead with the ground to continue to schedule U.S. science experiments, since we needed, more than ever before, to have something

positive to show for our efforts. At the end of a tough day, I could always tell Vasily that yes, we were working like slaves, yes, the ethylene glycol burned our skin and choked our lungs, but at least we had accomplished something productive.

The interaction among the crew changed radically because of the workload. We no longer had the luxury of eating together, but instead grabbed a quick bite individually whenever we could. We would update each other on our own progress with a few quick words in passing. Small talk, which was never vibrant in the first place, given our cultural differences and the language barrier, ground to a halt. Inevitably, we were continually rushing from one task to the next, always hours behind schedule. There was no free time, no weekends, no diversions—nothing but work for months on end. I laughed to myself that Annapolis and medical school were a piece of cake. I had never been so challenged in my life.

20

Broken Trust

THE COMMUNICATION SYSTEM on *Mir* was horrible. All radio conversations were static filled—the voice quality so scratchy that it reminded me of talking over a plastic walkie-talkie set that Santa Claus had given to me as a boy.

The satellite communication system was doubly crippled. Lack of cooling for the electronics box that controlled the pointing of *Mir*'s tracking antenna caused it to fail. That particular failure was not so critical because there were no satellites to communicate with. One of the two orbiting Russian communication satellites used by *Mir*, long past its design lifetime, was broken and the Russians could not find the money to replace it. The other satellite was being moved to a new location in space to cover for the broken satellite and could not be used during transit. Without the satellite communication system working, two-way video teleconferencing was out. We would not be seeing our families periodically. Kathryn, who chose to live alone with John in Star City during my flight in order to take advantage of the opportunity for us to see each other once a week, would be disappointed.

All radio communication was line of sight. We would only be able to communicate with the ground for five or six minutes each time we passed over a ground-based antenna. As a further cost-cutting measure, the Russians only maintained a couple of antenna stations.

Originally, we were to have periodic psychological support communications with family members throughout the flight. Because of our limited radio capability, these sessions were scheduled no more than once a week.

As trivial as a weekly five-minute conversation might sound, I can tell you that to an astronaut-cosmonaut cut off from the world, those five minutes are precious. Just hearing my wife's voice saying that our son was fine, that she was proud of what I was doing, and that everyone back home sent their love, would make my week. I would actually prepare for those five minutes by writing down on my kneeboard some questions that I wanted to ask Kathryn, so that in the excitement of the moment I would not forget them. I did not have the luxury of being able to call back again. If I had forgotten to ask, for example, how her latest pregnancy ultrasounds had gone, I would have to wait another week before knowing whether everything was fine.

The controllers at mission control in Moscow would normally schedule our family conferences on Sunday afternoons. One particular Sunday, after looking at the schedule and noting the time of my communication pass, I floated to the World Map program on the computer to see exactly where our orbit would be during that time period. Depending on where our orbital path would take us in relationship to the ground antennas, I could, based on previous experience, predict the amount of time that Kathryn and I would have to talk together.

I noted that the orbital path would take us over Lake Baikal. This meant that we would have two minutes of relatively good voice quality, followed by a two-minute hole of communication dropout, followed by two more minutes of static-filled, but readable communications.

"Okay," I thought, "we will be able to talk for about four minutes total. Better than usual. Don't forget to ask about the ultrasounds."

As the communication pass began, the first voice that I heard was the ground controller at mission control in Moscow. "Jerry, we have Kathryn on the line from Star City, but first we need to talk with Vasily."

I listened as my precious seconds ticked by. The controller and Vasily were having an idle conversation about nothing of particular importance. "How are things? Any new problems? Oh, by the way, there is about half a meter of fresh snow in Moscow today. How is the loading of the Progress going?"

I watched through the window as the western edge of Lake Baikal came into view. Just then the Russian ground controller said, "Go ahead, Jerry, it's all yours."

As I had predicted, the second he spit out his final words, loud static filled my headset.

I yelled to Kathryn, "Can you hear me?" I heard no reply, only static.

I did hear Kathryn's voice once. She was evidently asking me the same question because I heard the words "can," "hear," and "me" through the noise.

I waited as we moved further into Siberia, where I knew communications would clear and we could talk for the final two minutes. At the precise moment that the static lessened over my headset, I heard not Kathryn's voice, but that of the Russian controller once again interrupting.

"Jerry, we need to talk to Sasha for a minute, then you can continue."

The Russian controller proceeded to discuss with Sasha how the toilet repairs were going. Sasha and Vasily both gave me a look of disbelief and embarrassment, but had to respond. Vasily bravely interrupted and asked that Kathryn be put back on the line. The controller finally gave the communication pass back to Kathryn and me for about thirty seconds. We said hello, how are you, great to hear your voice. I squeezed in an "I love you, Kath," just before static overwhelmed our voices as we moved beyond the range of the ground antenna.

At least I heard her voice, I thought to myself. She is alive. The questions that I had written down on my kneeboard pad would remain unanswered for another week.

AFTER weeks of trying to repair leaking cooling lines, the futility of our effort became another irritant in a growing list of sore points between us and mission control in Moscow.

The lines carry antifreeze to cool the internal atmosphere of *Mir* as well as to remove heat from friction-producing machinery throughout the space station. Machinery—carbon dioxide scrubbers, oxygen generators, and condensers—all robbed of cooling, continued to break down at alarming rates.

Unfortunately, the lines were not designed to be repaired in orbit. The pipes weaved behind cable bundles and support beams, behind machinery and ventilation fans. Many of the lines were so enmeshed in the general machinery of *Mir* that we could not physically get to the pipe, let alone have adequate clearance to repair it. The pipes were so rusted that they were fragile. We had isolated hopelessly leaking pipes by shutting down valves and had plugged as many leaks as possible in order to stabilize the system.

Vasily very plainly told the ground that we had done as much as we could possibly do. To continue to open isolation valves, repressurize lines, and search for more leaks in the sievelike pipes was counterproductive. Every time we repressurized a line, Sasha Lazutkin's eyeballs would swell to the size of golfballs and we would all become congested. In fact, I could fly into the base block module from my sleeping area in Spektr and, without observing anything, know instantly whether or not we were once again repressurizing cooling lines—my nose would become immediately congested and my lungs would begin to wheeze.

In the face of weeks of blatant evidence to the contrary, the Russian controllers continued to insist that the antifreeze fumes were harmless. We disregarded their assessment. I finally got word to the U.S. contingent in Moscow that I wanted a thorough medical literature search done concerning the toxic effects of ethylene glycol. A week later, Tom Marshburn, my flight surgeon, responded with a short report. He stated that ethylene glycol is highly toxic if ingested, but the fumes were not known to cause significant health problems at concentration levels tested in work areas *over an eight-hour exposure.* That was as much as he could find, but he had some toxicologists looking into it further.

Knowing that each breath that we took could affect our long-term health gnawed at each of us. We learned that a prolonged but indirect low-level threat is much more unsettling than an acute high-risk event. One can face an acute danger head on, either win or lose, and move beyond it. But we could effect no such closure against the fumes. We felt defenseless. "How long can we safely breathe in these fumes, Dr. Jerry?" Vasily would ask. "Can't you give us something to protect us, some medicine?" Sasha would inquire. The only way that I knew to counter the effects of an exposure to a toxic substance was to limit the time of exposure to that substance and to move away from the contaminated environment. But we were stuck. There was nowhere to go, no windows that could be opened. Our only option was to stop contaminating the environment.

VASILY and I did leave once, near the end of the mission, to do a five-hour spacewalk. We breathed the fresh oxygen supplied by our spacesuits. At the completion of the walk, and the moment that we got out of our suits, we were both shocked at how strong the fumes smelled on *Mir*. We just stood there looking at each other, not wanting to breathe. Our sense of smell had obviously been deadened by the constant exposure. *Mir* smelled like a gas station where someone had not merely spilled a few drops of gasoline, but had taken the hose and sprayed it on the pavement.

Vasily had had enough. He argued with the ground that the cooling system was as stable as we could hope to make it and that we did not want to repressurize the lines anymore, or at least for a few more days. His request was ignored. When he asked whether there were any more air filters onboard that we could use to replace the already saturated and ineffective filters in the air cleaning units, he was told, "No, there are no spares."

In fact, there was one spare. This spare was "discovered" by the ground the day prior to the space shuttle docking, when the astronauts would arrive with a sniffing device that could determine the level of ethylene glycol in the air. Vasily was livid when the ground told him to replace the filter at that time. It was okay for the three of us to breathe in the fumes for months, but the implication was not to look bad to the arriving U.S. shuttle crew.

OUR WORK continued. Whenever another hole was found and plugged, we would repressurize the line. The pressure would inevitably not hold; another leak would sprout further down the pipe. More antifreeze would pour out into the atmosphere, eyeballs would swell, and the sound of coughing and hacking would fill the space station once again.

We continued to wear filter masks day and night, but our health was getting predictably worse. As *Mir* commander, Vasily repeatedly implored mission control in Moscow that we were becoming increasingly concerned about our health and strongly felt that we should discontinue the dangerous work. The ground continued to assert that the air was fine; the crew continued to remain concerned.

The Russian doctors on the ground tried a new tack. They assured Vasily that he had a very good American doctor onboard who could take care of him. But what was I supposed to do? Disgusted by Moscow's latest ploy at reassurance, I told Vasily that there was nothing that I could do to help any of us. When the doctors on the ground advised more vitamins and drinking dairy products in an attempt to bind any ingested chemical, I knew that they had no real solution to the problem either.

VASILY was becoming noticeably irritated with the ground, at times losing his composure and screaming at them over the radio. While working relationships among the crew remained good, relationships between the crew and the ground were dismal. I would later learn that during this period psychologists on the ground were having a field day dreaming up all sorts of schemes concerning the relationships among the crew, even going so far as to say that we were at each other's throats. It was simply not the case. It was the ground that Vasily had grown tired of, the controllers at mission control in Moscow who could not seem to fathom just how hard we were working, who could not understand that there was not another spare minute in the day to do anything additional.

The Russian medical support team in Moscow, by this time grasping at straws, suggested that we run some blood tests to see if we were having any physiological reactions to the fumes. We had a blood analyzer that could determine the value of twenty blood parameters. The doctors ordered me to draw blood, analyze the samples, and then call down the results of the tests.

Of the twenty tests, only a few seemed relevant—those that reflected liver and renal function. I knew, for example, that the cholesterol level had no bearing whatsoever on any diagnosis related to ethylene glycol fumes, and that only more sophisticated tests run in specialized laboratories could be definitive. But I also realized that the tests, if negative, could nonetheless be reassuring psychologically to Vasily and Sasha. Since I did not want to interfere with this possible benefit, I performed all of the tests.

I examined the results and noted that ten of the twenty blood-test values were either off-scale high or off-scale low. I do not mean merely above or below average. I mean that the test results were so much above or below normal that the recorded values were inconsistent with life. A typical adult, for example, should have a glucose value of about one hundred. Our values all showed zero. Zero blood glucose is incompatible with life, and we were obviously still alive. I figured that there must be a problem with the reagents on the test strips, probably caused by the chemicals on the strips being exposed to the high heat and humidity of the space station. The other ten results were compatible with life, but without knowing our preflight values, I could draw no conclusions concerning their significance.

During the next comm pass, Vasily read the raw blood-test results verbatim to mission control in Moscow from a list I had prepared. He did not mention my interpretation of the results, but only read the numbers. We were told that the doctors would take a look at the data and get back to us on the next comm pass.

Ninety minutes later, we received word from a cheerful Russian doctor that "all of your test results look fine!" He assured us that there was nothing to worry about, and that this was good news—the ethylene glycol had no effect on us whatsoever. We could continue working on the leaking pipes with impunity. "Now you can relax, Vasily, all is fine" was his closing comment.

Vasily was anything but relaxed. Fighting back his anger, he decided to make no comment to mission control in Moscow about their appraisal of our blood results before talking with me once again. Communication pass complete, he calmly signed off and then approached me. I told him that yes, I was absolutely sure. Ten of the twenty values were anything but normal. I then assured him that I was certain that those ten values did not reflect reality, but rather a failure of the testing equipment.

During the next comm pass, Vasily could not be restrained. He told them that Doctor Linenger, stressing the title doctor, says that the values are *not* normal, and that we would all be dead if we had such blood values. For the full six minutes of the comm pass, he screamed at the ground, ranting and raving, totally out of control. During the subsequent comm pass, with nerves somewhat calmed, the ground conceded that yes, after all, ten of the twenty values were not normal. But the ground controllers still stubbornly continued to prevaricate that in spite of the blood tests, they still felt that the ethylene glycol fumes were not a problem.

From that moment on, our crew no longer fully trusted what the controllers at mission control in Moscow told us. It was, in a sense, us against them. We would follow their instructions—this was not a mutiny by any means—but we would always question their intentions. An untoward effect of the ground's dishonesty was a strengthening of the bonds within the crew. We became even closer; and in spite of the speculations of the psychologists on the ground, any anger expressed by the crew, any frustration vented, was not caused by any conflict among the crew, but rather precipitated by the master-slave relationship that the ground sought to perpetuate over us.

One example of our pulling together as a crew and our pulling away from the Russian controllers on the ground occurred when my crewmates told me that they would depend entirely upon me for all of their medical needs. Furthermore, they asked me not to discuss any of the medical results with Moscow. They wanted everything kept private among us. So-called private medical conferences with the ground were anything but private, they reminded me. In fact, they said that during these supposedly one-on-one talks between the medical staff in Moscow and myself, everyone listens to get the dirt on the crew. I, of course, already knew that this was the case. I had always used discretion when deciding what to tell the ground.

We had gradually come to understand that, for the people at mission control in Moscow, the continued existence of the space station was paramount—more important than the health of the crew aboard the station. Their mantra was that *Mir* would survive at all costs, that we would do what we were told, and that all decisions were theirs to make. No input from us was solicited or desired. All trust between crew and ground was broken. We felt more isolated, more cut off, than ever.

WITH trust irreparably broken, Vasily, in the eyes of mission control in Moscow, but by no means in the eyes of his crew, began to become more and more a problem commander. In other words, he would no longer passively accept his role as slave in the master-peon relationship that Moscow sought to impose over all *Mir* crews. Vasily began to question orders and openly object over the radio when, in his judgment, mission control was asking us to tolerate a hazardous condition or perform an unsafe activity aboard his spacecraft.

Admittedly, Vasily was feeling the strain. I began to act the part of a psychiatrist, letting him vent his pent-up anger in my confidence. I had to keep one ear shut, however, not because what he was saying was senseless, but rather because much of what he was saying was correct. I was fearful that I, too, might join him on his psychological downward spiral.

But who would not decompensate somewhat under such extreme isolation and difficult working conditions, all the while being ridiculed by the ground *support* people, who, as their title indicates, are supposed to be supporting you, not chastizing you. Vasily had become quick to anger and always on edge in his dealings with the ground controllers. But he was not paranoid, nor were Sasha and I. The problems that he discussed and the objections that he raised were legitimate—even if Moscow did not care to hear about them.

LESS THAN a month after I left the space station, Vasily flatly refused to do a spacewalk which he felt was inappropriate and that he was not trained to do. He knew his limits. With only days remaining in his tenure, why not wait for the fresh, incoming crew that had rehearsed the steps of the spacewalk in the training pool in Star City? The ground openly criticized him, lambasted him, really. Under the pressure, Vasily's heart began to flutter irregularly. He was then declared not medically qualified. The Russian doctors on the ground urged him to take "the special medicine," vodka and cognac, more often. Use sleeping pills, use anxiolytics. They calmed Vasily to the point of incapacitating him.

IN THE office of the lead flight director at mission control in Moscow there is a poster showing a puppeteer pulling strings attached to Space Station *Mir*. This exemplifies how the Russian flight director views his relationship toward the crew. During my shuttle flights, I have seen how productive professional working relationships between the ground and the astronauts can be. The missions are enhanced. Teamwork becomes an essential part of all critical operations. During my time on *Mir*, I have also seen how awful, destructive, and counterproductive a puppeteer-pulling-the-strings relationship can be. Of my entire experience with the Russians, this blatant lack of respect that the Russian flight directors exhibited toward their cosmonauts in space was my greatest disappointment.

21

Taking a Stroll

I KNEW WHAT it was like to be in dangerous situations. I had years of experience under my belt. I had worked, protected by my spacesuit, in vacuum chambers. I dived, equipped with scuba gear, to ocean depths. In U.S. Navy cockpit crash training, I had been strapped into a mock ejection seat and then sent sliding down rails and into a pool. Eight feet underwater, the entire seat apparatus was inverted violently. Holding my breath and submerged in the turbulent water, I struggled to release my harness straps. Once free, I determined which way was up by observing the movement of rising bubbles, and then, following the bubbles, swam to the surface for air. I had sat in jets as they slammed onto the moving deck of an aircraft carrier in rough seas at night.

Monsoon raging, I had once been lowered onto a Chinese fishing boat in the middle of the North China Sea by a navy SH-3 helicopter. A Chinese fisherman had been crushed when the mast of the small vessel had snapped during the storm. I was sent in following their distress call. Rappelling down the superstructure of the bobbing ship in the midst of wind-driven rain and perilous seas, I lowered myself to the deck and unhooked my harness from the helicopter-suspended cable. Low on fuel, the helicopter left me behind among the entirely Chinese-speaking crew aboard the damaged ship. By bandaging the exposed femur of the fisherman's leg, splinting the leg, and then pouring IV fluids into his veins, I kept him alive. We were lifted—gurney spinning under the prop-wash—from the disabled ship by a second helicopter two hours later.

Through these life-threatening experiences I had trained myself to divorce my thoughts from the frightening realities of the moment, to remain calm, and to focus on the task at hand. But nothing had prepared me for the terror that came over me when dangling from the end of a telescoping pole outside the confines of the space station during my spacewalk.

ZERO gravity does not really exist in an orbiting spacecraft. Gravity is out there all right, a force between any two bodies that have mass. The earth has a lot of mass, the space station a little, and given no other competing forces, the *Mir* would indeed fall toward the earth. The force that keeps us from falling to the ground from our perch three hundred miles above the earth is the velocity of our movement.

Even though gravity is still a factor in space, we float because we are, in fact, free-falling. We fall and fall and fall, but because the earth is a sphere and our speed is in perfect equilibrium with the pull of gravity we keep falling over the edge of the earth, but never strike it. In the constant state of falling, we, onboard the space station, float, just as one would float inside a falling elevator should the cable of the elevator be severed. The difference between falling in an elevator and free-falling through space is that, because of our speed and because space is nearly a perfect vacuum, we never hit the bottom and we never slow due to air resistance. We just fall and fall and float and float. A falling elevator, on the other hand, inevitably comes to an abrupt halt.

OPENING the airlock hatch, I was greeted by the rising sun climbing up over the curvature of the earth. It was blindingly bright. I quickly pulled down my gold-flaked visor. For a moment, as the sun reflected directly off of my visor, I could see nothing through the glare. Feeling my way along, drawing more upon memory than actual sight, I crawled out of space-station airlock. I gingerly maneuvered myself onto a platform that extended outward from the nosecone and parallel to my body.

The platform resembled a six-step metal ladder, and I carefully climbed the ladder by first attaching my two carabiners—climbing hooks—over the first two rungs. I then inched my way to the end of the platform, swung my body around through the free and uncluttered space at the end of the ladder, and reversed my direction. The sun was now at my back and higher above the horizon. My vision sharpened as I backtracked and climbed up the blunt-end wall of the nosecone to the cylindrical side of the school bus–sized module.

Freedom! Inside my space suit, I was essentially a self-contained spacecraft. The world was spinning below, the space station sprawling in front of me, my view totally unobstructed. I could hear myself breathing; I could feel the uncomfortable coldness of the water circulating through my inner cooling garment. Looking down the length of the module, I saw solar panels—golden and glowing in the sunlight—extending perpendicular to the long axis of the module. Well-adapted to space, I was floating gracefully, moving almost effortlessly, but carefully, along the outer walls of the space station. I glanced at my spacesuit caution-and-warning panel. Reassuringly unremarkable; oxygen tank–level and suit-pressure needles both in the green range. All was going well.

I then worked my way along the circumference of the module and attached myself and the five-hundred-pound experiment package that I was dragging behind me to the end of a fifteen-meter telescoping pole. Vasily made his way to the base of the pole and, by turning a handle, swung me away from the space station. I was dangling on the end of a wavering pole, getting pushed out farther and farther from the space station. *Mir* began to look smaller and smaller—almost like a toy model in the distance. Suddenly, it hit me: the feeling of speed—pure, raw speed—faster than anything that I, who have gone supersonic a time or two, had ever experienced in my life.

Accompanying this overpowering sense of speed was the overwhelming sensation of falling. I felt as if I were falling off the station and catapulting toward the earth. Furthermore, and strangely, it felt as if the space station itself were plummeting earthward with me clinging to its surface.

My heart raced. I wanted to close my eyes in an effort to escape this dreadful and persistent sensation of falling. White-knuckled, I gripped the handrail on the end of the pole, holding on for dear life.

"This is not good," I said to myself, understating the obvious, and forcing myself to keep my eyes open and not scream.

I had been training in underwater tanks for this day for over a year, and I had important work to do. Somehow I would have to overcome the pure terror of falling back toward earth. But how?

I reasoned that this instantaneous sense and surge of orbital speed occurred because I had lost the stabilizing visual perspective provided by the protective interior walls of the space station. No longer confined within *Mir*, I was dangling on the end of a pole, flying almost independently. A difference of perspective would be expected. But, deprived from any strong visual clues of containment, I felt as if I were falling off a cliff that just kept falling away from me.

Inside the space station I had never, even for a moment, felt this sensation of raw speed. Oh, sure, I knew that we were traveling fast—about five miles every time I snapped my fingers. Snap, snap, snap—fifteen miles. Looking out the window, I could see places on the planet rapidly coming and going. "There's Chicago," and seconds later, "Ah, my hometown, Detroit. Hi, Mom!" Rationally, I knew that I was going Mach 25, twenty-five times faster than the speed of sound, but I never *felt* the speed at a gut level.

I also knew, from orbital mechanics, that the space station and, of course, I, attached to the space station, were in constant free-fall. I reasoned that my internal defense mechanism against the uncomfortable and crippling sensation of speed and falling had broken down now that I was no longer inside the confines of the station. The sensory input provided by my eyes could not dominate and counteract the input from my other body sensors. No longer surrounded by strong visual cues, my brain was unable to ignore the reality and fake me into believing that things were stable when they were, in fact, not stable at all. I *was* going 18,000 mph. I *was* free-falling. No longer looking at anything stable, namely the interior walls of the station, reality had finally hit.

I could not fake my brain into its previously comfortable state of being. I tried concentrating on the surface of the station far in front of me, attempting to use visual input to mask the reality. But despite my intense concentration, I could not fool myself. There is a saying in Texas that a cowboy standing in a pile of manure will never be able to convince himself the smell is a pleasant one. Try as I might, I could not trick my brain into distorting the reality. Outside the spacecraft, my senses were simply too fully attuned to the realities of speed and free-fall.

Despite my efforts to block the reality out, the sensations of raw speed and falling persisted. And not just falling, but falling at ten times or a hundred times faster than I had fallen when free-fall parachuting years earlier. Yet, in the midst of this, I knew I had a job to do.

Unable to block the sensation, I moved to plan B. I looked down at the earth, then looked back up. *"Adeen, dva, tre, chiteri, pyat,"* I counted in Russian. Then I looked back at the earth again.

"Jerry, you haven't hit and you are not going to hit," I told myself aloud. "It is okay to be falling at Mach 25 as long as you do not hit the bottom!" Falling inside an elevator from the hundredth floor is inconsequential until the first floor. In a like manner, I convinced myself that it was okay to fall and fall and fall, as long as I would never hit the bottom. I loosened my grip, tucked the fear away, and got to work.

On my return trip on the end of the same telescoping pole two hours later, I amazed myself with how well I had already adapted. I was acclimated to the screaming speed already. Swinging back on the pole was the ride of a lifetime, pure thrill, pure joy. After all, I was in space. I was spacewalking, hanging out like a satellite. I was having an experience few others would ever share. "Yahoo!" I found myself shouting to Vasily. This was great. What a view! What a ride!

AFTER I returned to earth from my *Mir* mission, I sheepishly described (did I have the right stuff?) the sensations of speed and falling which I experienced during the early moments of the spacewalk in a NASA debriefing for my fellow astronauts. To my knowledge, this sensation of falling rarely occurs during shuttle spacewalks, probably for two reasons. First, and probably most important, almost all shuttle spacewalks are conducted within the three-wall confines of the shuttle's payload bay. The concave surface surrounding the spacewalker is probably sufficient to maintain the illusion of being contained, of being surrounded by a stable frame of visual reference. Second, whenever the spacewalker moves out of this envelope of containment, he or she is usually firmly attached by footholds to either the end of the robotic arm or to the edge of the payload bay. As I found on *Mir*, whenever I was able to wiggle my bulky, boot-laden toes under a handrail, the stability provided lessened the sensation of falling.

Although everyone listening sat wide-eyed during my description, no one commented. After the talk, a friend of mine pulled me aside. He was an experienced astronaut who had worked to help repair the Hubble Space Telescope.

The Hubble is a huge telescope. To repair the telescope, the space shuttle rendezvous with the orbiting telescope, and then, using the shuttle's robotic arm, reaches out and retrieves the instrument. The telescope is then temporarily berthed, perpendicular to the long axis of the shuttle, in the open payload bay. Target secure, two space-suited astronauts then venture out of the shuttle's airlock to work on the telescope.

My friend admitted to me that although he had never before told anyone on the ground, he, too, had experienced the same frightening phenomenon. Feet securely in place on the robotic arm, he was being conveyed to the far end of the telescope, well out of the confines of the payload bay. So far, so good, he said. But in order to begin his repair work, he had to extricate himself from the stabilizing foot-loops and cross over to the telescope. Feet now free and reaching across the two-foot gap to the end of the telescope, he unexpectedly and overwhelmingly felt the sensation of falling off the edge of the world! Stunned by the unexpected sensation, he bear-hugged the convex surface of the telescope and hung on for dear life! Once he was stabilized on the end of the telescope, the sensation eased and he was able to continue working.

His spacewalking partner experienced the same phenomenon at precisely the same location. His reaction was the same: to cling to the Hubble. Later during the walk, this same astronaut, when asked by his partner to bring him a needed tool via this same route, politely declined. He declared that he did not care to go across no man's land again!

WHILE I was on *Mir*, I would write a short letter to my then fifteen-month-old son, John, every night. It might take weeks to get a batch of these letters to the ground via telemetry. While I knew that it would certainly be years before little John could ever read the letters, I persisted nonetheless. I wanted him to know that, even though I was in space and far from him, I was thinking about him, that I cared and worried about him.

At first, the letters were light and carefree, descriptive of my adventures. The notes were not dissimilar to what any father away on an extended business trip might write to his children. But as *Mir* malfunctions and high-risk space operations continued unabated, as a near collision, a fire, and oxygen-generator breakdowns became part of life onboard *Mir*, my letters became progressively more serious.

Although I refused to dwell on what-ifs, and despite the fact that I managed to sleep anxiety-free each night, I was not naive. I realized that space travel in general entailed risk, and that *Mir* held even greater risk. I had survived close calls and felt that another might be just around the corner. I had better say the things to my son that needed saying, and not wait for a future date that might not ever come to be.

In my letters to John, I would try to explain to him the experiences I was undergoing and the lessons I was learning. And I would try to share with him the ideals in which I strongly believed—honesty, moral courage, integrity, compassion, and love—ideals whose worth was of renewed importance to me aboard *Mir*. Through the letters, I wanted John to come to know what kind of man his father was.

In leadership classes at the U.S. Naval Academy, I had studied great leaders, individuals of courage and integrity. I knew the definition of courage, what courage, in essence, meant. But I could never unhesitatingly say that I possessed that quality I had so admired in others.

People assume because I have flown onto aircraft carriers or rocketed into space that I must be brave. So they have told me. But I never felt particularly brave or courageous doing these acts. Sure, they were dangerous undertakings, but I was trained to do them. They were part of my job. I felt confident in my own abilities and in the ability of the crew. Was that courage when the outcome, at least in my mind's eye, was determined?

During my spacewalk, I learned firsthand what courage was. Traveling at Mach 25 and dramatically experiencing, in an exponential way, the sensations of raw speed and falling, I found courage. Despite the seizure of terror that accompanied the phenomenon, within less than a minute, I was able to overcome my fear and proceed with the mission before me. To do so took courage, plain and simple.

The evening after my spacewalk I wrote another letter to John. I told him that his father had courage. I meant it sincerely. I also relayed to him a very important lesson that I had learned that day: that the ability of the human being to adapt, to rise to the occasion, to accomplish tasks against all odds, is immeasurable. No goal cannot be achieved. Determination can win over anything. I ended the letter in the usual manner. "Good night, my son. I'll be watching over you. Dad."

22

Going Home

I WAS ECSTATIC. The Space Shuttle *Atlantis* was in sight—perhaps a thousand miles away—glistening in the sunlight. My ride home to the planet.

All told, I was to spend 132 days, four hours, and one minute in space. The minutes were starting to matter. I had traveled the equivalent of 110 round trips to the moon. I had drawn big Xs through January, February, March, April, and most of May on my 1997 calendar. I had watched much of the Northern Hemisphere thaw and the Southern Hemisphere grow white. Lake Superior was transformed from a mass of solid ice to a deep blue lake.

I had grown weaker and my bones were softer. I was no longer an earthling but a fully adapted, lived-there-all-my-life spaceman. In the back of my mind was the nagging concern that my transition back to the planet might prove more difficult than my adaptation to space had been.

Atlantis kept getting closer and closer. I kept my nose pressed to the three-foot-diameter window located on the floor of module Kvant II as *Atlantis* approached. I began to make out the faces of the shuttle crew. "Hey, Charlie!" I shouted aloud to no one, when it became clear that the face in the overhead window of the approaching space shuttle was that of commander Charlie Precourt. He was at that moment bringing *Atlantis* closer to *Mir* by manually firing thrusters. His face wore the determined look of someone who would succeed at his task.

We were both traveling at nearly 17,500 miles per hour. The shuttle had to find its way up an ever-narrowing imaginary corridor to the *Mir*. At selected distances the crew of *Atlantis* would verify their position and distance to *Mir* to ensure that they were still within the corridor. If not, they would back away and try again. The rings on the docking ports of the vehicles needed to line up almost perfectly—the margin for error was no greater than an inch. Rotational orientation was also important—one did not want to dock off-center and risk bumping into a protruding solar panel.

In addition to proper alignment, closing speed was of critical importance. If the closure rate between the two vehicles was too slow, the mechanical docking mechanism—designed to hook and latch the vehicles together—would not activate properly. On the other hand, if the closure rate was too fast, the docking would be not a gentle meeting in space but instead a violent collision between two one-hundred-ton vehicles. In fact, the closing rate had to be precisely .10 foot per second; .07 fps was too slow, 1.3 fps too fast. It was show time for Charlie and his crew aboard *Atlantis*.

I was snapping pictures and changing film and lenses like a madman. The photos were all once-in-a-lifetime shots of the greatest, most complex flying machine ever built—the U.S. space shuttle—flying flawlessly through space. What the shuttle was doing, against the backdrop of the earth, was breathtaking to watch. Although I was on a headset and communicating with both the crew onboard the *Mir* and the incoming shuttle crew, there were many moments when I was simply too choked up to talk.

Let me be very frank. I love my country and am patriotic to a fault. To see the U.S. Space Shuttle *Atlantis* pirouetting through space, on a mission to pick me up from space station *Mir* and take me back to the planet, back to my country, back to my pregnant wife and infant son, was emotionally overwhelming. The arrival of *Atlantis* signaled that I had persevered and had met the challenge. At times, I would have to take my headset off because I could not restrain myself from whooping and screaming at the top of my lungs—a victory celebration of sorts.

The shuttle *Atlantis* contacted *Mir* with the gentlest touch. The resultant force could, nonetheless, be felt inside the normally placid space station. I counted one, two, three oscillations of the solar panels, gentle but definite. My ride home had arrived.

I IMMEDIATELY flew to the hatch between the vehicles and peered through the six-inch porthole window, hoping to catch a glimpse of the shuttle crew. After looking at the same two Russian faces for the past four months, I was not so much wanting to see anyone in particular, just a different human being. I saw the shuttle crew gathering on the other side of the window. How wondrous the variety of humans!

The *Atlantis* crew later told me that when they first looked through the window of the hatch that separated the two vehicles, they did not recognize me. Five months of uncut hair, no sun on my face, and some tough times and struggles had changed me physically. Imagine that! The *Atlantis* crew wondering, "Who is that guy, and how did he get up here?" Or maybe they even wondered whether they should open the hatch before identifying the stranger.

Eventually they did recognize me. The hatch opened and we bearhugged one another. Although I had not bathed in the past five months, none of the meticulously clean and freshly shaven members of the shuttle crew pulled away. Astronaut Jean-François Clervoy immediately offered to cut my hair so that I would look good for Kathryn when I got back. The shuttle had brought up a working vacuum cleaner to replace the broken-down one on *Mir*—a space haircut could now be given without having hair floating everywhere. Jean-François was a Frenchman with impeccable taste and style, so I accepted his offer.

But then shuttle pilot Eileen Collins told me that, although I sure looked different, I had a rough Robinson Crusoe-explorer look. I liked her comment, because I felt a bit like Crusoe—isolated on an island, needing to make do with what I had brought along, always improvising, and relying on my ingenuity. I told Jean-François that I had reconsidered.

My wife, when she saw me for the first time in months via a two-way video broadcast from the shuttle later the same day, commented that it looked like I was having a "bad hair day up there." The press loved her comment. Headlines the following day read: "Linenger Ready to Return After Having 'Bad Hair Days' on *Mir.*"

THE SHUTTLE remained docked to *Mir* for five days. Supplies—water, spare parts, food, clothing, new equipment, and science gear—were hand-carried over to the *Mir,* while results of my science experiments—metal samples, protein crystals, fungus-lined petri dishes, along with some discarded equipment—were transferred to the shuttle. During this overlap period, we also conducted experiments in the pressure-tight Spacehab module mounted in the payload bay of the shuttle.

While the docked phase was a productive and busy time, it was not, by any means, conducted at the hurried pace that I was accustomed to aboard *Mir.*

Life on *Mir* changed dramatically during the docked phase. The time represented a welcomed aberration from the daily grind. To begin with, the master alarm on *Mir* remained, for the most part, silent. Not because *Mir* had made a miraculous recovery, but rather because most of the life support systems were shut off. The air for the combined volume of shuttle and *Mir* was conditioned entirely by shuttle systems. The shuttle also supplied the oxygen and pressure to the complex; in fact, the pressure was pumped-up during the docked phase in order to boost the *Mir* reserves.

The thrusters aboard the shuttle maintained the position of the shuttle-*Mir* complex in space. Communications to the ground improved dramatically because we dragged communication cords from the shuttle into *Mir.* Television interviews with CNN and other networks became plentiful and were carried out on time and without interruption. One could actually hear the questions without accompanying static. *Mir* had become an appendage of the shuttle.

With ten people now floating around the complex, the mood became almost festive. In addition to the real work that needed to be accomplished, one of the major goals (certainly political) was to showcase the cooperative spirit between the Russians and Americans, who were now working together and not aiming nuclear missiles at one another. We restaged the welcoming ceremonies for the cameras. Charlie Precourt had some NASA-approved words to say. Vasily Tsibliev reciprocated in the same gushing manner. He was, at least for the cameras, a changed man—smiling and welcoming our guests to carefree Space Station *Mir.*

We all shook hands. We feasted on a specially prepared international meal that included Russian caviar, French paté, fresh bread, canned roast duck, Hawaiian macadamia nuts, and even a native Peruvian dish that I cannot properly describe or pronounce. This feast was topped off with ice cream. Real, frozen ice cream, not the dehydrated variety. The ice cream had been stuffed into a biological sample freezer onboard the shuttle that would eventually be filled with my frozen blood samples on the trip home. For five days, *Mir* became a different place.

Enjoyable as the time was, I felt that we were somehow being deceptive, that we were giving the shuttle crew a snow job. The transformation of *Mir* during the docked phase reminded me of a homeless shelter at Christmas—lots of volunteers helping out, the building spruced up and decorated, and ham and turkey set on the table. Likewise, the American visitors to *Mir* never saw the reality of life on the station.

To be sure, that the *Mir* looked and even smelled better than the astronauts had expected was not accidental. Every free moment during the weeks prior to the arrival of the shuttle was spent cleaning up. We received very strict orders from Russian space program leaders in Moscow that getting things shipshape was of the highest priority. We stuffed excess gear behind panels and scrubbed down the bulkheads with a special towel containing fungicide. We reattached panels, covering up broken-down machinery that had not yet been repaired. New filters were installed in air-cleaning units. With six Americans about to arrive who would be conducting interviews with the international press concerning their impressions of *Mir,* appearances counted for everything.

AT THE end of the uneventful five days of joint operations, it was time to say goodbye to Vasily and Sasha, and to my American replacement, Michael Foale. I knew how Mike felt—smiling on the outside, but sinking on the inside. Feeling like he wanted to close the door and get on with it, but at the same time feeling very insecure, with the nagging concern that he may have forgotten to bring something vitally important with him. On top of this, Mike suffered from an unrelenting headache that began the day he entered the space station, which he and other astronaut sufferers attributed to the poor air quality on *Mir.*

I alone knew exactly how Mike felt. What he needed was reassurance. I told him that he would be fine and do a great job. I knew then what a crusty U.S. Marine gunny sergeant in the field must feel like when ordering his unseasoned troops into battle for the first time—trying to instill confidence in them, but at the same time knowing that they would be in for more than they could possibly imagine. I was leaving behind a friend aboard a nearly worn-out space station and among a crew that had few reserves left.

I had been through it all and felt seasoned and battle-hardened. I had an almost cocky confidence that I could survive anything that *Mir* might throw at me. Mike was still bright-eyed, carefree and, quite honestly, naive. During in-flight press interviews he described how he was enjoying the slower pace of work on *Mir* and how he was looking forward to gathering nightly around the table with his Russian colleagues and enjoying their company over tea.

I knew better. Once the doors closed and the shuttle departed, *Mir* would have to stand on its own, and would, undoubtedly, continue to falter. There would be little leisure time, no ice cream or idle conversation. Life would be anything but carefree. I knew that during my time onboard, the crew rarely had the opportunity to eat a meal together, let alone sit around and talk after dinner. *Mir* was both demanding and unpredictable. Once one problem was solved, another would inevitably crop up.

When an interviewer asked for my take on what Mike should expect, I only said that Mike was in for a real challenge, and he was the kind of person who could handle challenges and rise to the occasion.

It is interesting how vocabulary changes during press conferences—my own included. I found myself using the words "challenges" and "difficulties" to substitute for more the accurate "dangerous" and "life-threatening." In response to legitimate, pointed questions about specific mechanical breakdowns and whether I had expected *Mir* to have so many problems, I responded vaguely that life was tough on the frontier and that I expected it to be so. On the other hand, I would comment that the frequency of breakdowns and their severity was not something that I had entirely anticipated.

While I answered truthfully, I was at the same time diplomatic in my response. I could tell the entire story to a closed group of NASA safety experts upon my return. I toned down my comments to CNN mainly because I knew that my family and Mike's family might be watching. I did not want to worry them.

Vasily Tsibliev was a master at controlling his answers during an interview. Clearly flustered with how the ground was handling and prioritizing our work and, at times, clearly concerned about whether we could continue to occupy the space station or even whether we would survive, he would voice his opinion to the ground by screaming at controllers during communication passes over Moscow. The next instant, this time responding to an interviewer's question concerning the condition of *Mir* or the toll that its continual breakdowns took on the crew, Vasily would smile and respond: "Oh, as you can see, I am alive and well. Surely, you are exaggerating the difficulties on *Mir*—it is really quite pleasant up here."

I did not blame Vasily for his less-than-straightforward response. He knew that the Russian space program *was* the *Mir,* and that positive public perception of its utility, both in Russia and in America, was important for its survival. In a sense, he was only following orders. He was also trying to protect his report card, written by mission control in Moscow. His flight bonus, money he needed to support his family, was dependent on his grades. Criticizing the teacher was a surefire way to get poor grades.

AFTER I returned to the planet, friends gave me a collection of newspaper articles and press reports concerning my stay on *Mir.* At times I thought that the press must have been talking about a different space station than the one I had been living aboard.

For example, one report, based on an official release from the Russian space agency, read, "Russian officials reported yesterday that a non-life-threatening fire occurred on *Mir,* which was easily put out in a matter of seconds by the crew. Oxygen masks were unstowed as a precaution, but were not needed. No one was injured." What space station were they talking about? The fire that we lived through aboard *Mir* burned uncontrollably for fourteen minutes, smoke filled the station with a density so thick that we could not count the fingers in front of our faces for nearly an hour, and without donning personal oxygen respirators we would all have suffocated. Any more life-threatening, even a smidgen, and we would have had six dead space explorers. Period.

SO, REGARDLESS of what Mike Foale thought or had heard back on the planet, I knew that the reality would be far different. I was in a quandry because on the one hand, I knew that he would need all the optimism and enthusiasm he could muster to get through the next four months. On the other hand, I needed to impress upon him how important it was for him to always be ready for the worst. Unless things changed dramatically—and I could think of no reason why they would—master alarms signaling critical system breakdowns would not be rare, and Mike needed to be alert and ready to respond at a moment's notice.

I tried to strike a middle ground. I insisted that he show me, physically, how he would don the respirator, find his way into the Soyuz capsule, and activate the fire extinguisher. In general, I wanted to see how he would respond in those situations where seconds, not minutes, matter. I sensed that Mike thought that maybe I had gotten too much radiation to the brain, with me insisting that we run through these fundamentals step by step, but to appease me he went along with the drills.

Once I had satisfied myself that Mike was prepared for the worst, we moved on to more mundane endeavors. I instructed him in how to use the toilet in its present patched-together state, which was an entirely different procedure from what he had been taught in Star City. We unpacked his personal gear and his experimental hardware. I described where power cables were located, how to unscrew panels behind which were located the intakes to circulation fans that needed weekly cleaning, and where to find the stash of spare food. I showed him as much as I could and as much as he could stand for the five days that we overlapped.

When the day came for my departure, I gave him a bear hug, whispered words of encouragement to him, told him he was one of the best there was and that he would do great. I meant the "best there was" part sincerely—Mike is as smart and capable as they come. He was an Oxford-trained physicist who, in addition to his exceptional mental powers, believed in his heart that Russian-American cooperation was vital not only to the space program, but to making the world a safer place strategically. While knowing that he was as good as they come, to be honest, I had my doubts about how well he would hold up on *Mir*; or, better put, I wondered how well anyone, including my two cosmonaut crewmates, who still had a month of duty to go before their replacements arrived, would do under the conditions existing on *Mir*.

Surprisingly, saying goodbye to Sasha Lazutkin and Vasily Tsibliev, my fellow space travelers for the last four months of my own five-month duty onboard, was not so difficult. Leaving *Mir* did not bother me. It was not like leaving the cottage on the lake after a summer's vacation, but more like graduating from college—feeling a sense of accomplishment, but ready to get on with the future. The thought of going home, of getting back to the planet and living once again among a mix of human beings, was so positively joyous that I had no regrets leaving. I had done my part. It was time to go.

I knew that Vasily and Sasha would be going home in less than a month. I told them I had been proud to serve with them and wished them luck in their remaining month onboard. I asked them to look out for Mike, especially during the early part of his stay. They assured me that they would. The last thing I said was that I was looking forward to seeing them back on the planet and that I would be praying for their safety.

Leaving was part of the plan, something expected. When the hatch closed between the vehicles, I was not particularly sad or glad; I remained emotionally neutral. I did exclaim that it sure was nice to be talking English once again and to hear news from home. Charlie Precourt, Eileen Collins, and I swapped stories in the middeck of *Atlantis* until well after midnight. I was going home.

23

Even the Air Tastes Sweet

As *Atlantis* PULLED AWAY from *Mir,* I was once again able to see the station in its entirety. Unlike five months earlier, when I had first seen the space station, *Mir* now looked very familiar. I did not have to look twice to identify the various modules and accessories of my orbiting home.

The shuttle crew was busy. Eileen Collins, the shuttle pilot, performed the undocking under the watchful eye of Charlie Precourt. I helped by acting as the Russian-language communicator on the radio, but since the *Mir* crew played no active role once the shuttle undocked, there was not much to say.

I did keep busy snapping photographs of the *Mir* complex as part of the planned *Mir* survey experiment. Experts on the ground would later carefully analyze these photos in order to detect such things as the extent of micrometeorite strike damage to the solar panels and the condition of *Mir*'s hull. Crew trainers at both Star City, Russia, and at Johnson Space Center, Houston, would select some of these photos to use for orienting future cosmonauts and astronauts to external landmarks on *Mir.*

As we moved farther away, the photographs I was taking became less technically useful, but at the same time more spellbinding. *Mir* was glittering gold against the backdrop of blue planet earth. I continued snapping photos, noting not only the majesty of *Mir,* but also the Caspian Sea, the Aral Sea, and the peaks of the Himalayan Mountains whirring by below the space station.

With time, *Mir* shrank until it resembled nothing more than a bright star and then disappeared into darkness. I peered into the darkness and felt a twinge of pain—a sort of homesickness. After a few seconds and a final sigh, I began to label the five rolls of 36-exposure film I had just taken and store them in a return-to-earth film bag.

I turned my full attention to *Atlantis,* and began to think about landing day. Although officially a part of the crew, I was primarily the return cargo. After all, the main goal of shuttle mission STS84 was to drop off my replacement and to bring me home safely. The shuttle crew had long ago carved out their assigned tasks during training on the ground which, of course, was done in my absence since I was at the time already in space aboard *Mir.* Therefore, I was a bonus, an extra set of hands, but not an integral, irreplaceable component during any particular shuttle operation.

In spite of this, I knew shuttle operations and the demanding schedule placed upon everyone. So I helped wherever I could, volunteering to clean intake vents and do other housekeeping tasks. But my priority was to get ready for the landing two days away. While confident that the *Atlantis* crew would get me home in one piece, how my weakened and space-adapted body would hold up under the strain of gravity during reentry and landing was questionable and thus worrisome.

Partially at my request, a newly designed treadmill was flown on *Atlantis.* I continued my exercise regimen of two one-hour-long workout sessions each day on the treadmill. After nearly five months of running on the Russian treadmill, coupled with my professional training in sports medicine, I was arguably the best subject that a treadmill designer would ever have aboard the shuttle to evaluate the equipment.

Recording my observations and suggestions on a microcassette recorder, I put the treadmill through a rigorous and thorough evaluation. I increased the tension on the pull-down load plates to equal a force equivalent to that of my body weight on earth, 165 pounds. The harness straps dug deeply into my shoulders, and the sensitive soles of my feet (soft and callous-free, since I had not walked on them in months) felt as if nails were being driven into them. I ignored the pain and pressed all the harder. I wanted to mimic now what I would soon be feeling under the strain of gravity. I wanted to assure myself that I would be prepared for the rigors of landing day. I wanted to be peaked and ready. Pleased with both the performance of the new U.S. treadmill and with my own performance, my confidence grew.

I next took a closer look at my reentry seat. It was not a standard shuttle seat; in fact, it was not much of a seat at all. Instead, it looked more like a couch. After five months of cardiac deconditioning, the medical experts decided that a returning long-duration astronaut was better off lying down, not sitting up. Pulling 1.5 Gs in the head-to-foot direction during reentry, all the while depending on the heart to keep a sufficient column of blood to the brain, was deemed imprudent. All long-duration crew members come back to the planet lying flat on their backs, feeling the Gs through the chest fore-to-aft, with the added precaution of having their legs elevated.

The seat expert on our crew was French astronaut Jean-François Clervoy, on his second shuttle flight. When he saw me looking at the seat, he did not hesitate to launch into a ten-minute demonstration of the seat components, actually strapping me into the seat. He continued my lesson by outlining the crew evacuation plan, to be acted out should the shuttle skid off of the runway or be forced to ditch. The complicating factor, he informed me, was my deadweight. Given the past experience with other long-duration travelers, the expectation was that I would not be able to stand on my own.

"Billy Bob," Jean-François's less-than-distinguished American nickname, then told me that the crew had trained on the ground lugging a 150-pound dummy out of the shuttle simulator, and it took three of them to do it successfully. Without the help of our bull-necked crewmate, U.S. Marine Carlos Noriega, the task was always unsuccessful. So in an emergency, look for Carlos. Billy Bob then told me that anything that I could do to avoid being total deadweight would be appreciated.

I had read in some newspaper clippings sent up in my care package on the Progress resupply vehicle that astronaut John Blaha, my predecessor on *Mir*, needed to be carried off the shuttle on a stretcher. He described the sensation as feeling "so heavy that there was no way I could move." John went on to say that he felt like he weighed a thousand pounds and was stuck to the deck. "I could not even lift my arm, let alone stand up and walk. No way."

I know John. John is a tough and determined person, and he has walked off the shuttle after shorter flights without difficulty. As I thought of my own impending landing day, I became concerned. Had my exercise been adequate? Had I pushed myself hard enough? And probably more meaningfully, would I just be one of those people who, for whatever reason, just does not do well?

Doing well on landing day is relative. Cosmonauts are generally lifted out of the capsule at landing and carried immediately to couches in a makeshift medical tent on the steppes of Kazakhstan. Some insist on walking. They shuffle two or three steps with bearish Russian men holding on to their arms and half-carrying them the entire time. At Star City, I would later hear one shuffling cosmonaut say that he had felt "just great at landing" and could have walked a kilometer. The film clips disputed those boastful words.

Other cosmonauts told me of crewmates who vomited throughout reentry and were essentially incapacitated even before the capsule parachute opened. The thud and tumble of hitting the ground, followed in some cases by the capsule flopping over with the cosmonauts inside hanging upside down from their seat straps, completed the misery. Even some American astronauts, after a mere ten days in space, have had a very hard time getting their bearings after landing, feeling weak and nauseous and needing to be helped off the vehicle.

The night before landing I talked individually with each member of the *Atlantis* crew concerning my plan for landing. I told each of them that, in my mind, my mission did not end when the wheels of *Atlantis* touched down on the runway at the Kennedy Space Center in Florida, but rather only after I had gotten off the vehicle, greeted my family, done the medical tests, talked to the press, shut the door to my room in crew quarters, and plopped into bed. As a member of the *Mir* crew I had overcome a lot of adversity over the past 132 days, and I would not give up on landing day. I wanted to get off the vehicle under my own power, even if it meant crawling. If they had to carry me off on a stretcher, fine, but it would only be after I had already passed out. I would finish what I started.

LANDING day arrived. I floated into my bright-orange launch-and-entry spacesuit, put on the parachute harness, and got into my seat. After fastening my parachute risers to the harness, I loosely fastened my shoulder straps and waist straps to keep from floating out of the seat. I then continued my fluid loading protocol, drinking my fourth packet of salty chicken broth. When in space, body fluids shift headward due to the weightlessness. The carotid artery pressure sensors in the neck tell the kidneys that there is a fluid overload. The kidneys dump the supposedly excess fluid as urine. The result is relative dehydration. Since gravity would soon prevail, it was important to refill my tank and reexpand my blood volume. Feeling bloated but comfortable in my seat, I closed my eyes and took a nap.

Not sleeping soundly, I was monitoring the radio conversation between Houston and Charlie Precourt on the flight deck. The weather at the cape was not good, and the decision was made to wave off one orbit and to try to land the next time around. That meant ninety more minutes. I decided that the prudent thing to do was to use the bathroom one more time, and then force down more broth. After another spin around the earth, and at the last possible moment, the decision was made that the weather at the cape was good enough and that we were "go for the burn." We all let out a yell at the good news.

In my mind, one of the most amazing aspects of spaceflight is deorbit burn and landing. While the brute force of launch offers quite a show, the finesse and accuracy of landing is truly amazing. The task is to go from Mach 25 in orbit to zero velocity on the end of a runway at the Kennedy Space Center. In order to accomplish the task, somewhere over Australia or the Pacific Ocean the engines of the shuttle are pointed in the direction that we are moving, then fired for a precise amount of time. The burn duration must be perfect, for we must decelerate a precise amount in order to enter the atmosphere at a safe angle and at the proper location. After completion of the burn, the shuttle is essentially a glider dropping from the sky. There are no further means to adjust our course or fly around the runway for a second landing attempt.

It is a one-shot deal. The burn must be precise, or we might not even hit the earth, let alone Florida or the approach-end of the runway at Kennedy Space Center on altitude and on airspeed.

ATLANTIS shudders as it decelerates in the thick atmosphere. We become enveloped inside a plasma fireball and surrounded by a sound resembling a speeding locomotive. As the altitude drops, clouds begin to whiz by below us faster and faster until they are just plain screaming by us. "Tally ho, on the West Coast," I hear Charlie bark over the radio. I cannot restrain myself at hearing these words and start whooping it up—just screaming with joy. Charlie, hearing my shouts trailing up through the hatch between the middeck and the flightdeck, reports to the ground that "Jerry is in good spirits."

In order to ease the tension of the flight surgeons on the ground, I mash my comm button and report to Houston that I am stable. Surprisingly, I *am* feeling fine. Sure, I keep dropping my pencil—for the first time in five months it falls—but I am feeling much better than I expected. As we pull 1.5 Gs—the maximum force that we will experience during landing—I am still able to lift my arm.

The Mississippi River flashes into view, and then, finally, the peninsula of Florida. Leaving behind the shattering sound of the last two sonic booms, we make our final 180-degree turn over the Kennedy Space Center runway. Barreling in, we come down precisely over the threshold of the runway, reporting to the ground, "On altitude and on airspeed." Diving at a twenty-degree glideslope—four times steeper than a commercial jet would use to land—Charlie pulls the nose up at the final moment, gliding in at over two hundred knots while Eileen lowers the landing gear. Touchdown. Eileen deploys the drag chute and we decelerate down the runway. As *Atlantis* stops, Charlie informs the controllers that we are "wheels stop."

ON THE middeck of the orbiter, and flat on my back, I have no view out the window. I feel the wheels strike the pavement and the slight pull of the shuttle drag chute as it fully deploys. At wheels stop, the whole crew lets out a stress-releasing cheer. Charlie asks for a status report on how I am doing; I am, after all, his cargo, colleague, and friend. Over the intercom I report to Charlie that I am doing just fine and will be going off comm.

The last thing I hear before disconnecting is someone in Houston welcoming the crew back to earth and me, specifically, back home. I thank him and then disconnect my comm cord and remove my helmet. Very methodically, I unstrap my shoulder and waist harnesses, and carefully place the now heavy straps to either side. I then pop the Koch fittings on the parachute risers and loosen the leg straps of my harness.

Free of the parachute, I swing my legs to the right and pull myself up to the sitting position. I can feel my heart respond—racing to keep the blood pumped up to my head. My heart is keeping up with gravity's demands, I think. I turn my head slightly to the right and down in order to place my helmet on the deck beside me. I immediately feel as if I am doing backward somersaults, spinning tight and fast.

I make a mental note not to move my head abruptly and to avoid any further bending or twisting. My inner ear is obviously not responding appropriately to gravity's pull. It is still set at its space-adapted threshold. But gravity is now pulling down on the otolith, the small stone in the inner ear, causing it to press down harder on the sensitive nerve fibers surrounding it than it has in months. In weightlessness, this much force would equate to acceleration—caused by my spinning. Now my body is fooled into thinking that I must be spinning.

Nausea cannot be far behind, I think to myself. I lock my neck.

Although I am facing with my back to the hatch and do not want to turn my head to confirm it, I know that someone has opened the side hatch because I can feel the fresh earth-air pouring in, surrounding me with its fragrance. My God, how wonderful! After breathing stale, "made" air for months, the air even *tastes* sweet. I feel invigorated by it.

Dr. Tom Marshburn, who has been part of my NASA team from the start, rushes onboard to see how I am holding up. He looks very surprised to see me sitting up, parachute already off. He suggests that I sit for as long as I care to, telling me that we can take an hour or more if I need it. He informs me that there are two people waiting outside whose job it is to lift me out of the shuttle—just let him know when I am ready for them to come and get me.

After telling Tom how great it is to see him, I inform him that I am ready to go now. I explain that while I appreciate his efforts, I would prefer to get out on my own, and that doing so is very important to me. Tom knows me well, knows that when I have my mind set on something it is wise to stay out of my way. He reluctantly agrees with my plan. With a smile, but only half-joking, I tell him that it is okay to pick me up if I collapse.

I get up. My heart races—trying to maintain a column of blood to my brain. I begin to gray out—the periphery of my vision darkening—but I do not black out. My chest is heaving, my heart pounding like never before. The gray clears and my heart settles.

You can do this, Jerry, I say to myself. *Finish this thing.*

I feel heavy, as if Tom were sitting on my shoulders, somewhat weak, but capable. I turn to the left and start shuffling toward the forward bulkhead with neck braced. The spacesuit feels heavy, but I am making progress. At the forward bulkhead I grab on and turn ninety degrees to the left again. Some spinning, but not severe. My seat is in the way; I have to step over it in order to get to the hatch. With great effort, I scale the seat and make my way past it. I shuffle to the hatch, bend down on my knees, and after momentarily feeling like I am tumbling again, I crawl out.

Two big men are standing ready on the other side. Surprised to see me, they offer, "Sir, we can carry you from here." I tell them thanks anyway, but I prefer to walk. I shake their hands and tell them that it is great being back on the planet. They are somewhat dumbfounded, but as I walk away they both start clapping for me. "Way to go, Captain Linenger. You make us all proud."

The air feels wonderful, I feel wonderful. Even though I am sure that my stride resembles a shuffle more than a walk, I think: Man, does it ever feel good to be walking again, feet planted firmly on the ground.

As I enter the medical vehicle attached to the end of the walkway, I am greeted by smiling faces and more applause. I shake hands with everyone I see and smile broadly. The NASA administrator, Dan Goldin, is there to greet me. He has the three gifts that I had requested when we talked via *Mir* radio a few weeks prior to landing. The gifts are tulips for my wife, Kathryn, her favorite; a NASA teddy bear for our son, John; and a rattle for our child to be.

AFTER two trips around the vehicle, and after contributing my first urine sample to science—the specimen must have been similar in composition to chicken broth—I changed from my spacesuit into medical scrubs. A photographer took a group picture of Mr. Goldin, the teddy bear, and me for NASA Public Affairs. I then took a seat on a reclining chair and the medics drew my blood. After the rest of the crew arrived, the van was driven to the medical building, where I could finally see my son and pregnant wife.

On the way I prayed that my strength would hold out. For the first time in five months, I cared again about my appearance. My face looked sallow and white. My five-month growth of hair had a bad case of helmet-head. I poured some of my drinking water on my head, borrowed a comb, and tried to make it look decent. Oh well, that's about all I can do, I thought. Most important: walk tall. Try to be strong. My heart was racing by the time the van stopped, this time not from orthostatic intolerance, but from nervous anticipation.

Kathryn stood, holding John, in the middle of a large, sterile-looking room. Around the perimeter of the room were onlookers who felt somewhat guilty that they were there, invading what should have been a private moment, but unable to resist the temptation of witnessing the reunion. Even the guards, whose duty it was to keep the people away, were standing inside of the room and watching.

I walked toward her with a huge smile on my face. She looked beautiful; she looked different, very pregnant! As I was giving her my best, unsteady hug, she lost it and began sobbing deeply. Seeing his mother cry upset John, who, although vaguely remembering me, became defensive and started to cry too. I also probably had a tear of joy in my eye, so the floor was quite slippery by the time we walked together, as a family, down the hall to a more private area.

We were allowed to be alone for a few minutes before further medical testing would begin. We started to catch up—an impossible task. We mainly just sat and admired John. Kathryn would hand him to me, and he would call me "Mommy." He felt like he weighed a ton. Fearful that I might forget that I was back on the planet and set him in front of me to float, I cautioned Kathryn to help hold on to him whenever I held him. He amazed me. Whenever I was surprised by what he was now able to do, as compared to what he was doing five months prior, Kathryn would proudly tell me another story about one of his accomplishments. I told her that I was sorry that I wasn't there to share those moments with them. She jokingly told me, "Don't worry, Jerry. You now have the duty for the next five months!"

After a short ten minutes I was led away, this time on a stretcher, to begin my hour-long medical testing. It felt good to get off my feet, and even better to be home again.

PART THREE

BACK ON THE PLANET

24

Home at Last

My MISSION did not end on landing day. Five months of weightlessness had taken a toll on my body. My bones were softer, my muscles weaker, and my reflexes slower than when I had left earth. I needed to recuperate.

It took tremendous determination for me to stand erect and to walk off *Atlantis*. Even the enormously gratifying experience of once again being able to give my wife a big hug was a struggle against the force of gravity for me. And I admit to being rather proud of myself when I was even able to hold my son during a short press conference just an hour after the shuttle landing.

Despite feeling unstable, and the fact that my body felt like a five-hundred-pound barbell, I was able to get through an hour or so of medical testing by the NASA flight surgeons and medical researchers. Following the testing, I went to astronaut crew quarters at the Kennedy Space Center for dinner.

The small dining area in the crew quarters had thoughtfully been prepared for my first meal back on earth. Each of the two dining tables was adorned with flowers, the fragrance of which mingled with the smell of freshly baked bread. Oatmeal cookies, my favorite, filled the cookie jars along the kitchen countertops. Per my request, the staff had prepared vegetable lasagna and a fresh salad. The only thing missing was my appetite.

I had not slept in almost a day and I was exhausted. Because the force of earth's gravity was still very new to me, I felt as though I were spinning and tumbling whenever I moved my head abruptly or leaned forward. These sensations were mildly nauseating.

More out of courtesy than desire, I politely ate a few bites of lasagna and drank some juice. After nibbling at the food for as long as I could, I thanked the staff profusely and then told them that I would be back for the milk and oatmeal-raisin cookies for my midnight snack. As I left the dining room, I carefully turned the corner—going around any corner provoked the sensation of a delayed tumble—and headed down the corridor to my room. Finally, I would be able to get off my feet and relax.

Within ten minutes of getting to my room, Tom Marshburn knocked on the door. Already quite groggy, I had to force myself to get up out of bed and to answer the door. Tom told me that about thirty family members and friends had arrived and were waiting to greet me in the crew quarters conference room. He suggested that I signal him with a wink when I found it physically difficult to continue with the get-together. When I signaled, Tom would know that I had reached the limits of my endurance and would announce that he was sorry, but visiting hours were over.

I looked forward to seeing my family and friends, but I knew, too, that the signal was a good idea. The last thing I wanted to do on my first evening back on earth was to collapse from exhaustion. Walking down the hall, Kathryn, John, and I must have resembled a drunken trio. Kathryn, only a few weeks away from delivery, waddled at my unsteady side, while John, now eighteen months old, had barely mastered the skill of walking and stumbled and fell twice.

I saw my mom first. There was no doubt by the look on her face that she was very glad to see me back home safe and sound. She began sobbing with joy—the terrible worries we sons put our mothers through—as we hugged. Over her shoulder, I saw the broad smiles of my brother, Ken, and my sisters Karen, Barbara, and Susan. All looked at me with pride, but also with a look of . . . was it curiosity? Kathryn's parents were there, too. Rounding out the crowd were some of my aunts, my uncles, my cousins, and other friends. All of them wanted to share in my triumph over the odds and to welcome me back to the planet.

I made my way around the room, embracing everyone. My senses were overwhelmed by colorful dresses, the smell of perfume, and unencumbered and carefree laughter. To be with my family and friends was a blessing for which I was very grateful.

It was difficult for me to keep my emotions in check. My eyes welled up with relief and joy as I hugged those dear to me. And if my hugs were a bit protracted it was, in part, because hugging another human being was something that I had been deprived of for months; besides, my body found special respite in hugging others, for the struggle against gravity was made considerably easier by leaning on them!

In addition to the crowd jammed into the conference room, the flash of cameras overwhelmed me. Ken led the charge; in fact, I cannot recall seeing his face unobstructed the entire time. He dedicated himself to taking home movies. Admittedly, I was not wild about the cameras. After a day without much sleep and with greasy hair not properly washed for five months, I knew I probably resembled a space alien more than my old self.

But I tried to smile. One by one, people moved in behind my chair to get a picture with their astronaut. What they did not realize was that, as they positioned themselves behind me for each photo, they would inevitably put their hand on the back of the chair which was designed to respond to such pressure by tilting back an inch or two. This slight chair tilt caused my inner ear sensors to think that I was doing a back flip. Thirty somersaults later, everyone had a souvenir picture, and I signaled Dr. Marshburn with a wink.

Tom ordered everyone out of the room except for my mom and my brother and sisters. Now able to speak more intimately, my family expressed to me their concern about my health. I told them that I was doing far better than I had expected. Dr. Marshburn chimed in that I was doing exceptionally well given the circumstances and that, frankly, he was surprised by my stamina. His comments did much to relieve my family's concerns and, to a certain extent, my own. After everyone departed, I drank another fruit drink and headed to my room.

My brother later confided in me that he had been shocked by my appearance the first time he saw me after the flight. To him I looked thin and weak, my flesh pale. I moved unsteadily and looked like I had not slept in weeks. My handshake was a rather feeble one, more like that of a terminal cancer patient saying his final goodbyes than that of his normally active and robust younger brother. Ken told me that my seeming fragility had worried him a lot.

His anxiety over my health solved one mystery for me. Apparently, Ken had stayed perched behind his camera because he had wanted to capture my last living moments on film!

Although I knew that I was doing better than expected after being weakened by the effortlessness of living in space, to be honest, I did feel fragile.

KATHRYN, John, and I remained in crew quarters overnight. Although anticipating the most wonderful sleep of my life, under clean sheets and in a room where no master alarms would awaken me, I was disappointed. My first night's sleep back on earth was a struggle. So was my first shower.

The spray of water from the shower was like pellets bombarding my body. I felt as if I would be sent tumbling. My mind was not yet earth-adjusted, and such a force in space would have caused a reaction—pushing me away from the stream of water. Furthermore, in the back of my space-adapted mind, I kept expecting the water in the shower stall to float back up and possibly drown me.

For a while I braced and tried to withstand the power of the shower pellets. I eventually gave up. I resorted to taking my often dreamed of first glorious shower back on the planet sitting on the shower floor with the water dribbling out of the showerhead.

Clean for the first time in five months, I crawled into bed. Ah, the clean fragrance and crisp feel of fresh sheets!

While in space, I floated, day and night. To move, I would push off a bulkhead or ceiling or floor using a force no greater than a gentle push of my finger.

Gravity now yanked me down into the mattress. Rolling from my back over onto my side took great effort. Getting smashed into the mattress in turn created a sensation of pressure on my body, and hot spots developed that remained unrelieved no matter how I positioned myself.

If I were still in space, such pressure would translate into a propulsive force. It felt to my not-yet-earth-adapted senses that I would, at any moment, be thrust out of bed and toward the ceiling.

I knew, of course, that I would remain on the bed and *not* go flying toward the ceiling. But whenever I would drift closer to sleep, my space instincts—no longer relevant on earth—would warn me to hold on!

I finally gave up. I rolled the sheet into a sort of rope, positioned it firmly across my waist, and tucked the loose ends of the sheet under the mattress. With the sheet now holding me in place as an improvised restraint, that stubbornly insurgent part of my mind was put at ease and I relaxed enough to fall asleep.

The next morning the shuttle crew, accompanied by our spouses and my son John (an exception was made in deference to my long time away), boarded two NASA passenger planes at Patrick Air Force Base, Cape Canaveral, to fly home to Houston. The appetite I had lost the night before now returned with a vengeance. I gorged myself, eating nonstop during the entire three-hour flight back to Houston. Upon landing at Ellington Field near the Johnson Space Center, I felt remarkably rejuvenated.

Although it was only late May, the tropical heat and sweltering humidity of Houston greeted us along with a sizable and enthusiastic crowd gathered to welcome us home. I felt much improved since landing the previous day, but now contending with the sizzling Houston temperatures, I made a mental note to avoid standing for too long a period of time. "Whatever you do Jerry," I thought, "don't pass out."

A small platform was set up on the tarmac. In front of the platform were some seats for VIPs and family. Behind them stood the general public, mostly made up of Johnson Space Center employees and autograph seekers. We took our seats on the platform, and then, sequentially, stepped up to the microphone to say a few words.

"It was a great flight!" and "Thanks to everyone who helped to train us for this mission!" was the general theme of the comments. I was mesmerized just looking at the crowd, thinking how wonderful it was to see so many diverse human beings again. I spoke last. I told the audience what an honor and privilege that it had been for me to represent them, the U.S. Navy, our country, and all of the people of the earth on Space Station *Mir,* and that I always tried my best to represent them well. I told them that our planet was indeed precious and that we are blessed to be living in such an extraordinary place.

I let them know that I would never again take anything for granted—fresh air, green grass, swaying trees. Then I thanked them for their support and prayers.

Afterward, we all shook hands with the crowd and signed autographs. Kathryn, John, and I were then escorted to a waiting police car by two Houston police officers and whisked home, with sirens blaring and streets blocked for our passage. Although I felt as if I had all the time in the world and did not need to rush, I could sense that the officers were giving us special treatment to show their appreciation for my sacrifice. Once we arrived at our house, the police officers informed us that they would be patrolling our neighborhood for the next twenty-four hours to make sure that we were left alone and that we could spend a quiet family evening together.

Home, sweet home.

25

Getting Back on My Feet

IMAGINE GOING TO BED in January and getting out of bed, for the first time, at the end of May. This was how inactive my body had become in space. As I had found during my first restless night at the crew quarters, bed rest on earth is actually strenuous since it takes effort to roll over. My postflight bone scan showed that I had lost a disturbing 13 percent of my bone density in the weight-bearing areas of the hip and lower spine. That result, although not unusual, was disappointing. I had worked very hard in orbit, exercising diligently each day in spite of how hard it was. But the exercise had obviously not been enough to counteract the effects of merely floating for the remaining twenty-two hours of the day.

TRAINER Beth Shepherd was knocking at my door at 5 A.M. sharp the morning after my return to Houston.

On the advice of experts in sports medicine, Beth and I had planned an extensive rehabilitation program. The first month I would train exclusively in the water. With my bones now weakened to a level similar to the bone loss experienced by an older woman with osteoporosis, I was prone to fracture. Furthermore, my muscles had atrophied somewhat and would not be able to protect my bones from repeated low-level impact. From my work with the SEALs, I

237

knew that a tibial stress fracture or other overuse injury was a very real possibility. Low-impact water workouts made sense.

So I plunged into the pool bright and early every day. Upon entering the water for the first time, I thought that I was going to drown. The water felt as thick as mud, like quicksand trying to pull me under. I slugged my way through the dense medium for a couple of laps, breathing heavily. By the beginning of the second week, the water felt more like mercury, by the third week it felt like water should.

In addition to swimming laps, I would exercise in the water. Strapping on a restraining harness attached by a line to the side of the pool, I would run in place. In the shallow end, I would squat and explosively lunge from the bottom of the pool, first with both feet planted, then alternating on each leg. I also used Styrofoam dumbbells to restrengthen my upper body.

Emulating a protocol used by the Russian trainers for returning cosmonauts, I always finished the workout with a therapeutic massage. During those early days of rehabilitation therapy, Beth, who happens to be a power lifter, could easily coerce me into crying uncle during my massage anytime she wanted. My paraspinal muscles—the small muscle group running longitudinally on either side of the spine and responsible in large part for posture—were downright sore. The muscles had grown accustomed to not having to maintain an upright posture. Usually Beth restrained herself, but as a precaution I always tried to stay on her good side.

While I could not *feel* anything unusual in my demineralized bones, I did have a strong sense that I could very easily injure myself. So strong was this feeling of vulnerability that if someone had offered me a thousand dollars to stand on a three-foot platform and jump to the floor, I would have staunchly refused.

I was impressed with the ability of the human body to instinctively know its vulnerabilities and needs. Pregnant women crave ice cream—a source of needed calcium—and pickles—the salt is needed for the blood volume expansion of pregnancy. Long-duration space travelers with weakened bones know innately not to jolt their spines.

My muscles had also weakened, but their recovery was rapid. By the end of the first month of training, I felt that I was at roughly 70 percent of my full strength. Looking in the mirror at myself after a workout, I did not notice any severe atrophy.

On the other hand, it felt as if I had short-circuited the wires leading to the muscles. While my muscles were probably adequate in strength to respond to the impact of a jump, they were not quick enough to tense up in time. That is to say, I felt as if my muscles would respond too late to the impact—tensing up to cushion the fall only *after* my vertebrae had absorbed the shock. I also noticed that I could not do a pull-up. I have been able to do fifteen or twenty pull-ups with ease since I was a kid. I hung on the bar, trying to yank myself up, but I could not budge. I had noticed a similar, though less severe deficit after returning from space after my first ten-day shuttle flight. I had to concentrate hard before I could eke out even three or four pull-ups, even though I am certain that my biceps and triceps had not weakened to that extent over ten days.

Although no medical tests were done on me to document this deficit in my response time, I am quite certain of its existence. In fact, even after I had regained all of my strength, I still felt sluggish and slow, like a batter who has lost his sense of timing. Reestablishing the nerve-to-muscle conduction paths seemed to be the most stubborn deficit of all following my space flight. I did not feel fluid and natural running for almost a year after my return to earth.

By the end of the first month, I could swim laps, but by no means with the endurance and speed to which I was accustomed. During the second month, Beth and I added walking to our rehab routine. Perhaps still not used to doing only one task at a time, I would usually push my son, John, also an early riser, in his stroller. After our walk, I would do classic interval training in the pool—timed sets of a given number of laps, repeated eight or ten times. My high school swim coach would have been proud.

By the end of the second month of rehab, Beth commented that I was now training *her* during the lap swimming exercises. Her comment was needed encouragement, since my progress, although steady, was too slow for my impatient desire.

And so we fell into a routine. After the morning's massage, I would shower—no longer feeling as if bullets were riddling my body—and Beth and I would drive to work. Beth did the driving. NASA flight surgeons advised me not to drive for the first month after my return to earth because turning corners sometimes leaves returning astronauts disoriented and spinning. I rather liked Beth's chauffeur treatment and her airy convertible, so I adhered strictly to the flight surgeon's advice.

BETH and I trained together for four months regularly. At the end of four months, I was jogging slowly, still swimming, and beginning to do some weight training. The weight training was thought to be especially important for me in order to recover some of my lost bone mass.

Unusual for me, I could not seem to rekindle the aggressiveness that is necessary to make progress in weight training. It felt as if my testosterone level had dropped. I could not get myself to grunt and groan and push out one more repetition on the bench press. Growing physically tired, I could not summon the needed willpower. Whatever it was (male ego?) that I had before the flight which allowed me to aggressively push myself was now sorely lacking. I knew that the weight training was more important than ever, but I was flat. I thought perhaps I had pushed myself as hard as I could for five months and I just did not have any push left in me.

AFTER a year of rehabilitation, my repeat bone scans showed that I had recovered about half of my lost bone density, with my hips and lower spine showing a 6 percent deficit. Whether full recovery is possible is not yet known. I finally felt the return of my reserve willpower. Over the summer I began bicycling aggressively past the cherry orchards of northern Michigan, gradually building up to nonstop, eighty-five-mile rides three times a week. I did an occasional hundred-miler and ran a half marathon just to convince myself that I was, indeed, back to normal. A year and a half after flight and back in shape, I declared myself recovered.

26

Aftershock

I AM SEEING THINGS. Eerie and elusive images, lots of people, all swirling. There are dull colors and ghastly forms, and now the bow of a powerboat rushing at me. The boat is going to run me over! "Look out!" I scream at the driver, frantically waving my arms. My next thought is of Pope John Paul II. I had met him a few weeks earlier, in December 1997, after being invited to Italy for postflight appearances. Dignity and presence. I was impressed by this man of virtue and quiet piety. The film running in my head puts me back in the Vatican, and I once again see the Pope kissing and blessing our six-month-old son, Jeffrey. What a presence His Holiness has! My Vatican world begins to blur as I feel my thoughts tumbling away.

I wake up. Where am I? I look around and notice the clock radio at my bedside. Four o'clock. Curtains drawn, I wonder whether it is morning or night. My T-shirt, like the bedsheet, is soaking wet. I am perspiring as heavily as if I had just played an hour-long game of one-on-one basketball at high noon. I realize that I still have a high fever. I wonder if the hallucinations are side effects from the antibiotics? No, I never heard of such side effects. Maybe they gave me the wrong pills, some kind of stimulant, perhaps.

The doctor in me notes that if what I am suffering from is the 1997 strain of the flu, many older people afflicted will not survive. I try to recall through the mental haze if I had gotten my flu shot this year. I vaguely remember doing so, but my time since the *Mir* flight has been filled with so many medical proddings and probings that I cannot recall with certainty. I seem to remember the nurse giving me the vaccination, but was it *this* year or *last* year?

I try to categorize the time of the shot within the new framework of thirds that my life has been divided into. Living in space was so shockingly different that the experience redefined my life forever into three segments: on the planet before space, off the planet during space, and back on the planet after space. Yes, I think the shot came in the latter third of my life. Unable to recall with certainty, the nagging concern of whether I have lost some brain cells to radiation crosses my mind once again.

If I do have the flu, the antigens in the virus must have shifted big time, because my immunization, if I had indeed gotten it, has proven worthless. Then again, maybe it is *Legionella* pneumonia, as the doctor suggested earlier today at the flight medicine clinic. How the heck could I have acquired that illness? Think. Legionnaire's disease. A lot of people getting pneumonia at some convention—Philadelphia, I think—something to do with the ventilation system in an old hotel. And some people died from it.

Uncomfortably wet and now beginning to feel chilled, I reach over and grab the unused pillow and draw it to my forehead. As I wipe away the sweat, the coldness of the cloth excites a body-shaking chill. I pull the covers up to my neck. Clear your mind, I tell myself. Try to figure out what is happening. Be the doctor that you are, and heal thyself.

I begin my self-assessment. I can hear my lungs wheezing even without a stethoscope. Okay, Doctor Jerry, cough and see if your lungs clear. I cough feebly, my head splitting. The gurgling does not clear, especially on the left side. This makes sense, I think to myself, as I recall what my chest X ray had looked like earlier today: puffy infiltrates at the bases of both lungs, but predominantly on the left side.

As I begin to concentrate on my physiology, I become aware of the fact that not only am I soaking wet, but that I am actively and profusely sweating. I can feel the perspiration pouring out of every pore. Rather strangely, I become fascinated by it. So this is what classic chills and fever feel like. Water just pouring out as if someone turned on a faucet. As bad as this pneumonia is, the doctor and researcher in me sort of relish the fact that I can now experience, firsthand, what pneumonia does to a person.

Breaking through my curiosity, it dawns on me that I am *really* sick! People regularly die from pneumonia. It was the number-one killer before antibiotics. The hallucinations were probably fever-induced, and even though I feel bitterly cold, I had better get out from underneath these covers. I reach over to the nightstand, flick on the lamp, and grab the thermometer. A minute later, I roll the glass tube until I can make out the meniscus of mercury and, reading the scale, see that my temperature has once again topped 104 degrees. I realize that I must get up whether I want to or not.

I remove the covers, and my body responds with uncontrollable full-body shaking chills. I rush to the closet to get some dry clothes. I am shivering and shaking and hacking. I spit up some thick green nasty stuff. I make my way to the medicine cabinet and take my next dose of antibiotics and Tylenol. I decide that I had better go to the hospital emergency room. The hospital, I chuckle to myself, is the proper place to die.

On my way there, I wonder how I could go from perfect health to pneumonia in one day? I have hardly ever been sick in my entire life. Something related to my time on *Mir* must be the culprit. I am now and forevermore held hostage by my time in space.

To be sure, my crewmates and I were exposed to ethylene glycol fumes for months on end. The antifreeze fumes originated from leaks in the *Mir*'s cooling lines. Each of us would cringe every time the Russian ground controllers ordered us to repressurize the cooling loops. At the very least, the fumes must have wreaked havoc with my immune system and damaged my lungs. Maybe that is why I now have pneumonia.

I arrive at the emergency room. Intravenous fluids relieve my aching head and intravenous antibiotics kill the fever. This was not to be the most pleasant Christmas day that I had ever spent, but I was thankful to still be alive. By New Year's Day, I recovered from whatever it was that had ruined my holidays, and I resolved to have a less eventful 1998.

No doubt about it, my illness might have just been coincidental, something that I would have had regardless of my prior activities. Doctors had conducted pulmonary function tests a month after my return to earth, and everything appeared normal. Repeat tests taken a month after I recovered from the pneumonia were once again normal. Toxicologists continue to assure me that inhaling ethylene glycol fumes does not generally result in lung damage or other illness, although they admit that no one to their knowledge has ever been exposed to such high levels for as prolonged a period of time as I was.

Drinking ethylene glycol can result in serious pathology, however, and postflight testing of water samples showed that some of the chemical found its way into our water supply. Maybe I just plain caught something, and this pneumonia had nothing to do with my time on *Mir*. But in my mind, I cannot help but think that the tribulations of *Mir* contributed, and that it was not letting go of me just yet.

To be sure, there are recognized long-term health risks associated with long-duration spaceflight. While in the closed environment of a space station, the human body is not challenged by any new bacteria or viruses. Consequently, the immune system goes into low gear. Oh sure, the dank and dark environment of *Mir* invites the growth of molds, but there are no *new* pathogens introduced once the hatch is closed.

Radiation exposure is another unavoidable risk associated with space travel. Some nights while on *Mir,* I would be awakened by bright flashes in my eyes, caused by heavy particles penetrating my closed lids and then striking and exciting the nerve endings on my retina. Turning my head ninety degrees, the particles would move right-to-left and leave behind temporary, ghostly contrails. Although I would try to reposition myself behind lead-filled batteries for protection, more often than not the light show would continue unabated, and I would be irradiated.

Feeling helpless from the onslaught, I would return to my sleeping wall and try to fall asleep despite the disturbing flashes. After ten minutes or so, the space station would zoom away from the defect in the Van Allen magnetic belts that surround the earth. Reentering the belt, we would once again be shielded by their deflective force field, and my closed eyelids would once again provide darkness.

At the flight medicine clinic at the Johnson Space Center in Houston, medical researchers are conducting a long-term study on astronaut health. For each astronaut, three age-matched and screened-healthy control subjects are selected and followed. Everyone then receives yearly physicals, including lab studies. I will be returning to NASA every year until I die for a flight physical. The study is designed to determine whether being an astronaut increases one's morbidity and mortality.

Do astronauts have a higher frequency of say, bone cancer, than normal? Although it is still early in the study, no major differences between astronauts and the control subjects have been found. I hope that my data will not change that conclusion.

AFTER fourteen days in bed and too many feverish episodes to count, I recovered—just in time for the new year. When I reflected on the past year, noteworthy for all the challenges, it seemed that for the year to end quietly would have been inappropriate. Raging pneumonia was a more appropriate closing.

But I had learned a lot over that year. I would never again take for granted the elemental treasures of the earth. I would never again assume good health, daily comfort, or assured existence. These were blessings.

Vincent Van Gogh once commented that he used colors in his art not to try to imitate precisely the hues of nature, but rather to represent the feelings that nature evoked in him. For Van Gogh, the color green represented restfulness, tranquillity, and peacefulness.

How right Van Gogh was! I can attest to the fact that after my return to earth, there was nothing more calming and serene than the color green. There was nothing more relaxing for me than to spend time in my backyard, just lying in the grass looking up at the leaves swaying in the trees overhead. Savoring the simple beauty of the earth. Relishing in nothing more spectacular than a cool breeze, sunshine on my face, and the rustle of leaves.

27

"Are You Glad You Flew on *Mir?*"

AFTER I RETURNED to earth, I was frequently asked this question about my *Mir* experience: "Was it fun?"

I always wanted to answer with a firm yes, but could never quite bring myself to respond that way. I felt like a party pooper saying "No, not really." But the honest answer to the question "Was it fun on *Mir?*" is "No, not really."

I was busy. Everything was riding on our shoulders, the pressure unrelenting. It was not playtime up there. In fact, I have never worked so hard in my life. When we were not repairing broken-down life-support equipment, we were executing spacewalks and a myriad of experiments—more than a hundred. I slept with sensors stuck to my eyelids to record my rapid eye movement sleep and electrodes plastered to my scalp to record my brain-wave patterns.

But if the question were phrased, "Are you glad you flew on *Mir?*" my answer would be an unequivocal yes. We were pioneers, colonizing space. I was in the heavens with a view of the earth and our universe that was incredible, unforgettable. The launch and landing in the shuttle, the spacewalk, flying in the Soyuz capsule, the sense of scientific accomplishment, and yes, even the fire and near-collision, were experiences of such remarkable proportions that they will forever be with me. My experience changed me profoundly.

I was forced to acknowledge the fact that life is precarious. I knew that, very abruptly, my life could end. I now try to make each moment count.

Viewing the earth in its entirety broadened my perspective. I saw the beautiful blue Adriatic Sea and the uninterrupted Balkan mountain range. I wished that I could whisk the leaders in war-torn Bosnia and Yugoslavia up to space with me so that they could see the beauty of their land, so that they could understand that no natural borders separate them, only artificial ones. I have been a U.S. naval officer for twenty years. I understand the necessity of armed forces. But I have also seen the undivided earth from space. When viewed from this perspective, the fighting amongst ourselves makes no sense whatsoever. Now, whenever I witness conflict in any form, I try to step back and examine the problem from a broader perspective. Understanding follows.

I learned not to take anything for granted. During delays at airports, I now sit content. I can grab a tasty sandwich and no longer have to suck dehydrated food through straws. The chair is comfortable and stays on the floor. The air is *there,* I do not have to replenish it, filter it, analyze its oxygen content or pressure, or worry about whether it will be sufficient to keep me alive for the next few hours. I can look into the faces of not just two, but *scores* of people walking by or, better yet, strike up a conversation with someone whom I have never talked to before and learn something new.

I have learned that we are 99.9 percent alike. Why we earthlings chose to concentrate on the .1 percent difference makes no sense. We should celebrate our diversity, understand it for what it is—a blessing, not a curse. Prejudice in any form separates us and should never be tolerated. We are all on the earth together, and the earth when viewed from space is not divided up piecemeal, but exists as a wondrous whole. We need to recognize that our almost insane preoccupation with identifying and fighting over our differences is absurd. We should be counting our blessings daily, not squabbling among ourselves.

Aboard *Mir* I was transformed into a nearly fearless being, confident that if it were humanly possible to survive a given circumstance, I would do so. I would not panic; my heart would not race. Instead, I would calmly evaluate the situation and react to the emergency as I was trained to do. That confidence remains. No challenge is too great. I have learned that we can overcome any obstacle, any setback, live through any difficulty, and emerge better for it.

I no longer listen to people who say that we cannot change. Whenever I hear a businessman say, "We have always run our business like that; it would be too hard to change now," or someone else state that "I can't change; I've always been this way," I reject the premise. After living for forty-two years on the planet, in less than a month I changed from earthling to spaceman. Flying seemed as natural to me as walking had been. The ability of the human being to adapt is immeasurable. We can change.

Finally, I lived side by side with two former cold war enemies inside school bus–sized modules under the most difficult living conditions imaginable for five inescapable months—and we got along. No fighting; not an argument worth mentioning. We shared a common goal. Adversity taught us that only by working together could we survive. Human beings can get along. We can work together with people of different cultures, with people who might have different viewpoints than our own. I no longer accept the contrary view.

I learned a great deal about myself and about human nature. We can indeed go far beyond what most of us deem practical or even possible.

AFTER my return from *Mir* to earth, I was asked by numerous safety review committees, "Is it safe to send the next American astronaut to *Mir?*"

I always answered that I did not have enough information to respond properly to the question. I indicated that I was not at a high enough level in the NASA organization or, I suspect, in the U.S. government to assess fully all of the benefits, including political benefits, associated with an affirmative response to that question.

Perhaps regardless of the degree of important science or operational knowledge to be gained by the American space program, the U.S. government perceived that engaging the Russians in a cooperative space undertaking was reason enough to stick by *Mir*. Or perhaps having a means for our government to funnel millions of dollars in foreign aid to Russia under the guise of "rent money" so the United States can send astronauts to *Mir* is a valuable political stratagem.

I have read newspaper accounts claiming that American dollars sent to the Russian space program were being provided as leverage to keep the Russian government from sending arms to Iran or missiles to India. Although I am not privy to such dealings, nothing about these accounts conflicts with anything I observed in the trenches, as we continually tried to accommodate the Russians regardless of unkept promises, late delivery of hardware, or failed commitments.

While unable to answer the question of continuing the U.S. presence on *Mir* with a simple yes or no, I could comment, with some authority, about the risks entailed on *Mir*. When I was on the space station, that risk level climbed dramatically and was substantial. After I returned to earth, I told numerous NASA safety-review teams and independent safety teams that I thought the risk level on *Mir* was substantially higher than advertised by the Russian Space Agency, and that the risk level was significantly higher than understood, or officially acknowledged, by NASA. *Mir* had originally been designed to last for five years. During my stay there, it had been in space for more than twice that time.

High risk, however, does not necessarily equate to "no go" or "not safe." Going to the moon was a high-risk venture, but worth it. Risk is only one component of the equation. Benefit is the other half.

On the benefit side, it was clear to me that the science capability and the ability to use *Mir* to improve our operational expertise in the areas of docking and long-duration space experience were diminishing. After the collision between the Progress spacecraft and *Mir*, more than half of the *Mir* electrical power supply was lost. Also gone, sealed off, was Spektr, one of only two scientifically capable modules on *Mir*.

These losses contributed in two ways to the future diminished science productivity. First, without adequate, reliable electrical power to run the science equipment in the remaining modules, many meaningful experiments could no longer be performed. Second, without Spektr, access to over half of the scientific gear was no longer possible. Furthermore, because so much time was needed to make repairs to simply keep the space station alive, the astronauts and cosmonauts were left with little time to conduct experiments.

We had long ago proven that man can live in space and that life support systems can be made reliable enough to keep humans in space for prolonged periods of time. We, the Russians and Americans together, had moved beyond mere survival in space to the point where useful work—conducting experiments—could be done. To regress to merely trying to keep three people alive in space was to move backward, not forward.

Concerning space operations experience, by the time I departed the space station, we already had enough space shuttle dockings with *Mir* under our belt to feel confident about performing these dockings competently. We already knew the problems that crew members would encounter living for prolonged periods of time in isolation. We already understood that working cooperatively with the Russians would be forever difficult, but we had demonstrated that it could be done, despite the difficulties.

That we were operationally prepared to use the space shuttle for future dockings with the proposed International Space Station (ISS)—the next generation space station, to be built primarily by the United States and Russia, whose first components were launched in 1998—was an opinion I heard expressed many times by ISS top-level managers. The shuttle had proven itself—there was really nothing more to be gained operationally by repeating further dockings to *Mir.* In fact, these managers, for the most part, wished that we would stop the *Mir* flights so that the cash-strapped Russians would concentrate all their resources on building new modules for the International Space Station.

If the benefit to be gained from a venture is high enough to justify the risk, and the person volunteering for the duty is fully aware of the risks involved, then going to *Mir,* or partaking in any other risky endeavor for that matter, may be considered safe enough. There is a crossover point in the risk-benefit curve, however, when the risk outweighs the benefit. This point should be precisely defined prior to the venture. If that point is crossed, and the risk far outweighs the benefit, then a person or an organization has to make the very courageous decision to call a halt to the venture.

I want to emphasize the word *courageous* because it is often a tougher call to stop doing something than to continue with the status quo, especially when that status quo is reinforced by political and bureaucratic momentum. Less courageous is to change the stated goals of an endeavor to fit the new circumstances. Electrical power now inadequate? More than half the science gear sealed in a now airless, dead module? Well, scientific advancement is not all that important after all. It is important to learn how to fix modules when punctured, as well as to learn how to fight fires in space, and do impromptu spacewalks to try to reattach cables to dead solar panels.

After my flight experiences aboard the Russian space station,

American astronaut Jim Lovell of *Apollo 13* fame stepped forward to say that he thought *Mir* should be "retired with dignity." Lovell, to be sure, is not one to shy away from justifiably risky ventures. He has put his own life on the line as a test pilot and astronaut. But according to Lovell, we had already learned what we needed to learn and the benefit was no longer sufficient to justify further risk. Knowing when to abandon a spacecraft is also a lesson to be learned and, said Lovell, we should stop sending our astronauts to *Mir*.

Whether right or wrong in his analysis, Jim Lovell's conclusion was a tougher one to arrive at, and took more courage to express, than the opposite view, which propounded simply going along with the status quo. When viewed by an astronaut in the trenches, and not taking into consideration any political benefits, it was clear that on *Mir* risks were dramatically up and benefits were dramatically down. In my mind, the best indicators of future performance by *Mir* were its then-current and past performance. In the face of that reality, it became difficult for an astronaut like me to argue with Lovell's conclusion.

Americans and Russians continued on *Mir*. Choosing to throw the dice, three more joint missions were flown after my mission ended. The last U.S. astronaut returned in June 1998. The Russians continued flying, but after trying to court movie directors, advertisers, and rich thrill seekers to spend $20 million a month to visit *Mir* without getting any takers, it appears that the space station will finally be deorbited. Most of it will burn up reentering the atmosphere, but large chunks are expected to clunk down on earth—hopefully into the ocean.

I WENT to Chicago and visited Jim Lovell at his home. There was something about what he had said that struck me as not only right, but profound. About knowing when to stop being so very difficult. Having been spectacularly successful, it was time to retire *Mir* with dignity—not abandon *Mir* in the middle of a collision or a fire or some other catastrophic circumstance. It was time to move on to other endeavors.

I had flown with three U.S. shuttle crews and with two long-duration *Mir* crews. I flew in a Russian Soyuz capsule and the most incredible spacecraft ever built by mankind, the U.S. Space Shuttle. I had walked and lived in space and had been treated to a heavenly view of the earth. Many others have done more. Astronaut John Young, with his two Gemini, two Apollo, and two shuttle missions, and more than thirty-five years and counting at NASA, is a shining example of dedication to duty and love of country. But I am satisfied that I did my part and that I gave it my best shot. I know that others can ably take over where I left off.

After getting reestablished on earth, I was called into the office of the chief of the astronauts. He more or less told me that I should let him know what mission I was interested in doing in the future and he would do his best to make sure that I was assigned to that mission. This was far from typical, but he said that my performance and the sacrifice that I had made were not typical, either.

I thanked him but told him that I thought that my time was up and that I should move on. I was only forty-two, but had twenty years of service in the U.S. Navy and was eligible to retire. I had just completed an unforgettable space mission. My second son was born. I had flown fifty million miles and felt a bit worn, traveled-out. I had done the things in space that I dreamed about when I was a teen, lying on my back on a sand dune, looking at the moon, and knowing that we human beings were up there at that very moment. My chapter had ended. I decided to "retire with dignity."

SOME months later, University of Michigan football coach Lloyd Carr, coming off a national championship season, invited me to give a motivational talk to his players. After I spoke, Coach Carr and I talked in his office. He asked me about my future plans. I told him that I was taking some time off, spending time with my family.

"Jerry, you are at halftime. You had a good first half, you are solidly in the lead, and you can now alter the game plan to your liking. I am sure that you will have a great second half."

I liked the analogy. It was, indeed, a good first half, one in which I was privileged to play.

I NOW live in a quiet town in northern Michigan. I am content, not restless. I am not trying to top anything. I am happy to be back on the planet. Any new adventures will be shared adventures with my wife, our two sons, and our latest newborn.

A long time ago, my father told me, "Jerry, you can be an astronaut or anything else that you want to be if you set your mind to it and work hard. This is America." Those words of encouragement changed my life, spoken as they were by someone whom I respected. I spend most of my free time playing with my sons and letting them know that the sky is not the limit and that they, too, can do anything that they set their minds to.

I know that is so.

Index

Abbey, George, 24
Aldrin, Buzz, 4
Armstrong, Neil, 4
Astronaut
    long-term study on health of,
        244–45
    procedure on return to earth,
        223
    selection process, 14–16
    training, 17–18
Atlantis, 211–212
    docked with *Mir*, 84, 122,
        214–15
    journey to *Mir*, 76–79
    launch procedure, 59–68
    treadmill on, 221–22
    undocking from *Mir*, 220
    water production, 77–78
Attitude control computer, 185–
        86, 188–89

Baker, Ellen, 33, 35
Baker, Mike, 78–82, 87
Bartmann, Kathryn, 11
Blaha, John, 22, 45, 83–84, 86,
        88–89, 91, 123–27, 129,
        152, 222–23

Carbon dioxide scrubber, 190
Carr, Lloyd, 252
Challenger, 68
Clark, Mark, 11–12
Clervoy, Jean-Francois, 213, 222
Collins, Eileen, 213, 219–20, 225
Cosmonaut
    job viewed by Russian people,
        29
    procedure on return to earth,
        223
    psychological support group,
        128–30
    training, 41–43
Cronkite, Walter, 4
Culbertson, Frank, 45

Defense Language Institute, 24–25

Earth-observation studies, 135–
        36, 142, 147
Energia, 107
Ethylene glycol
    blood tests regarding, 199–200
    exposure to, 243–44
    level in air on *Mir*, 198
    toxic effects of, 197, 199

Ewald, Reinhold 92, 97, 105

Film in space, 136, 147–48
Foale, Mike, 35–36, 175, 189,
    215–19

Gibson, Robert "Hoot," 20–21,
    24
Glenn, John, 69, 140
Goldin, Dan, 227
Gravity, 226–27, 232, 234
    in space, 204
Grunsfeld, John, 61, 76–78, 82
Gunderson, E. K. K., 150–51

Hale-Bopp, 145–46
Hubble telescope, 147, 208

Inclination of orbit, 75–76
International Space Station (ISS),
    32, 44–45, 250
Ipperwash Provincial Park,
    Canada, 3
Isolation, 150–159
Ivins, Marsha, 62, 80, 85, 155

Jett, Brent, 87
Johnson Space Center, Houston,
    13, 15

Kaleri, Alexander "Sasha"
    Yurievich, 88, 90–92, 94,
    96, 105, 113–14, 127–28
Korzun, Valeri Grigorievich, 35,
    88–89, 91–92, 94, 96,
    104–108, 111–12, 126–28,
    132
    micromanagement, 126
Kregel, Kevin, 62

Laser use in space, 19
Lazutkin, Sasha, 92, 99, 105,
    114–16, 133, 167–70,
    189, 197, 215, 219
Linenger, Jerry M., 6
    astronaut application, 13
    daily schedule on *Mir*, 133
    letters to son, 209
    pneumonia, 241–43
    Russian psychological
        assessment of, 121–22
    selection as astronaut, 16–17
    shuttle mission, 18–20
Long-duration space flight, 151,
    238, 244, 249
Lovell, Jim, 251
Lucid, Shannon, 22, 91

MAGs, 61
Mafia, Russian, 37
Marshburn, Tom, 129, 197, 226,
    232–33
Max Q, 20, 65–66
Melroy, Pam, 62
Mir-22 mission, 92, 122
Mir-23 mission, 92, 122
    relationship between crew
        members, 130, 134, 193
    relationship with mission
        control in Moscow, 131–34
Mir space station, 22–23, 78–79,
    112–13
    air quality on, 215
    American science program on,
        135
    antifreeze leaks, 185, 191–92,
        196, 198
    bathing on, 181–82
    cause of fire on, 114–15
    clothing on, 180–81
    collision on, 175–77, 249

Mir space station, *(continued)*
    communication system, 124,
        127, 194, 214
    cooling system failure,
        190–92
    daily life on, 90–91
    docking with, 79–82, 95–96,
        212, 249–50
    electrical power-system
        failures, 116, 186–89
    exercise on, 178–80, 191
    fire on, 101–110, 114–15,
        217
    gyrodynes, 186–87, 189
    internal-communication sys-
        tem, 168
    junk accumulated on, 85–86
    Kvant I docking port, 95
    life support systems, 152, 214
    master alarms on, 84, 100
    near-collision with Progress,
        168–75
    orbital path, 141, 184
    out-dated condition of, 123
    oxygen-system failures, 116
    partnership with U.S. space
        program, 22
    plan to deorbit, 251
    press conference from, 83–84,
        216
    Priroda module, 192
    publicity regarding, 115
    radio communication system,
        194
    repair of cooling lines,
        196–98, 200
    risk-benefit curve, 250
    risks on, 249, 251
    satellite communication sys-
        tem, 194
    science modules, 79
    shaving on, 182
    sleeping on, 182–83
    smoke from fire on, 107–109
    solar panels, 186
    Spektr module, 192
    tooth-care on, 182
    undocking from, 86–87
    U.S. funding of, 125
    U.S. presence on, 249
Mir survey experiment, 220
Mission Control, Moscow, 126–
        27, 153, 158, 162, 177,
        189, 191, 195, 198–202,
        217
    micromanagement of *Mir*,
        132
    NASA contingent, 172, 197

NASA
    and fire on *Mir*, 115, 217
    management of shuttle-*Mir*
        program, 34
    psychologists, 157
NASA/*Mir* Earth-Observations
        Project
    Physiographic Atlas, 142
NASA-3/*Mir*-22 mission, 21
    launch procedure, 59–63
    pre-launch quarantine, 48–56
    training for, 26
NASA Shuttle-*Mir*
    management, 45
    program, 113
Naval Health Research Center,
        9–10, 150
Nedzi, Lucian, 5
Noriega, Carlos, 222

Orbital inclination, 139–41

People's Ten Sexiest Men, 183

Pilot-astronauts, 121
Postflight
   bone scans, 237, 240
   rehabilitation program,
      237–40
   response time deficit, 239
   weight training, 240
Pravda, 174
Precourt, Charlie, 211–212, 214,
   219–20, 224–25
Progress resupply/garbage vehicle,
   154–55, 160–63, 222
   manual docking with, 165–66
   near-collision with *Mir,* 168–
      74
   redocking with, 162–64, 167–
      68, 172–75
Puddy, Mr. Donald, 13

Radiation exposure, 244
Redundancy, built-in, 165, 175
Richards, Richard "Dick," 19
Russia
   foreign aid to, 36, 248
   space program of, 29–30,
      113, 164, 217

SEALs, 9–10, 12
Sagan, Carl, 146–47
Scatter-plot maps, 137–38
Schembechler, Bo, 156
Service, Jim, 7
Shepard, Alan, 140
Shepherd, Beth, 237, 239–40
Sheremetyevo airport, 30–31, 35
Shuttle Aircraft, 54
   Deorbit burn, 224
   docking, 165
   landing, 223–25
   launch safety procedures, 67–
      69

Skylab, 131–33
Solid-fueled oxygen canisters,
   100, 116
Solid rocket boosters, 66
Soyuz spacecraft, 92–93, 112,
   114, 128
   docking of, 92–93, 95
   undocking, 94
   using to stabilize *Mir,* 188
   water survival training, 119–21
Space motion sickness, 57–58, 97
Space suit
   launch-and-entry, 59–60
Spacehab, 76, 214
Spacewalk, 198, 204–208
   and sensation of falling, 205–
      208
Star City, Russia, 28–29, 31–33
   American living quarters in,
      32–34
   cosmonaut gymnasium, 41
   lack of written training
      materials, 43–44
   life in, 37
   Russian administration of, 43
   Russian/American relations
      in, 35–36
   training in, 34, 38–47, 118

Technology
   Russian, 23
Thagard, Norm, 21
Thermal stress, 184–85
Toilet procedures in space, 58–59
Tsibliev, Vasily, 92, 97–99, 101,
      105, 111, 114, 116, 129,
      154, 163, 166–69,
      171–72, 189, 197, 201,
      214–15, 217, 219
   and docking with Progress,
      166–71

Tsibliev, Vasily, *(continued)*
    frustration with Mission
        Control, Moscow, 131,
        199–202

U.S. Naval Academy, Annapolis,
    5, 7
University of North Carolina,
    Chapel Hill, 8
Urine-derived water, 190

Van Allen magnetic belts, 244
Van Gogh, Vincent, 245

Water, recycled, 190
Wayne State University, 6
Weightlessness, ill effects of,
    179, 231
Winfrey, Oprah, 183
Wisoff, Jeff, 82
World Map, 142–43

Yeltsin, Boris, 177
Young, John, 24, 252
Yzerman, Steve, 156